CASES AND MATERIALS ON EMPLOYMENT DISCRIMINATION

1990 Supplement

EDITORIAL ADVISORY BOARD

Little, Brown and Company
Law Book Division

Richard A. Epstein
James Parker Hall Distinguished Service Professor of Law
University of Chicago

E. Allan Farnsworth
Alfred McCormack Professor of Law
Columbia University

Ronald J. Gilson
Professor of Law
Stanford University

Geoffrey C. Hazard, Jr.
Sterling Professor of Law
Yale University

James E. Krier
Earl Warren DeLano Professor of Law
University of Michigan

Elizabeth Warren
William A. Schnader Professor of Commercial Law
University of Pennsylvania

Bernard Wolfman
Fessenden Professor of Law
Harvard University

CASES AND MATERIALS ON EMPLOYMENT DISCRIMINATION

Second Edition

1990 Supplement

MICHAEL J. ZIMMER
Professor of Law
Seton Hall University School of Law

CHARLES A. SULLIVAN
Professor of Law
Seton Hall University School of Law

RICHARD F. RICHARDS
Professor of Law
University of Arkansas, Fayetteville

Little, Brown and Company
Boston   Toronto   London

Copyright © 1990 by Michael Grant Moses Zimmer, Moira G. Sullivan, and Joyce A. Richards, Trustee.

All rights reserved. No part of this book may be reproduced in any form or by any electronic or mechanical means including information storage and retrieval systems without permission in writing from the publisher, except by a reviewer who may quote brief passages in a review.

Library of Congress Catalog Card No. 81-84828
ISBN 0-316-98820-0
Second Printing

ICP

Published simultaneously in Canada
by Little, Brown & Company (Canada) Limited

Printed in the United States of America

CONTENTS

Table of Cases   *xi*
Table of Selected Secondary Authorities   *xvii*
Preface   *xix*

PART 1

THE CONCEPT OF DISCRIMINATION   1

Chapter 1

Legal Approaches to the Employment Relation   3

A. The General Outline of Employment Law
   1. The Reassessment of Contract Law   3
   2. Reassessment of Tort Law   4
B. The Policy Bases for Antidiscrimination Law   4

Chapter 2

The Definition of Disparate Treatment Discrimination Under Title VII   7

B. Individual Disparate Treatment   7
   1. "Direct" Evidence of Discriminatory Intent   7
   3. Causation   9
       Price Waterhouse v. Hopkins   9
       Notes   38

v

D.	Defenses to Disparate Treatment Cases	41
	2. Bona Fide Occupational Qualifications	41
	3. Voluntary Affirmative Action	42

Chapter 3

The Definition of Systemic Disparate Impact Discrimination Under Title VII   45

A.	The Structure of Disparate Impact Discrimination	45
	Wards Cove Packing Company, Inc. v. Atonio	46
	Notes	63
C.	Statutory Exceptions	66
	1. Professionally Developed Tests	66

Chapter 4

The Interrelation of the Disparate Treatment and Disparate Impact Theories of Discrimination   67

B.	The Relationship Between Disparate Impact and Treatment Where the Prima Facie Case Is Based on Statistical Showing of Effects	67
	Notes	68

PART II

TITLE VII: SPECIAL PROBLEMS, PROCEDURES, AND REMEDIES   71

Chapter 5

Special Problems in Applying Title VII   73

B.	Coverage of Title VII	73
C.	Gender Discrimination	76
	1. Pregnancy	76
	United Automobile Workers v. Johnson Controls, Inc.	76
	Notes	113

Contents

	2. Sexual Harassment	118
	3. Affectional Preferences	122
D.	Religious Discrimination	123
	2. The Special Duty to Accommodate Employees' Religious Practices	123
E.	National Origin and Alienage Discrimination	124
	1. National Origin Discrimination	125
	2. Alienage Discrimination	125
F.	Retaliation	125
	Jennings v. Tinley Park Community Consolidated School District No. 146	126
	Notes	133

Chapter 6

Procedures for Enforcing Title VII — 139

A.	Introduction	139
B.	Private Enforcement of Title VII: The Administrative Phase	139
	2. Filing a Timely Charge	139
	c. Continuing Violations	139
	Lorance v. AT&T Technologies, Inc.	140
	Notes	149
	3. Filing a Timely Charge: Deferral Status	151
	b. Coordination of State and Federal Remedies	151
C.	Private Enforcement of Title VII: Filing Suit	152
D.	Private Enforcement of Title VII: Relationship of the EEOC Charge to the Private Suit	153
	1. Proper Plaintiffs	153
K.	Title VII Suit Against State and Local Governments	153
L.	Title VII Enforcement Against Federal Employers	154
M.	Settlement of Title VII Suits	155
	Martin v. Wilks	155
	Notes	170

Chapter 7

Title VII Remedies — 177

B.	Types of Relief	177
F.	Attorneys' Fees	178

vii

PART III

OTHER ANTIDISCRIMINATION STATUTES   181

Chapter 8

The Equal Pay Act   183

D.	Breaking a Prima Facie Case	183
F.	Beyond the Equal Pay Act: Using Title VII to Attack Gender-Based Wage Discrimination	185
	2. Structuring Title VII Attacks in Gender-Based Wage Discrimination	185
	a. Where the Work Is Equal	185
	b. Where the Work Is Unequal	185
H.	Equal Pay Act Remedies	186

Chapter 9

The Age Discrimination in Employment Act of 1967   191

A.	Introduction	191
B.	Coverage of the ADEA	192
C.	The Concept of Age Discrimination	192
	1. Individual Treatment Wage Discrimination	192
	3. Systemic Disparate Treatment	194
	4. The Interaction of the Theories	195
	Metz v. Transit Mix, Inc.	195
	Notes	214
D.	Statutory Exceptions	217
	2. Seniority Systems	217
	3. Bona Fide Benefit Plans	218
	Public Employees Retirement System of Ohio v. Betts	218
	Notes	231
	7. Temporary Exception for Police and Firefighters	235
F.	Enforcement Procedures for ADEA Rights	235
	1. Private Suit	235
	4. Federal Employee Suits Under the ADEA	237
G.	Remedies	238

Contents

Chapter 10

Reconstruction-Era Civil Rights Legislation — 239

B.	Section 1981	239
	2. The Meaning of Discrimination Under Section 1981	239
	Patterson v. McLean Credit Union	239
	Notes	255
	4. The Relationship of Section 1981 and Patterson	256
D.	Section 1983	256
E.	Remedies	258
	1. Legal and Equitable Relief	258
	3. The Eleventh Amendment	259

PART IV

ANTIDISCRIMINATION EFFORTS THROUGH GOVERNMENT CONTRACTS — 261

Chapter 12

Handicap Discrimination — 263

B.	The Substantive Provisions of the Rehabilitation Act of 1973	263
	2. The Concept of Handicap Discrimination	263

Appendix — 265

TABLE OF CASES

Italics indicate principal cases.

Abraham v. Graphic Arts Intl. Union, 371
Agee v. Seidman, 220
Alford v. City of Lubbock, 846
Anderson v. Creighton, 935
Apkin v. Treasurer and Receiver General, 800
Arnold v. United States Postal Service, 844, 845
Ayala v. Mayfair Molder Products Corp., 845

Bailey v. USX Corp., 422
Barnes v. Small, 471
Bartelt v. Berlitz School, 517
Bates v. Tennessee Valley Authority, 586
Batts v. NLT Corp., 395
Beard v. Whitley Cty. REMC, 768
Ben-Shalom v. Marsh, 406
Bennett v. Corroon and Black Corp., 394
Betts v. Hamilton County Bd. of Mental Retardation, 846
Bienkowski v. American Airlines, Inc., 816, 818
Bodnar v. Synpol, 817
Boeing Corporation, EEOC v., 155
Bordens, EEOC v., 846
Bornholdt v. Brady, 869, 870
Boureslan v. Aramco, 343
Branson v. Price River Coal Co., 816
Brown v. Board of Trustees of Boston University, 46, 605
Brown v. M & M/Mars, 816
Bryant v. International School Services, Inc., 343

Caruso v. Peat, Marwick, Mitchell & Co., 341
Castro v. United States, 869
Chalk v. U.S. District Court, 1004
Chambers v. Omaha Girls Club, 156, 354
City of. See name of city
Cleveland Newspaper Guild, Local No. 1 v. Plain Dealer Publishing Co., 527
Cody v. Marriott Corp., 395
Cohen v. West Haven Bd., 612
Colby v. J.C. Penney, 230
Commercial Office Products Co., EEOC v., 520, 866
Commonwealth. See name of state
Connecticut v. Teal, 220, 844
Conrad v. Robinson, 472
Cook v. Pan Am. World Airways, Inc., 517
Cosmair, EEOC v., 472
Covington v. Southern Illinois University, 728
Crown Zellerbach Corp., EEOC v., 472
Culbreath v. Dukakis, 592
Cygnar v. City of Chicago, 935

Davis v. Monsanto Chem. Co., 394
Delaware Dept. of Health and Soc. Servs., EEOC v., 727
Detroit Police Officers Assn. v. Young, 592
Diggs v. Harris Hospital-Methodist, Inc. 343
Dornhecker v. Malibu Grand Prix Corp., 394
Dubbs v. CIA, 406

Edwards v. Jewish Hospital, 938
EEOC. See name of other party
Eisenstadt v. Baird, 396
Employment Division v. Smith, 457
Evans v. City of Evanston, 220, 272

Fallon v. State of Illinois, 727, 753
Fite v. First Tennessee Prod. Cred. Assn., 881
Foley v. Interactive Data Corp., 14, 16, 22
Fort Halifax Packing Co. v. Coyne, 846
Foster v. Board of School Comm. of Mobile Cty., Ala., 921
Fragrante v. City and County of Honolulu, 460
Francis v. AT&T Co., 472
Fullilove v. Klutznik, 207

Table of Cases

Gilardi v. Schroeder dba Gary Schroeder Trucking, 395
Gilmer v. Interstate/Johnson Lane Corp., 524
Glenn v. General Motors, 728
Gondelman v. Commonwealth of Pennsylvania, 800
Gonzalez v. Secretary of the Air Force, 586
Goodman v. Lukens Steel Co., 921
Gray v. University of Arkansas at Fayetteville, 48, 68
Griswold v. Connecticut, 396
Grohs v. National Gypsum Co., Gold Bond Build. Prod. Div., 818

Hall v. Gus Constr. Co., 393-395
Hansard v. Pepsi Cola Metro. Bottling Co., 881
Harness v. Hartz Mountain Corp., 368
Harris v. Brock, 586
Harris v. McRae, 371
Harris v. U.S. Dept. of Transp., 586
Hayes v. Shelby Mem. Hosp., 371
Healy v. New York Life Ins. Co., 816
Hebert v. Mohawk Rubber Co., 817
Hefner v. New Orleans Pub. Serv., Inc., 592
Hicks v. Brown Group, Inc., 516
Hicks v. Gates Rubber Co., 393
Hill v. Seaboard Coast Line R.R., 220
Hoffman-La Roche, Inc. v. Sperling, 867
Honeycutt v. Long, 586
Howlett v. Rose, 934

Independent Fedn. of Flight Attendants v. Zipes, 592

J.C. Penney, EEOC v., 730, 754
Jennings v. Tinley Park Community Consolidated School District No. 146, 472
Jett v. Dallas Ind. School Dist., 583, 934, 939
Johnson v. General Electric, 517
Johnson v. United States Postal Service, 586
Johnson Controls, Inc. v. Cal. Fair Empl. & Housing Comm., 371
Johnston v. Harris Cty. Flood Control Dist., 469
Jordan v. Clark, 586

Karlen v. City Colleges of Chicago, 846
Kitchen v. Chippewa Valley Schools, 936

Lander v. Lujon, 603
Langford v. U.S. Army Corps of Engineers, 869

xiii

Table of Cases

Larkin v. Pullman, Inc., Pullman Standard Div., 531, 921
Lavrov v. NCR Corp., 343
Linn v. United Plant Guard Workers, 472
Lipsett v. University of Puerto Rico, 393-396
Loeffler v. Frank, 612
Lorance v. AT&T Technologies, Inc., 517, 592
Lowe v. Commack Union Free School Dist., 844
Lowe v. Philadelphia Newspapers, Inc., 395
Lusardi v. Lechner, 867

Machinists v. NLRB, 592
MacNamara v. Korean Air Lines, 343
Madison School District, EEOC v., 796
Maher v. Roe, 371
Malhotra v. Cotter & Co., 469, 921
Mallory v. Booth Refrigeration Service Supply Co., Inc., 220
Maresca v. Cuomo, 800
Martin v. Wilks, 592
Mas Maques v. Digital Equip. Corp., 343
Massachusetts, Commonwealth of, EEOC v., 802, 854
Mauter v. Hardy Corp., 845
McDonald v. Santa Fe Trail Transp. Co., 915
McKelvy v. Metal Container Corp., 521, 866
McKinney v. Dole, 396
McLaughlin v. Richland Shoe Co., 792
McLean v. Satellite Technology Serv., 395
Mechnig v. Sears, Roebuck & Co., 818
Menard v. First Security Servs. Corp., 818
Mester Manufacturing Co. v. INS, 466
Metz v. Transit Mix, Inc., 844
Missouri v. Jenkins, 663, 665
Mitchell v. Frank R. Howard Mem. Hosp., 341
Mitchell v. Hutchings, 395

NAACP v. Detroit Police Officers Assn., 592
National Conference of Catholic Bishops v. Bell, 371
New York State Club Assn. v. City of New York 343
New York Times Co. v. Sullivan, 472
Ngiraingas v. Sanchez, 935
Nicholson v. CPI, Intl., Inc., 524

Overby v. Chevron USA, Inc., 469
Owens v. Okure, 921

Table of Cases

Palucki v. Sears, Roebuck & Co., 43
Pardazi v. Cullman Med. Cent., 343
Paroline v. Unisys. Corp., 394
Patterson v. McLean Credit Union, 395, 469, 816, 915, 936
Paulk v. Department of the Air Force, 586
Pendleton v. Rumsfeld, 472
Penton Indust. Publishing Co., EEOC v., 517, 797
Perez v. Laredo Junior College, 517
Pettway v. American Cast Iron Pipe Co., 472
Plumbers Local 189, EEOC v., 472
Poe v. Haydon, 935
Price v. Lockheed Space Operations, 754
Price Waterhouse v. Hopkins, 47, 68, 517, 612, 820
Proud v. United States, 869
Public Employees Retirement Sys. of Ohio v. Betts, 846

Quern v. Jordan, 939

Rabidue v. Osceola Ref. Co., 393
Richmond, City of, v. J.A. Croson Co., 207
Riordan v. Kempiners, 727, 936
Rivera v. United States Postal Serv., 869
Robinson v. Jacksonville Shipyards, Inc., 395
Rodriquez v. Taylor, 612
Roe v. Wade, 371
Rowlett v. Anheuser-Busch, 921, 938
Rushton v. Nebraska Pub. Power Dist., 527

Santa Barbara, County of, EEOC v., 846
Santiago-Negron v. Castro-Davila, 937
Schiavone v. Fortune, 586
Schlitz v. Commonwealth of Virginia, 802
Schuler v. Polaroid Co., 817
Seville v. Martin Marietta Corp., 343
Sias v. City Demonstration Agency, 472
Skinner v. Total Petroleum, Inc., 937
Sparks v. Pilot Freight Carriers, 394
Starrett v. Wadley, 396, 469
Steele v. Offshore Shipbuilding, Inc., 394
St. Francis College v. Al-Khazraji, 921
Stillians v. State of Iowa, 802
Swenson v. Management Recruiters Intl., Inc., 524
Swentik v. USAIR, Inc., 394-395

Texas State Teachers Assn. v. Garland, 663
Torres v. Wisconsin Dept. of Health and Human Servs., 156

United Automobile Workers of America v. Johnson Controls, Inc., 371
United States v. Board of Ed. for School Dist. of Philadelphia, 442
University of Pennsylvania v. EEOC, 48
US Steel Corp., EEOC v., 472
Utley v. Goldman, Sacks & Co., 524

Venegas v. Mitchell, 665
Vinson v. Superior Court, 395
Volk v. Coler, 396

Wards Cove Packing Company, Inc., v. Atonio, 220, 272, 314, 322, 844
Warner v. Graham, 935
Watkins v. U.S. Army, 406
Watson v. Fort Worth Bank & Trust, 220, 314, 322
Ways v. City of Lincoln, 395
White v. Westinghouse Electric Co., 844
Will v. Michigan Dept. of State Police, 934, 939
Williams v. Army & Air Force Exchange Serv., 586
Williamson v. Handy Button Machine Corp., 886
W.R. Grace & Co. v. Rubber Workers, 592
Wright v. Olin, 371
Wright v. South Arkansas Regional Health Center, Inc., 935
Wu v. Thomas, 531

Yatvin v. Madison Metropolitan School Dist., 469
Yellow Freight System v. Donnelly, 525

Zabkowicz v. West Bend Co., 395
Zaklama v. Mt. Sinai Med. Cent., 343
Zombro v. Baltimore Police Dept., 800

TABLE OF SELECTED SECONDARY AUTHORITIES

Becker, From *Muller v. Oregon* to Fetal Vulnerability Policies, 53 U. Chi. L.Rev. 1219 (1986)

Belton, Causation in Employment Discrimination Law, 34 Wayne L. Rev. 1235 (1988)

Brodin, Reflections on the Supreme Court's 1988 Term: The Employment Discrimination Decisions and the Abandonment of the Second Reconstruction, 31 B.C.L. Rev. 1 (1989)

Comment, Administrative Res Judicata and the Age Discrimination in Employment Act, 89 Colum. L. Rev. 1111 (1989)

Comment, Collateral Attacks on Employment Discrimination Consent Decrees, 53 U. Chi. L. Rev. 147 (1983)

Comment, The Meaning of "Sex" in Title VII: Is Favoring an Employee Lover a Violation of the Act?, 83 Nw. U. L. Rev. 612 (1989)

Comment, Partners as Employees Under the Federal Employment Discrimination Statutes: Are the Roles of Partner and Employee Mutually Exclusive?, 42 U. Miami L. Rev. 699 (1988)

Comment, Title VII—The Doctrine of Laches as a Defense to Private Plaintiff Title VII Employment Discrimination Claims, 11 W.N. Eng. L. Rev. 235 (1989)

Comment, Voluntary Acceptance of Early Retirement Offers: Golden Handshake or Gilded Shove, 20 Ariz. St. L.J. 797 (1988)

Comment, When Prior Pay Isn't Equal Pay: A Proposed Standard for the Identification of "Factors Other Than Sex" Under the Equal Pay Act, 89 Colum. L. Rev. 1085 (1989)

Constitutional Scholars' Statement on Affirmative Action After *City of Richmond v. J. A. Croson Co.*, 98 Yale L. J. 1171 (1989)

Devins, Affirmative Action after Reagan, 68 Tex. L. Rev. 353 (1989)

Donahue, Prohibiting Sex Discrimination in the Workplace: An Economic Perspective, 56 U. Chi. L. Rev. 1337 (1989)

Table of Selected Secondary Authorities

Fried, Affirmative Action After *City of Richmond v. J. A. Croson Co.:* A Response to the Scholars' Statement, 99 Yale L. J. 155 (1989)

Laycock, Consent Decrees Without Consent: The Rights of Nonconsenting Third Parties, 1987 U. Chi. Leg. Forum 103 (1987)

Maltz, Affirmative Action and Employer Autonomy: A Comment on *City of Richmond v. Croson*, 68 Ore. L. Rev. 459 (1989)

McMorrow, Retirement and Worker Choice: Incentives to Retire and the Age Discrimination in Employment Act, 29 B.C.L. Rev. 347 (1988)

Mengier, Consent Decree Paradigms: Models Without Meaning, 29 B.C.L. Rev. 291 (1988)

Note, Early Retirement Incentives: "Golden Handshake" for Some, Age Discrimination for Others, 54 Brooklyn L. Rev. 927 (1988)

Note, English-Only Rules and "Innocent" Employers: Clarifying National Origin Discrimination and Disparate Impact Theory Under Title VII, 74 Minn. L. Rev. 587 (1989)

Note, Equal Employment Opportunity for Americans Abroad, 62 N.Y.U.L. Rev. 1289 (1987)

Note, Sending Notice to Potential Plaintiffs in Class Actions Under the Age Discrimination in Employment Act: The Trial Court's Role, 54 Fordham L. Rev. 631 (1986)

Note, Summary Judgment and the ADEA Claimant: Problems and Patterns of Proof, 21 Conn. L. Rev. 99 (1988)

Player, Is *Griggs* Dead? Reflections (Fearfully) on *Wards Cove Packing Co. v. Atonio*, 17 Fla. St. L. Rev. 1 (1989)

Posner, An Economic Analysis of Sex Discrimination Laws, 56 U. Chi. L. Rev. 1311 (1989)

Radford, Sex Stereotyping and the Promotion of Women to Positions of Power, 41 Hastings L.J. 471 (1990)

Ross, The Richmond Chronicles, 68 Tex. L. Rev. 381 (1989)

Scherer, Affirmative Action Doctrine and the Conflicting Messages of *Croson*, 38 Kan. L. Rev. 281 (1990)

Scholars' Reply to Professor Fried, 99 Yale L. J. 163 (1989)

Silver, The Uses and Abuses of Informal Procedures in Federal Civil Rights Enforcement, 55 Geo. Wash. L. Rev. 482 (1987)

Torrey, Indirect Discrimination Under Title VII: Expanding Male Standing to Sue for Injuries Received as a Result of Employer Discrimination Against Females, 64 Wash. L. Rev. 365 (1989)

Underkuffler, "Discrimination on the Basis of Religion: An Examination of Attempted Value Neutrality in Employment, 30 Will. & Mary L. Rev. 581 (1989)

Walterscheid, A Question of Retaliation: Opposition Conduct as Protected Expression Under Title VII of the Civil Rights Act of 1964, 29 B.C.L. Rev. 391 (1988)

Weber, Beyond *Price Waterhouse v. Hopkins*: A New Approach to Mixed Motive Discrimination, 68 N. Car. L. Rev. 495 (1990)

PREFACE

Preparing employment discrimination supplements has typically been a demanding task because of the pace of new developments that has characterized the field since the enactment of Title VII in 1964. However, the year 1989—the 25th anniversary of the Civil Rights Act of 1964—represented an unusually tumultuous period, even for a field that has accommodated itself to rapid change. Some of the changes had been presaged. For example, the Supreme Court's emasculation of Title VII's disparate impact theory in *Wards Cove* had been portended by the plurality opinion in *Watson*, decided the year before. Similarly, the Court action setting down Patterson v. McLean Credit Union for reargument at least signalled the possibility of a reassessment of §1981.

But other changes had been largely unforeseen. The Supreme Court's decision in *Betts* essentially immunizing employee benefit schemes from ADEA review had been predicted by few. Similarly, the revival in *Lorrance* of the Court's hostility to the continuing violation theory was not readily foreseeable in light of the recent decisions which had been far more hospitable to this method of mitigating the rigors of Title VII's short filing periods. And even decisions that had been presaged by earlier cases, such as *Wards Cove* and *Patterson*, were resolved in opinions that added sometimes baroque refinements to the law. Surely, no one could have predicted that §1981's application to racial discrimination in private contracts would be ringingly reaffirmed in *Patterson* by an opinion which also held that that statute forbade only discrimination in the formation of contracts, not in their performance.

Perhaps as surprising was the failure of the decisions to fit into a coherent pattern. While the bulk of the Supreme Court's decisions clearly cut back on plaintiff's procedural or substantive rights, Hopkins v. Price Waterhouse was widely heralded as a liability-expanding decision insofar as it shifted the burden of persuasion to defendant in certain situations.

Nor was the rapid pace of change confined to the Supreme Court. The circuits were busy developing and refining important aspects of employment discrimination law, and Congress, in addition to enacting some relatively minor changes, was working on the first major initiative in federal discrimination legislation in a number of years, a bill that would broadly prohibit employment and other discrimination against handicapped persons. As this is written, that effort seems likely to culminate in the passage of such legislation. There is also pending legislation that would reverse many of the Supreme Court's 1989 decisions, although the prospects for enactment of such legislation are less certain.

The time frames governing publication of this Supplement have limited the extent to which the changes during this year could be analyzed. Although the bulk of the manuscript was prepared by March 15, 1990, we have endeavored to incorporate later developments to the extent the publication process permitted.

Charles A. Sullivan
Michael J. Zimmer
Richard F. Richards

July 1990

CASES AND MATERIALS ON EMPLOYMENT DISCRIMINATION

1990 Supplement

PART I

THE CONCEPT OF DISCRIMINATION

Chapter 1

Legal Approaches to the Employment Relation

A. THE GENERAL OUTLINE OF EMPLOYMENT LAW

1. The Reassessment of Contract Law

Page 14. Add at end of paragraph under "Oral Contracts":

E.g., Foley v. Interactive Data Corp., 47 Cal. 3d 654, 254 Cal. Rptr. 211, 765 P.2d 373 (1988).

Page 16. Add at end of first paragraph under "Good Faith":

See Foley v. Interactive Data Corp., 47 Cal. 3d 654, 254 Cal. Rptr. 211, 765 P.2d 373 (1988).

2. Reassessment of Tort Law

Page 22. Add new text before last paragraph:

In Foley v. Interactive Data Corp., 47 Cal. 3d 654, 254 Cal. Rptr. 211, 765 P.2d 373 (1988), the California Supreme Court articulated a test for determining the scope of the public policy exception to the at-will doctrine. Plaintiff, citing the duty of an employee to report relevant business information to his employer, claimed a violation of public policy after his discharge for telling management that his supervisor was under federal investigation for embezzlement from a prior employer. The Court found plaintiff's claim outside the protection of public policy because any duty to report ran to his employer, not to the public. Under this approach, the employer can discharge an employee for failing to provide relevant business information and can discharge him because he did provide that information. That may not seem fair, but it is the essence of the at-will doctrine. In justifying its result, the court wrote:

> The absence of a distinctly "public" interest in this case is apparent when we consider that if an employer and employee were *expressly* to agree that the employee has no obligation to, and should not, inform the employer of any adverse information the employee learns about a fellow employee's background, nothing in the state's public policy would render such an agreement void. By contrast, in the previous cases asserting a discharge in violation of public policy, the public interest at stake was invariably one which could not properly be circumvented by agreement of the parties. For example, . . . a contract provision purporting to obligate the employee to comply with an order of the employer directing the employee to violate the antitrust laws would clearly have been void as against public policy, and . . . a contract provision which purported to obligate the employee to commit perjury at the employer's behest would just as obviously have been invalid. Because here the employer and employee could have agreed that the employee had no duty to disclose such information, it cannot be said that an employer, in discharging an employee on this basis, violates a fundamental duty imposed on all employers for the protection of the public interest.

765 P.2d at 380 n.12.

B. THE POLICY BASES FOR ANTIDISCRIMINATION LAW

Page 32. Add at end of first full paragraph:

Judge Posner returned to the question in Posner, An Economic Analysis of Sex Discrimination Law, 56 U. Chi. L. Rev. 1311 (1989). Professor Donahue responded with a very different economic slant. Donahue, Prohibiting Sex Discrimination in the Work Place: An Economic Perspective. 56 U. Chi. L. Rev. 1337 (1989).

Chapter 2

The Definition of Disparate Treatment Discrimination Under Title VII

B. INDIVIDUAL DISPARATE TREATMENT

1. *"Direct" Evidence of Discriminatory Intent*

Page 43. Add at end of Note 1:

In one case, Judge Posner colorfully described the interaction of the at-will rule with the antidiscrimination statutes:

> The employee doesn't get to write his own job description. An employer can set whatever performance standards he wants, provided they are not a mask for discrimination on forbidden grounds such as race or age. He can set unrealistic standards and fire an employee for not being able to meet them; he can (as perhaps happened here) try to force a square peg into a round hole — and throw away the peg when it doesn't fit. He can be as arbitrary as

he wants — he just cannot treat an older employee more harshly than a younger one.

Palucki v. Sears, Roebuck & Co., 879 F.2d 1568, 1571 (7th Cir. 1989).

Page 46. Add at end of Note 6:

Stereotyping is not confined to low level or uneducated people. In a recent case, a professor was awarded tenure, in large part because of the statements of the President of one of the nation's best-known educational institutions. In Brown v. Trustees of Boston University, 891 F.2d 337 (1st Cir. 1989), the President of Boston University, John Silber, was quoted by a witness as saying: "I don't see what a good woman in your department is worried about. The place is a damned matriarchy." At the time, the department in question had a female chairman, but a total of only seven women out of 26 tenured faculty. With respect to another woman candidate who inquired about her prospects for tenure, Silber was quoted as saying that he had never worried about job security "and your husband is a parachute, so why are you worried[?]."

Page 47. Add at end of carryover Note 7:

At the Supreme Court, in *Price Waterhouse v. Hopkins*, 109 S. Ct. 1775 (1989), reproduced below at page 9, the justices divided. Essentially, six justices agreed that a plaintiff established a prima facie case by showing that race or gender was a substantial factor in the employer's decision, although four justices would also approve a less demanding standard. Further, evidence of stereotypical thinking as applied to the plaintiff's application for promotion sufficed to carry this burden. At that point, the six agreed, the employer may nevertheless escape liability if it can prove by a preponderance of the evidence that the same decision would have been made if it had not taken plaintiff's gender or race into account.

Page 48. Add to end of Note 11:

The Supreme Court has decided that a university enjoys no special privilege, grounded in either common law or in academic freedom protected by the First Amendment, against disclosure of faculty peer review materials to EEOC in course of investigation into tenure decisions. University of Pennsylvania v. Equal Employment Opportunity Commission, 110 S. Ct. 577 (1990).

2. Disparate Treatment Discrimination under Title VII

Page 48. Add a new Note 13:

13. In Gray v. University of Arkansas at Fayetteville, 883 F.2d 1394 (8th Cir. 1989), plaintiff, who had been dismissed as academic coordinator for the Razorbacks, presented tape recordings in which the Associate Academic Director, Dr. Farrell, told her that the football coach wanted a man in her position. Farrell explained, "He wanted somebody to go up there [the athletic dormitory] and jack 'em [the players] out of bed, and that's all he said." Id. at 1399. Tape recordings would seem a very effective way to prove admissions of discriminatory intent, but the majority in *Gray* was critical of plaintiff's surreptitious taping. Judge McMillan, in dissent, believed that the district court erroneously discounted the recordings because he disapproved of secret taping. The dissent noted that such evidence was admissible under the Federal Rules of Evidence, R. 1101-1104, and that taping was "a practical response to the exigencies of the situation" in which plaintiff found herself. "Gray did nothing illegal or immoral." Id. at 1405.

3. Causation

Page 68. Move Blalock v. Metal Trades, Inc. to page 417 and add:

PRICE WATERHOUSE v. HOPKINS
109 S. Ct. 1775 (1989)

Justice BRENNAN announced the judgment of the Court and delivered an opinion, in which Justice MARSHALL, Justice BLACKMUN, and Justice STEVENS join. . . .

I

At Price Waterhouse, a nationwide professional accounting partnership, a senior manager becomes a candidate for partnership when the partners in her local office submit her name as a candidate. All of the other partners in the firm are then invited to submit written comments on each candidate — either on a "long" or a "short" form, depending on the partner's degree of exposure to the candidate. Not every partner in the firm submits comments on every candidate. After reviewing the comments and interviewing the partners who submitted them, the firm's Admissions Committee makes a recommendation to the Policy Board. This recommendation will be either that the firm accept the candidate for partnership, put her application on "hold," or deny her the promotion outright. The Policy Board then decides whether to submit the candidate's name to the entire partnership for a vote, to "hold" her candidacy, or to reject her. The recommendation of the Admissions Committee, and the decision of the Policy Board, are not controlled by fixed guidelines: a certain number of positive comments from partners will not guarantee a candidate's admission to the partnership, nor will a specific quantity of negative comments necessarily defeat her application. Price Waterhouse places no limit on the number of persons whom it will admit to the partnership in any given year.

Ann Hopkins had worked at Price Waterhouse's Office of Government Services in Washington, D.C., for five years when the partners in that office proposed her as a candidate for partnership. Of the 662 partners at the firm at that time, 7 were women. Of the 88 persons proposed for partnership that year, only 1—Hopkins—was a woman. Forty-seven of these candidates were admitted to the partnership, 21 were rejected, and 20—including Hopkins—were "held" for reconsideration the following year.[1] Thirteen of the 32 partners who had submitted comments on Hopkins supported her bid for partnership. Three partners recommended that her candidacy be placed on hold, eight stated that they did not have an informed opinion about her, and eight recommended that she be denied partnership.

In a jointly prepared statement supporting her candidacy, the partners in Hopkins' office showcased her successful 2-year effort to secure a $25 million contract with the Department of State, labeling it "an outstanding performance" and one that Hopkins carried out "virtually at the partner level." Despite Price Waterhouse's attempt at trial to minimize her contribution to this project, Judge Gesell specifically found that Hopkins had "played a key role in Price Waterhouse's successful effort to win a multi-million dollar contract with the Department of State." Indeed, he went on, "[n]one of the other partnership candidates at Price Waterhouse that year had a comparable record in terms of successfully securing major contracts for the partnership."

The partners in Hopkins' office praised her character as well as her accomplishments, describing her in their joint statement as "an outstanding professional" who had a "deft touch," a "strong character, independence and integrity." Clients appear to have agreed with these assessments. At trial, one official from the State Department described her as "extremely competent, intelligent," "strong and forthright, very productive, energetic and creative." Another high-ranking official praised Hopkins' decisiveness, broadmindedness, and "intellectual clarity"; she was, in his words, "a stimu-

---

1. Before the time for reconsideration came, two of the partners in Hopkins' office withdrew their support for her, and the office informed her that she would not be reconsidered for partnership. Hopkins then resigned. Price Waterhouse does not challenge the Court of Appeals' conclusion that the refusal to repropose her for partnership amounted to a constructive discharge. . . . We are concerned today only with Price Waterhouse's decision to place Hopkins' candidacy on hold. Decisions pertaining to advancement to partnership are, of course, subject to challenge under Title VII. Hishon v. King & Spalding, 467 U.S. 69 (1984).

lating conversationalist." Evaluations such as these led Judge Gesell to conclude that Hopkins "had no difficulty dealing with clients and her clients appear to have been very pleased with her work" and that she "was generally viewed as a highly competent project leader who worked long hours, pushed vigorously to meet deadlines and demanded much from the multidisciplinary staffs with which she worked."

On too many occasions, however, Hopkins' aggressiveness apparently spilled over into abrasiveness. Staff members seem to have borne the brunt of Hopkins' brusqueness. Long before her bid for partnership, partners evaluating her work had counseled her to improve her relations with staff members. Although later evaluations indicate an improvement, Hopkins' perceived shortcomings in this important area eventually doomed her bid for partnership. Virtually all of the partners' negative remarks about Hopkins—even those of partners supporting her—had to do with her "interpersonal skills." Both "[s]upporters and opponents of her candidacy," stressed Judge Gesell, "indicated that she was sometimes overly aggressive, unduly harsh, difficult to work with and impatient with staff."

There were clear signs, though, that some of the partners reacted negatively to Hopkins' personality because she was a woman. One partner described her as "macho"; another suggested that she "overcompensated for being a woman"; a third advised her to take "a course at charm school". Several partners criticized her use of profanity; in response, one partner suggested that those partners objected to her swearing only "because it[']s a lady using foul language." Another supporter explained that Hopkins "ha[d] matured from a tough-talking somewhat masculine hard-nosed mgr to an authoritative, formidable, but much more appealing lady ptr candidate." But it was the man who, as Judge Gesell found, bore responsibility for explaining to Hopkins the reasons for the Policy Board's decision to place her candidacy on hold who delivered the coup de grace: in order to improve her chances for partnership, Thomas Beyer advised, Hopkins should "walk more femininely, talk more femininely, dress more femininely, wear make-up, have her hair styled, and wear jewelry."

Dr. Susan Fiske, a social psychologist and Associate Professor of Psychology at Carnegie-Mellon University, testified at trial that the partnership selection process at Price Waterhouse was likely influenced by sex stereotyping. Her testimony focused not only on the overtly sex-based comments of partners but also on gender-neutral remarks, made by partners who knew Hopkins only slightly, that were intensely critical of her. One partner, for example, baldly stated that Hopkins was "universally disliked" by staff, and another described her as "consistently annoying and irritating"; yet these were people who had had very little contact with Hopkins. According to Fiske, Hopkins' uniqueness (as the only woman in the pool of candidates) and the subjectivity of the evaluations made it likely that sharply critical remarks such as these were the product of sex stereotyping—although Fiske admitted that she could not say with certainty whether any particular comment was the result of stereotyping. Fiske based her opinion on a review of the submitted comments, explaining that it was commonly accepted practice for social psychologists to reach this kind of conclusion without having met any of the people involved in the decisionmaking process.

In previous years, other female candidates for partnership also had been evaluated in sex-based terms. As a general matter, Judge Gesell concluded, "[c]andidates were viewed favorably if partners believed they maintained their femin[in]ity while becoming effective professional managers"; in this environment, "[t]o be identified as a 'women's lib[b]er' was regarded as [a] negative comment." In fact, the judge found that in previous years "[o]ne partner repeatedly commented that he could not consider any woman seriously as a partnership candidate and believed that women were not even capable of functioning as senior managers—yet the firm took no action to discourage his comments and recorded his vote in the overall summary of the evaluations."

Judge Gesell found that Price Waterhouse legitimately emphasized interpersonal skills in its partnership decisions, and also found that the firm had not fabricated its complaints about Hopkins' interpersonal skills as a pretext for discrimination. Moreover, he concluded, the firm did not give decisive emphasis to such traits only because Hopkins was a woman; although there were male candidates who lacked these skills but who were admitted to partnership, the judge found that these candidates possessed other, positive traits that Hopkins lacked.

The judge went on to decide, however, that some of the partners' remarks about Hopkins stemmed from an impermissibly cabined view of the proper behavior of women, and that Price Waterhouse had done nothing to disavow reliance on such comments. He held that Price Waterhouse had unlawfully discriminated against Hopkins on the basis of sex by consciously giving credence and effect to partners' comments that resulted from sex stereotyping. Noting that Price Waterhouse could avoid equitable relief by proving by clear and convincing evidence that it would have placed Hopkins' candidacy on hold even absent this discrimination, the judge decided that the firm had not carried this heavy burden.

The Court of Appeals affirmed the District Court's ultimate conclusion, but departed from its analysis in one particular: it held that even if a plaintiff proves that discrimination played a role in an employment decision, the defendant will not be found liable if it proves, by clear and convincing evidence, that it would have made the same decision in the absence of discrimination. Under this approach, an employer is not deemed to have violated Title VII if it proves that it would have made the same decision in the absence of an impermissible motive, whereas under the District Court's approach, the employer's proof in that respect only avoids equitable relief.

We decide today that the Court of Appeals had the better approach, but that both courts erred in requiring the employer to make its proof by clear and convincing evidence.

II

The specification of the standard of causation under Title VII is a decision about the kind of conduct that violates that statute. According to Price Waterhouse, an employer violates Title VII only if it gives decisive consideration to an employee's gender, race, national origin, or religion in making a decision that affects that employee. On Price Waterhouse's theory, even if a plaintiff shows that her gender played a part in an employment decision, it is still her burden to show that the decision would have been different if the employer had not discriminated. In Hopkins' view, on the other hand, an employer violates the statute whenever it allows one of these attributes to play any part in an employment decision. Once a plaintiff shows that this occurred, according to Hopkins, the employer's proof that it would have made the same decision in the absence of discrimination can serve to limit equitable relief but not to avoid a finding of liability. We conclude that, as often happens, the truth lies somewhere in-between.

A

In passing Title VII, Congress made the simple but momentous announcement that sex, race, religion, and national origin are not relevant to the selection, evaluation, or compensation of employees.[3] Yet, the statute does not purport to limit the other qualities and characteristics that employers may take into account in making employment decisions. The converse, therefore, of "for cause" legislation,[4] Title VII eliminates certain bases for distinguishing among employees while otherwise preserving employers' freedom of choice. This balance between employee rights and employer prerogatives turns out to be decisive in the case before us.

Congress' intent to forbid employers to take gender into account in mak-

---

3. We disregard, for purposes of this discussion, the special context of affirmative action.
4. Congress specifically declined to require that an employment decision have been "for cause" in order to escape an affirmative penalty (such as reinstatement or backpay) from a court. As introduced in the House, the bill that became Title VII forbade such affirmative relief if an "individual was . . . refused employment or advancement, or was suspended or discharged *for cause.*" H.R. 7152, 88th Cong., 1st Sess. 77 (1963) (emphasis added). The phrase "for cause" eventually was deleted in favor of the phrase "for any reason other than" one of the enumerated characteristics. See 110 Cong. Rec. 2567-2571 (1964). Representative Celler explained that this substitution "specif[ied] cause"; in his view, a court "cannot find any violation of the act which is based on facts other . . . than discrimination on the grounds of race, color, religion, or national origin." Id., at 2567.

ing employment decisions appears on the face of the statute. In now-familiar language, the statute forbids an employer to "fail or refuse to hire or to discharge any individual, or otherwise to discriminate with respect to his compensation, terms, conditions, or privileges of employment," or to "limit, segregate, or classify his employees or applicants for employment in any way which would deprive or tend to deprive any individual of employment opportunities or otherwise adversely affect his status as an employee, *because of* such individual's . . . sex." 42 U.S.C. §§2000e-2(a)(1), (2) (emphasis added).[5] We take these words to mean that gender must be irrelevant to employment decisions. To construe the words "because of" as colloquial shorthand for "but-for causation," as does Price Waterhouse, is to misunderstand them.

But-for causation is a hypothetical construct. In determining whether a particular factor was a but-for cause of a given event, we begin by assuming that that factor was present at the time of the event, and then ask whether, even if that factor had been absent, the event nevertheless would have transpired in the same way. The present, active tense of the operative verbs of §703(a)(1) ("to fail or refuse"), in contrast, turns our attention to the actual moment of the event in question, the adverse employment decision. The critical inquiry, the one commanded by the words of §703(a)(1), is whether gender was a factor in the employment decision *at the moment it was made.* Moreover, since we know that the words "because of" do not mean "solely because of,"[7] we also know that Title VII meant to condemn even those decisions based on a mixture of legitimate and illegitimate considerations. When, therefore, an employer considers both gender and legitimate factors at the time of making a decision, that decision was "because of" sex and the other, legitimate considerations—even if we may say later, in the context of litigation, that the decision would have been the same if gender had not been taken into account.

To attribute this meaning to the words "because of" does not, as the dissent asserts divest them of causal significance. A simple example illustrates the point. Suppose two physical forces act upon and move an object, and suppose that either force acting alone would have moved the object. As the dissent would have it, neither physical force was a "cause" of the motion unless we can show that but for one or both of them, the object would not have moved; to use the dissent's terminology, both forces were simply "in the air" unless we can identify at least one of them as a but-for cause of the

---

5. In this Court, Hopkins for the first time argues that Price Waterhouse violated §703(a)(2) when it subjected her to a biased decisionmaking process that "tended to deprive" a woman of partnership on the basis of her sex. Since Hopkins did not make this argument below, we do not address it.

7. Congress specifically rejected an amendment that would have placed the word "solely" in front of the words "because of." 110 Cong. Rec. 2728, 13837 (1964).

object's movement. Events that are causally overdetermined, in other words, may not have any "cause" at all. This cannot be so.

We need not leave our commonsense at the doorstep when we interpret a statute. It is difficult for us to imagine that, in the simple words "because of," Congress meant to obligate a plaintiff to identify the precise causal role played by legitimate and illegitimate motivations in the employment decision she challenges. We conclude, instead, that Congress meant to obligate her to prove that the employer relied upon sex-based considerations in coming to its decision.

Our interpretation of the words "because of" also is supported by the fact that Title VII does identify one circumstance in which an employer may take gender into account in making an employment decision, namely, when gender is a "bona fide occupational qualification [(BFOQ)] reasonably necessary to the normal operation of th[e] particular business or enterprise." 42 U.S.C. §2000e-2(e). The only plausible inference to draw from this provision is that, in all other circumstances, a person's gender may not be considered in making decisions that affect her. Indeed, Title VII even forbids employers to make gender an indirect stumbling block to employment opportunities. An employer may not, we have held, condition employment opportunities on the satisfaction of facially neutral tests or qualifications that have a disproportionate, adverse impact on members of protected groups when those tests or qualifications are not required for performance of the job. See Watson v. Fort Worth Bank & Trust, 108 S. Ct. 2777 (1988); Griggs v. Duke Power Co.

To say that an employer may not take gender into account is not, however, the end of the matter, for that describes only one aspect of Title VII. The other important aspect of the statute is its preservation of an employer's remaining freedom of choice. We conclude that the preservation of this freedom means that an employer shall not be liable if it can prove that, even if it had not taken gender into account, it would have come to the same decision regarding a particular person. The statute's maintenance of employer prerogatives is evident from the statute itself and from its history, both in Congress and in this Court.

To begin with, the existence of the BFOQ exception shows Congress' unwillingness to require employers to change the very nature of their operations in response to the statute. And our emphasis on "business necessity" in disparate-impact cases, see *Watson* and *Griggs*, and on "legitimate, nondiscriminatory reason[s]" in disparate-treatment cases, see McDonnell Douglas Corp. v. Green; Texas Dept. of Community Affairs v. Burdine, results from our awareness of Title VII's balance between employee rights and employer prerogatives. In *McDonnell Douglas*, we described as follows Title VII's goal to eradicate discrimination while preserving workplace efficiency: "The broad, overriding interest, shared by employer, employee, and consumer, is efficient and trustworthy workmanship assured through fair and racially neutral employment and personnel decisions. In the implementation of such decisions, it is abundantly clear that Title VII tolerates no racial discrimination, subtle or otherwise."

When an employer ignored the attributes enumerated in the statute, Congress hoped, it naturally would focus on the qualifications of the applicant or employee. The intent to drive employers to focus on qualifications rather than on race, religion, sex, or national origin is the theme of a good deal of the statute's legislative history. . . . An interpretive memorandum entered into the Congressional Record by Senators Case and Clark, comanagers of the bill in the Senate, is representative of this general theme. According to their memorandum, Title VII "expressly protects the employer's right to insist that any prospective applicant, Negro or white, must meet the applicable job qualifications. Indeed, the very purpose of Title VII is to promote hiring on the basis of job qualifications, rather than on the basis of race or color."[9] 110 Cong. Rec. 7247 (1964). . . .

The central point is this: while an employer may not take gender into account in making an employment decision (except in those very narrow circumstances in which gender is a BFOQ), it is free to decide against a woman for other reasons. We think these principles require that, once a plaintiff in a Title VII case shows that gender played a motivating part in an employment decision, the defendant may avoid a finding of liability[10] only by

---

9. Many of the legislators' statements . . . focused specifically on race rather than on gender or religion or national origin. We do not, however, limit their statements to the context of race, but instead we take them as general statements on the meaning of Title VII. The somewhat bizarre path by which "sex" came to be included as a forbidden criterion for employment—it was included in an attempt to defeat the bill, see C. & B. Whalen, The Longest Debate: A Legislative History of the 1964 Civil Rights Act 115-117 (1985)—does not persuade us that the legislators' statements pertaining to race are irrelevant to cases alleging gender discrimination. The amendment that added "sex" as one of the forbidden criteria for employment was passed, of course, and the statute on its face treats each of the enumerated categories exactly the same.

By the same token, our specific references to gender throughout this opinion, and the principles we announce, apply with equal force to discrimination based on race, religion, or national origin.

10. Hopkins argues that once she made this showing, she was entitled to a finding that Price Waterhouse had discriminated against her on the basis of sex; as a consequence, she says, the partnership's proof could only limit the relief she received. She relies on Title VII's §706(g), which permits a court to award affirmative relief when it finds that an employer "has intentionally engaged in or is intentionally engaging in an unlawful employment practice," and yet forbids a court to order reinstatement of, or backpay to, "an individual . . . if such individual was refused . . . employment or advancement or was suspended or discharged *for any reason other than* discrimination on account of race, color, religion, sex, or national origin." 42 U.S.C. §2000e-5(g) (emphasis added). We do not take this provision to mean that a court inevitably can find a violation of the statute without having considered whether the employment decision would have been the same absent the impermissible motive. That would be to interpret §706(g)—a provision defining remedies—to influence the substantive commands of the statute. We think that this provision merely limits courts' authority to award affirmative relief in those circumstances in which a violation of the statute is not dependent upon the effect

proving that it would have made the same decision even if it had not allowed gender to play such a role. This balance of burdens is the direct result of Title VII's balance of rights.

Our holding casts no shadow on *Burdine*, in which we decided that, even after a plaintiff has made out a prima facie case of discrimination under Title VII, the burden of persuasion does not shift to the employer to show that its stated legitimate reason for the employment decision was the true reason. We stress, first, that neither court below shifted the burden of persuasion to Price Waterhouse on this question, and in fact, the District Court found that Hopkins had not shown that the firm's stated reason for its decision was pretextual. Moreover, since we hold that the plaintiff retains the burden of persuasion on the issue whether gender played a part in the employment decision, the situation before us is not the one of "shifting burdens" that we addressed in *Burdine*. Instead, the employer's burden is most appropriately deemed an affirmative defense: the plaintiff must persuade the factfinder on one point, and then the employer, if it wishes to prevail, must persuade it on another. See NLRB v. Transportation Management Corp., 462 U.S. 393 (1983).[11]

Price Waterhouse's claim that the employer does not bear any burden of proof (if it bears one at all) until the plaintiff has shown "substantial evidence that Price Waterhouse's explanation for failing to promote Hopkins was not the 'true reason' for its action" merely restates its argument that the plaintiff in a mixed-motives case must squeeze her proof into *Burdine*'s framework. Where a decision was the product of a mixture of legitimate and illegitimate motives, however, it simply makes no sense to ask whether the legitimate reason was "*the* 'true reason' " for the decision — which is the question asked

---

of the employer's discriminatory practices on a particular employee, as in pattern-or-practice suits and class actions. "The crucial difference between an individual's claim of discrimination and a class action alleging a general pattern or practice of discrimination is manifest. The inquiry regarding an individual's claim is the reason for a particular employment decision, while 'at the liability stage of a pattern-or-practice trial the focus often will not be on individual hiring decisions, but on a pattern of discriminatory decisionmaking.' " Cooper v. Federal Reserve Bank of Richmond, 467 U.S. 867, 876(1984). . . .

11. Given that both the plaintiff and defendant bear a burden of proof in cases such as this one, it is surprising that the dissent insists that our approach requires the employer to bear "the ultimate burden of proof." It is, moreover, perfectly consistent to say both that gender was a factor in a particular decision when it was made and that, when the situation is viewed hypothetically and after the fact, the same decision would have been made even in the absence of discrimination. Thus, we do not see the "internal inconsistency" in our opinion that the dissent perceives. Finally, where liability is imposed because an employer is unable to prove that it would have made the same decision even if it had not discriminated, there is not an imposition of liability "where sex made no difference to the outcome." In our adversary system, where a party has the burden of proving a particular assertion and where that party is unable to meet its burden, we assume that that assertion is inaccurate. Thus, where an employer is unable to prove its claim that it would have made the same decision in the absence of discrimination, we are entitled to conclude that gender did make a difference to the outcome.

by *Burdine*. See *Transportation Management*.[12] Oblivious to this last point, the dissent would insist that *Burdine*'s framework perform work that it was never intended to perform. It would require a plaintiff who challenges an adverse employment decision in which both legitimate and illegitimate considerations played a part to pretend that the decision, in fact, stemmed from a single source—for the premise of *Burdine* is that either a legitimate or an illegitimate set of considerations led to the challenged decision. To say that *Burdine*'s evidentiary scheme will not help us decide a case admittedly involving both kinds of considerations is not to cast aspersions on the utility of that scheme in the circumstances for which it was designed.

B

In deciding as we do today, we do not traverse new ground. We have in the past confronted Title VII cases in which an employer has used an illegitimate criterion to distinguish among employees, and have held that it is the employer's burden to justify decisions resulting from that practice. When an employer has asserted that gender is a bona fide occupational qualification within the meaning of §703(e), for example, we have assumed that it is the employer who must show why it must use gender as a criterion in employment. See Dothard v. Rawlinson. In a related context, although the Equal Pay Act expressly permits employers to pay different wages to women where disparate pay is the result of a "factor other than sex," see 29 U.S.C. §206(d)(1), we have decided that it is the employer, not the employee, who must prove that the actual disparity is not sex-linked. See Corning Glass Works v. Brennan, 417 U.S. 188, 196 (1974). . . .

We have reached a similar conclusion in other contexts where the law announces that a certain characteristic is irrelevant to the allocation of burdens and benefits. In Mt. Healthy City School Dist. Board of Education v. Doyle, 429 U.S. 274 (1977), the plaintiff claimed that he had been dis-

---

12. Nothing in this opinion should be taken to suggest that a case must be correctly labeled as either a "pretext" case or a "mixed motives" case from the beginning in the District Court; indeed, we expect that plaintiffs often will allege, in the alternative, that their cases are both. Discovery often will be necessary before the plaintiff can know whether both legitimate and illegitimate considerations played a part in the decision against her. At some point in the proceedings, of course, the District Court must decide whether a particular case involves mixed motives. If the plaintiff fails to satisfy the factfinder that it is more likely than not that a forbidden characteristic played a part in the employment decision, then she may prevail only if she proves, following *Burdine*, that the employer's stated reason for its decision is pretextual. The dissent need not worry that this evidentiary scheme, if used during a jury trial, will be so impossibly confused and complex as it imagines. Juries long have decided cases in which defendants raise affirmative defenses. The dissent fails, moreover, to explain why the evidentiary scheme that we endorsed over ten years ago in *Mt. Healthy* has not proved unworkable in that context but would be hopelessly complicated in a case brought under federal antidiscrimination statutes.

2. Disparate Treatment Discrimination under Title VII   Page 68

charged as a public school teacher for exercising his free-speech rights under the First Amendment. Because we did not wish to "place an employee in a better position as a result of the exercise of constitutionally protected conduct than he would have occupied had he done nothing," we concluded that such an employee "ought not to be able, by engaging in such conduct, to prevent his employer from assessing his performance record and reaching a decision not to rehire on the basis of that record." We therefore held that once the plaintiff had shown that his constitutionally protected speech was a "substantial" or "motivating factor" in the adverse treatment of him by his employer, the employer was obligated to prove "by a preponderance of the evidence that it would have reached the same decision as to [the plaintiff] even in the absence of the protected conduct." A court that finds for a plaintiff under this standard has effectively concluded that an illegitimate motive was a "but-for" cause of the employment decision. See Givhan v. Western Line Consolidated School District, 439 U.S. 410, 417 (1979). See also Arlington Heights v. Metropolitan Housing Corp., 429 U.S. 252, 270-271, n.21 (1977) (applying *Mt. Healthy* standard where plaintiff alleged that unconstitutional motive had contributed to enactment of legislation); Hunter v. Underwood, 471 U.S. 222, 228 (1985) (same).

In *Transportation Management,* we upheld the NLRB's interpretation of §10(c) of the National Labor Relations Act, which forbids a court to order affirmative relief for discriminatory conduct against a union member "if such individual was suspended or discharged for cause." 29 U.S.C. §160(c). The Board had decided that this provision meant that once an employee had shown that his suspension or discharge was based in part on hostility to unions, it was up to the employer to prove by a preponderance of the evidence that it would have made the same decision in the absence of this impermissible motive. In such a situation, we emphasized, "[t]he employer is a wrongdoer; he has acted out of a motive that is declared illegitimate by the statute. It is fair that he bear the risk that the influence of legal and illegal motives cannot be separated, because he knowingly created the risk and because the risk was created not by innocent activity but by his own wrongdoing."

We have, in short, been here before. Each time, we have concluded that the plaintiff who shows that an impermissible motive played a motivating part in an adverse employment decision has thereby placed upon the defendant the burden to show that it would have made the same decision in the absence of the unlawful motive. Our decision today treads this well-worn path.

C

In saying that gender played a motivating part in an employment decision, we mean that, if we asked the employer at the moment of the decision what its reasons were and if we received a truthful response, one of those reasons would be that the applicant or employee was a woman.[13] In the specific context of sex stereotyping, an employer who acts on the basis of a belief that a woman cannot be aggressive, or that she must not be, has acted on the basis of gender.

Although the parties do not overtly dispute this last proposition, the placement by Price Waterhouse of "sex stereotyping" in quotation marks throughout its brief seems to us an insinuation either that such stereotyping was not present in this case or that it lacks legal relevance. We reject both possibilities. As to the existence of sex stereotyping in this case, we are not inclined to quarrel with the District Court's conclusion that a number of the partners' comments showed sex stereotyping at work. As for the legal relevance of sex stereotyping, we are beyond the day when an employer could evaluate employees by assuming or insisting that they matched the stereotype associated with their group, for " '[i]n forbidding employers to discriminate against individuals because of their sex, Congress intended to strike at the entire spectrum of disparate treatment of men and women resulting from sex stereotypes.' " Los Angeles Dept. of Water & Power v. Manhart, 435 U.S. 702, 707, n.13 (1978). An employer who objects to aggressiveness in women but whose positions require this trait places women in an intolerable and impermissible Catch-22: out of a job if they behave aggressively and out of a job if they don't. Title VII lifts women out of this bind.

Remarks at work that are based on sex stereotypes do not inevitably prove that gender played a part in a particular employment decision. The plaintiff must show that the employer actually relied on her gender in making its decision. In making this showing, stereotyped remarks can certainly be evidence that gender played a part. In any event, the stereotyping in this case did not simply consist of stray remarks. On the contrary, Hopkins proved that Price Waterhouse invited partners to submit comments; that some of the comments stemmed from sex stereotypes; that an important part of the Policy Board's decision on Hopkins was an assessment of the submitted comments; and that Price Waterhouse in no way disclaimed reliance on the sex-linked evaluations. This is not, as Price Waterhouse suggests, "discrimination in the air"; rather, it is, as Hopkins puts it, "discrimination brought to ground and visited upon" an employee. By focusing on Hopkins' specific proof, however, we do not suggest a limitation on the possible ways of proving that stereotyping played a motivating role in an employment decision, and we refrain from

---

13. After comparing this description of the plaintiff's proof to that offered by the concurring opinion, we do not understand why the concurrence suggests that they are meaningfully different from each other. Nor do we see how the inquiry that we have described is "hypothetical." It seeks to determine the content of the entire set of reasons for a decision, rather than shaving off one reason in an attempt to determine what the decision would have been in the absence of that consideration. The inquiry that we describe thus strikes us as a distinctly nonhypothetical one.

deciding here which specific facts, "standing alone," would or would not establish a plaintiff's case, since such a decision is unnecessary in this case. But see (Justice O'CONNOR, concurring in judgment).

As to the employer's proof, in most cases, the employer should be able to present some objective evidence as to its probable decision in the absence of an impermissible motive.[14] Moreover, proving "that the same decision would have been justified . . . is not the same as proving that the same decision would have been made." *Givhan*. An employer may not, in other words, prevail in a mixed-motives case by offering a legitimate and sufficient reason for its decision if that reason did not motivate it at the time of the decision. Finally, an employer may not meet its burden in such a case by merely showing that at the time of the decision it was motivated only in part by a legitimate reason. The very premise of a mixed-motives case is that a legitimate reason was present, and indeed, in this case, Price Waterhouse already has made this showing by convincing Judge Gesell that Hopkins' interpersonal problems were a legitimate concern. The employer instead must show that its legitimate reason, standing alone, would have induced it to make the same decision.

III

The courts below held that an employer who has allowed a discriminatory impulse to play a motivating part in an employment decision must prove by clear and convincing evidence that it would have made the same decision in the absence of discrimination. We are persuaded that the better rule is that the employer must make this showing by a preponderance of the evidence.

Conventional rules of civil litigation generally apply in Title VII cases, see, e.g., United States Postal Service Bd. of Governors v. Aikens, 460 U.S. 711, 716 (1983) (discrimination not to be "treat[ed] . . . differently from other ultimate questions of fact"), and one of these rules is that parties to civil litigation need only prove their case by a preponderance of the evidence. . . .

Although Price Waterhouse does not concretely tell us how its proof was preponderant even if it was not clear and convincing, this general claim is implicit in its request for the less stringent standard. Since the lower courts required Price Waterhouse to make its proof by clear and convinving evidence, they did not determine whether Price Waterhouse had proved by a preponderance of the evidence that it would have placed Hopkins' candidacy on hold even if it had not permitted sex-linked evaluations to play a part in

---

14. Justice WHITE's suggestion that the employer's own testimony as to the probable decision in the absence of discrimination is due special credence where the court has, contrary to the employer's testimony, found that an illegitimate factor played a part in the decision, is baffling.

the decision-making process. Thus, we shall remand this case so that that determination can be made.

IV

The District Court found that sex stereotyping "was permitted to play a part" in the evaluation of Hopkins as a candidate for partnership. Price Waterhouse disputes both that stereotyping occurred and that it played any part in the decision to place Hopkins' candidacy on hold. In the firm's view, in other words, the District Court's factual conclusions are clearly erroneous. We do not agree.

In finding that some of the partners' comments reflected sex stereotyping, the District Court relied in part on Dr. Fiske's expert testimony. Without directly impugning Dr. Fiske's credentials or qualifications, Price Waterhouse insinuates that a social psychologist is unable to identify sex stereotyping in evaluations without investigating whether those evaluations have a basis in reality. This argument comes too late. At trial, counsel for Price Waterhouse twice assured the court that he did not question Dr. Fiske's expertise and failed to challenge the legitimacy of her discipline. Without contradiction from Price Waterhouse, Fiske testified that she discerned sex stereotyping in the partners' evaluations of Hopkins and she further explained that it was part of her business to identify stereotyping in written documents. We are not inclined to accept petitioner's belated and unsubstantiated characterization of Dr. Fiske's testimony as "gossamer evidence" based only on "intuitive hunches" and of her detection of sex stereotyping as "intuitively divined." Nor are we disposed to adopt the dissent's dismissive attitude toward Dr. Fiske's field of study and toward her own professional integrity.

Indeed, we are tempted to say that Dr. Fiske's expert testimony was merely icing on Hopkins' cake. It takes no special training to discern sex stereotyping in a description of an aggressive female employee as requiring "a course at charm school." Nor, turning to Thomas Beyer's memorable advice to Hopkins, does it require expertise in psychology to know that, if an employee's flawed "interpersonal skills" can be corrected by a soft-hued suit or a new shade of lipstick, perhaps it is the employee's sex and not her interpersonal skills that has drawn the criticism.

Price Waterhouse also charges that Hopkins produced no evidence that sex stereotyping played a role in the decision to place her candidacy on hold. As we have stressed, however, Hopkins showed that the partnership solicited evaluations from all of the firm's partners; that it generally relied very heavily on such evaluations in making its decision; that some of the partners' comments were the product of stereotyping; and that the firm in no way disclaimed reliance on those particular comments, either in Hopkins' case or in the past. Certainly a plausible—and, one might say, inevitable—conclusion to draw from this set of circumstances is that the Policy Board in making its decision did in fact take into account all of the partners' comments, including the comments that were motivated by stereotypical notions about women's proper deportment.[16] . . .

Nor is the finding that sex stereotyping played a part in the Policy Board's decision undermined by the fact that many of the suspect comments were made by supporters rather than detractors of Hopkins. A negative comment, even when made in the context of a generally favorable review, nevertheless may influence the decisionmaker to think less highly of the candidate; the Policy Board, in fact, did not simply tally the "yes's" and "no's" regarding a candidate, but carefully reviewed the content of the submitted comments. The additional suggestion that the comments were made by "persons outside the decisionmaking chain"—and therefore could not have harmed Hopkins—simply ignores the critical role that partners' comments played in the Policy Board's partnership decisions.

Price Waterhouse appears to think that we cannot affirm the factual findings of the trial court without deciding that, instead of being overbearing and aggressive and curt, Hopkins is in fact kind and considerate and patient. If this is indeed its impression, petitioner misunderstands the theory on which Hopkins prevailed. The District Judge acknowledged that Hopkins' conduct justified complaints about her behavior as a senior manager. But he also concluded that the reactions of at least some of the partners were reactions to her as a woman manager. Where an evaluation is based on a subjective assessment of a person's strengths and weaknesses, it is simply not true that each evaluator will focus on, or even mention, the same weaknesses. Thus, even if we knew that Hopkins had "personality problems," this would not tell us that the partners who cast their evaluations of Hopkins in sex-based terms would have criticized her as sharply (or criticized her at all) if she had been a man. It is not our job to review the evidence and decide that the negative reactions to Hopkins were based on reality; our perception of Hopkins' character is irrelevant. We sit not to determine whether Ms. Hopkins is nice, but to decide whether the partners reacted negatively to her personality because she is a woman.

V

We hold that when a plaintiff in a Title VII case proves that her gender played a motivating part in an employment decision, the defendant may avoid a finding of liability only by proving by a preponderance of the evi-

---

16. We do not understand the dissenters' dissatisfaction with the District Judge's statements regarding the failure of Price Waterhouse to "sensitize" partners to the dangers of sexism. Made in the context of determining that Price Waterhouse had not disclaimed reliance on sex-based evaluations, and following the judge's description of the firm's history of condoning such evaluations, the judge's remarks seem to us justified.

dence that it would have made the same decision even if it had not taken the plaintiff's gender into account. Because the courts below erred by deciding that the defendant must make this proof by clear and convincing evidence, we reverse the Court of Appeals' judgment against Price Waterhouse on liability and remand the case to that court for further proceedings.

Justice WHITE, concurring in the judgment.

In my view, to determine the proper approach to causation in this case, we need look only to the Court's opinion in Mt. Healthy City School District Bd. of Ed. v. Doyle. . . .

It is not necessary to get into semantic discussions on whether the *Mt. Healthy* approach is "but for" causation in another guise or creates an affirmative defense on the part of the employer to see its clear application to the issues before us in this case. As in *Mt. Healthy*, the District Court found that the employer was motivated by both legitimate and illegitimate factors. And here, as in *Mt. Healthy*, and as the Court now holds, Hopkins was not required to prove that the illegitimate factor was the only, principal, or true reason for the petitioner's action. Rather, as Justice O'Connor states, her burden was to show that the unlawful motive was a substantial factor in the adverse employment action. The District Court, as its opinion was construed by the Court of Appeals, so found, and I agree that the finding was supported by the record. The burden of persuasion then should have shifted to Price Waterhouse to prove "by a preponderance of the evidence that it would have reached the same decision . . . in the absence of" the unlawful motive. *Mt. Healthy*.

I agree with Justice Brennan that applying this approach to causation in Title VII cases is not a departure from and does not require modification of the Court's holdings in Texas Dept. of Community Affairs v. Burdine, and McDonnell Douglas Corp. v. Green. . . . I also disagree with the dissent's assertion that this approach to causation is inconsistent with our statement in *Burdine* that "[t]he ultimate burden of persuading the trier of fact that the defendant intentionally discriminated against the plaintiff remains at all times with the plaintiff."

Because the Court of Appeals required Price Waterhouse to prove by clear and convincing evidence that it would have reached the same employment decision in the absence of the improper motive, rather than merely requiring proof by a preponderance of the evidence as in *Mt. Healthy*, I concur in the judgment reversing this case in part and remanding. With respect to the employer's burden, however, the plurality seems to require, at least in most cases, that the employer submit objective evidence that the same result would have occurred absent the unlawful motivation. In my view, however, there is no special requirement that the employer carry its burden by objective evidence. In a mixed motive case, where the legitimate motive found would

2. Disparate Treatment Discrimination under Title VII

have been ample grounds for the action taken, and the employer credibly testifies that the action would have been taken for the legitimate reasons alone, this should be ample proof. This would even more plainly be the case where the employer denies any illegitimate motive in the first place but the court finds that illegitimate, as well as legitimate, factors motivated the adverse action.*

Justice O'CONNOR, concurring in the judgment.

I agree with the plurality that on the facts presented in this case, the burden of persuasion should shift to the employer to demonstrate by a preponderance of the evidence that it would have reached the same decision concerning Ann Hopkins' candidacy absent consideration of her gender. I further agree that this burden shift is properly part of the liability phase of the litigation. I thus concur in the judgment of the Court. My disagreement stems from the plurality's conclusions concerning the substantive requirement of causation under the statute and its broad statements regarding the applicability of the allocation of the burden of proof applied in this case. The evidentiary rule the Court adopts today should be viewed as a supplement to the careful framework established by our unanimous decisions in McDonnell Douglas Corp. v. Green, and Texas Dept. of Community Affairs v. Burdine, for use in cases such as this one where the employer has created uncertainty as to causation by knowingly giving substantial weight to an impermissible criterion. . . .

I

. . . The legislative history of Title VII bears out what its plain language suggests: a substantive violation of the statute only occurs when consideration of an illegitimate criterion is the "but-for" cause of an adverse employment action. The legislative history makes it clear that Congress was attempting to eradicate discriminatory actions in the employment setting, not mere discriminatory thoughts. Critics of the bill that became Title VII labeled it a "thought control bill," and argued that it created a "punishable crime that does not require an illegal external act as a basis for judgment." 100 Cong. Rec. 7254 (1964). Senator Case, whose views the plurality finds so persuasive elsewhere, responded:

> The man must do or fail to do something in regard to employment. There must be some specific external act, more than a mental act. Only if he does the act because of the grounds stated in the bill would there be any legal consequences.

---

*I agree with the plurality that if the employer carries this burden, there has been no violation of Title VII.

Thus, I disagree with the plurality's dictum that the words "because of" do not mean "but-for" causation; manifestly they do. We should not, and need not, deviate from that policy today. The question for decision in this case is what allocation of the burden of persuasion on the issue of causation best conforms with the intent of Congress and the purposes behind Title VII.

The evidence of congressional intent as to which party should bear the burden of proof on the issue of causation is considerably less clear. No doubt, as a general matter, Congress assumed that the plaintiff in a Title VII action would bear the burden of proof on the elements critical to his or her case. . . . But in the area of tort liability, from whence the dissent's "but-for" standard of causation is derived, the law has long recognized that in certain "civil cases" leaving the burden of persuasion on the plaintiff to prove "but-for" causation would be both unfair and destructive of the deterrent purposes embodied in the concept of duty of care. Thus, in multiple causation cases, where a breach of duty has been established, the common law of torts has long shifted the burden of proof to multiple defendants to prove that their negligent actions were not the "but-for" cause of the plaintiff's injury. See e.g., Summers v. Tice, 33 Cal. 2d 80, 84-87, 199 P.2d 1, 3-4 (1948). The same rule has been applied where the effect of a defendant's tortious conduct combines with a force of unknown or innocent origin to produce the harm to the plaintiff. See Kingston v. Chicago & N.W.R. Co., 191 Wis. 610, 616, 211 N.W. 913, 915 (1927) ("Granting that the union of that fire [caused by defendant's negligence] with another of natural origin, or with another of much greater proportions, is available as a defense, the burden is on the defendant to show that . . . the fire set by him was not the proximate cause of the damage"). See also 2 J. Wigmore, Select Cases on the Law of Torts, §153, p. 865 (1912) ("When two or more persons by their acts are possibly the sole cause of a harm, or when two or more acts of the same person are possibly the sole cause, and the plaintiff has introduced evidence that one of the two persons, or one of the same person's two acts, is culpable, then the defendant has the burden of proving that the other person, or his other act, was the sole cause of the harm").

While requiring that the plaintiff in a tort suit or a Title VII action prove that the defendant's "breach of duty" was the "but-for" cause of an injury does not generally hamper effective enforcement of the policies behind those causes of action, "at other times the [but-for] test demands the impossible. It challenges the imagination of the trier to probe into a purely fanciful and unknowable state of affairs. He is invited to make an estimate concerning facts that concededly never existed. The very uncertainty as to what might have happened opens the door wide for conjecture. But when conjecture is demanded it can be given a direction that is consistent with the policy

2. Disparate Treatment Discrimination under Title VII

considerations that underlie the controversy." Malone, Ruminations on Cause-In-Fact, 9 Stan. L. Rev. 60, 67 (1956).

Like the common law of torts, the statutory employment "tort" created by Title VII has two basic purposes. The first is to deter conduct which has been identified as contrary to public policy and harmful to society as a whole. . . . The second goal of Title VII is "to make persons whole for injuries suffered on account of unlawful employment discrimination."

Both these goals are reflected in the elements of a disparate treatment action. There is no doubt that Congress considered reliance on gender or race in making employment decisions an evil in itself. . . . Reliance on such factors is exactly what the threat of Title VII liability was meant to deter. While the main concern of the statute was with employment opportunity, Congress was certainly not blind to the stigmatic harm which comes from being evaluated by a process which treats one as an inferior by reason of one's race or sex. . . . At the same time, Congress clearly conditioned legal liability on a determination that the consideration of an illegitimate factor caused a tangible employment injury of some kind.

Where an individual disparate treatment plaintiff has shown by a preponderance of the evidence that an illegitimate criterion was a *substantial* factor in an adverse employment decision, the deterrent purpose of the statute has clearly been triggered. More importantly, as an evidentiary matter, a reasonable factfinder could conclude that absent further explanation, the employer's discriminatory motivation "caused" the employment decision. The employer has not yet been shown to be a violator, but neither is it entitled to the same presumption of good faith concerning its employment decisions which is accorded employers facing only circumstantial evidence of discrimination. Both the policies behind the statute, and the evidentiary principles developed in the analogous area of causation in the law of torts, suggest that at this point the employer may be required to convince the factfinder that, despite the smoke, there is no fire.

We have given recognition to these principles in our cases which have discussed the "remedial phase" of class action disparate treatment cases. . . . Teamsters v. United States. See also Franks v. Bowman Transportation Co.

The individual members of a class action treatment case stand in much the same position as Ann Hopkins here. There has been a strong showing that the employer has done exactly what Title VII forbids, but the connection between the employer's illegitimate motivation and any injury to the individual plaintiff is unclear. At this point calling upon the employer to show that despite consideration of illegitimate factors the individual plaintiff would not have been hired or promoted in any event hardly seems "unfair" or contrary to the substantive command of the statute. In fact, an individual plaintiff who has shown that an illegitimate factor played a substantial role in the decision in her case has proved more than the class member in a *Teamsters* type action. The latter receives the benefit of a burden shift to the defendant based on the *likelihood* that an illegitimate criterion was a factor in the individual employment decision. . . .

Moreover, placing the burden on the defendant in this case to prove that the same decision would have been justified by legitimate reasons is consistent with our interpretation of the constitutional guarantee of equal protection. . . .

If the strong presumption of regularity and rationality of legislative decisionmaking must give way in the face of evidence that race has played a significant part in a legislative decision [in the equal protection cases], I simply cannot believe that Congress intended Title VII to accord more deference to a private employer in the face of evidence that its decisional process has been substantially infected by discrimination. Indeed, where a public employee brings a "disparate treatment" claim under 42 U.S.C. §1983 and the Equal Protection Clause the employee is entitled to the favorable evidentiary framework of [the equal protection cases]. See, e.g., Hervey v. City of Little Rock, 787 F.2d 1223, 1233-1234 (CA8 1986). Under the dissent's reading of Title VII, Congress' extension of the coverage of the statute to public employers in 1972 has placed these employees under a less favorable evidentiary regime. . . .

II

The dissent's summary of our individual disparate treatment cases to date is fair and accurate, and amply demonstrates that the rule we adopt today is at least a change in direction from some of our prior precedents. We have indeed emphasized in the past that in an individual disparate treatment action the plaintiff bears the burden of persuasion throughout the litigation. Nor have we confined the word "pretext" to the narrow definition which the plurality attempts to pin on it today. . . . *McDonnell Douglas* and *Burdine* assumed that the plaintiff would bear the burden of persuasion as to both these attacks, and we clearly depart from that framework today. Such a departure requires justification, and its outlines should be carefully drawn.

First, *McDonnell Douglas* itself dealt with a situation where the plaintiff presented no direct evidence that the employer had relied on a forbidden factor under Title VII in making an employment decision. . . . I do not think that the employer is entitled to the same presumption of good faith where there is direct evidence that it has placed substantial reliance on factors whose consideration is forbidden by Title VII. . . .

[T]he entire purpose of the *McDonnell Douglas* prima facie case is to compensate for the fact that direct evidence of intentional discrimination is hard to come by. That the employer's burden in rebutting such an inferential

2. Disparate Treatment Discrimination under Title VII

case of discrimination is only one of production does not mean that the scales should be weighted in the same manner where there is direct evidence of intentional discrimination. Indeed, in one Age Discrimination in Employment Act case, the Court seemed to indicate that "the *McDonnell Douglas* test is inapplicable where the plaintiff presents direct evidence of discrimination." Trans World Airlines, Inc. v. Thurston, 469 U.S. 111, 121 (1985). See also East Texas Motor Freight System, Inc. v. Rodriguez, 431 U.S. 395, 403-404, n.9 (1977).

Second, the facts of this case, and a growing number like it decided by the Courts of Appeals, convince me that the evidentiary standard I propose is necessary to make real the promise of *McDonnell Douglas* that "[i]n the implementation of [employment] decisions, it is abundantly clear that Title VII tolerates no . . . discrimination, subtle or otherwise." In this case, the District Court found that a number of the evaluations of Ann Hopkins submitted by partners in the firm overtly referred to her failure to conform to certain gender stereotypes as a factor militating against her election to the partnership. The District Court further found that these evaluations were given "great weight" by the decisionmakers at Price Waterhouse. In addition, the District Court found that the partner responsible for informing Hopkins of the factors which caused her candidacy to be placed on hold, indicated that her "professional" problems would be solved if she would "walk more femininely, talk more femininely, wear make-up, have her hair styled, and wear jewelry." As the Court of Appeals characterized it, Ann Hopkins proved that Price Waterhouse "permitt[ed] stereotypical attitudes towards women to play a significant, though unquantifiable, role in its decision not to invite her to become a partner."

At this point Ann Hopkins had taken her proof as far as it could go. She had proved discriminatory input into the decisional process, and had proved that participants in the process considered her failure to conform to the stereotypes credited by a number of the decisionmakers had been a substantial factor in the decision. It is as if Ann Hopkins were sitting in the hall outside the room where partnership decisions were being made. As the partners filed in to consider her candidacy, she heard several of them make sexist remarks in discussing her suitability for partnership. As the decisionmakers exited the room, she was told by one of those privy to the decisionmaking process that her gender was a major reason for the rejection of her partnership bid. If, as we noted in *Teamsters*, "[p]resumptions shifting the burden of proof are often created to reflect judicial evaluations of probabilities and to conform with a party's superior access to the proof," one would be hard pressed to think of a situation where it would be more appropriate to require the defendant to show that its decision would have been justified by wholly legitimate concerns. . . .

Finally, I am convinced that a rule shifting the burden to the defendant where the plaintiff has shown that an illegitimate criterion was a "substantial factor" in the employment decision will not conflict with other congressional policies embodied in Title VII. Title VII expressly provides that an employer need not give preferential treatment to employees or applicants of any race, color, religion, sex, or national origin in order to maintain a work force in balance with the general population. See 42 U.S.C. §2000e-2(j). . . .

Last Term, in Watson v. Fort Worth Bank & Trust, the Court unanimously concluded that the disparate impact analysis first enunciated in Griggs v. Duke Power Co., should be extended to subjective or discretionary selection processes. At the same time a plurality of the Court indicated concern that the focus on bare statistics in the disparate impact setting could force employers to adopt "inappropriate prophylactic measures" in violation of §2000e-2(j). . . .

I believe there are significant differences between shifting the burden of persuasion to the employer in a case resting purely on statistical proof as in the disparate impact setting and shifting the burden of persuasion in a case like this one, where an employee has demonstrated by direct evidence that an illegitimate factor played a substantial role in a particular employment decision. First, the explicit consideration of race, color, religion, sex, or national origin in making employment decisions "was the most obvious evil Congress had in mind when it enacted Title VII." *Teamsters*. While the prima facie case under *McDonnell Douglas* and the statistical showing of imbalance involved in an impact case may both be indicators of discrimination or its "functional equivalent," they are not, in and of themselves, the evils Congress sought to eradicate from the employment setting. Second, shifting the burden of persuasion to the employer in a situation like this one creates no incentive to preferential treatment in violation of §2000e-2(j). To avoid bearing the burden of justifying its decision, the employer need not seek racial or sexual balance in its work force; rather, all it need do is avoid substantial reliance on forbidden criteria in making its employment decisions.

While the danger of forcing employers to engage in unwarranted preferential treatment is thus less dramatic in this setting than in the situation the Court faced in *Watson*, it is far from wholly illusory. Based on its misreading of the words "because of" in the statute, the plurality appears to conclude that if a decisional process is tainted" by awareness of sex or race in any way, the employer has violated the statute, and Title VII thus commands that the burden shift to the employer to justify its decision. The plurality thus effectively reads the causation requirement out of the statute, and then replaces it with an "affirmative defense."

In my view, in order to justify shifting the burden on the issue of causation to the defendant, a disparate treatment plaintiff must show by direct evidence that an illegitimate criterion was a substantial factor in the decision. . . . Requiring that the plaintiff demonstrate that an illegitimate factor played a

2. Disparate Treatment Discrimination under Title VII

substantial role in the employment decision identifies those employment situations where the deterrent purpose of Title VII is most clearly implicated. As an evidentiary matter, where a plaintiff has made this type of strong showing of illicit motivation, the factfinder is entitled to presume that the employer's discriminatory animus made a difference to the outcome, absent proof to the contrary from the employer. Where a disparate treatment plaintiff has made such a showing, the burden then rests with the employer to convince the trier of fact that it is more likely than not that the decision would have been the same absent consideration of the illegitimate factor. The employer need not isolate the sole cause for the decision, rather it must demonstrate that with the illegitimate factor removed from the calculus, sufficient business reasons would have induced it to take the same employment action. This evidentiary scheme essentially requires the employer to place the employee in the same position he or she would have occupied absent discrimination. Cf. Mt. Healthy Board of Education v. Doyle. If the employer fails to carry this burden, the factfinder is justified in concluding that the decision was made "because of" consideration of the illegitimate factor and the substantive standard for liability under the statute is satisfied.

Thus, stray remarks in the workplace, while perhaps probative of sexual harassment, see Meritor Savings Bank v. Vinson, 477 U.S. 57, 63-69 (1986), cannot justify requiring the employer to prove that its hiring or promotion decisions were based on legitimate criteria. Nor can statements by nondecisionmakers, or statements by decisionmakers unrelated to the decisional process itself suffice to satisfy the plaintiff's burden in this regard. In addition, in my view testimony such as Dr. Fiske's in this case, standing alone, would not justify shifting the burden of persuasion to the employer. Race and gender always "play a role" in an employment decision in the benign sense that these are human characteristics of which decisionmakers are aware and may comment on in a perfectly neutral and nondiscriminatory fashion. For example, in the context of this case, a mere reference to "a lady candidate" might show that gender "played a role" in the decision, but by no means could support a rational factfinder's inference that the decision was made "because of" sex. What is required is what Ann Hopkins showed here: direct evidence that decisionmakers placed substantial negative reliance on an illegitimate criterion in reaching their decision.

It should be obvious that the threshold standard I would adopt for shifting the burden of persuasion to the defendant differs substantially from that proposed by the plurality, the plurality's suggestion to the contrary notwithstanding. The plurality proceeds from the premise that the words "because of" in the statute do not embody any causal requirement at all. Under my approach, the plaintiff must produce evidence sufficient to show that an illegitimate criterion was a substantial factor in the particular employment decision such that a reasonable factfinder could draw an inference that the decision was made "because of" the plaintiff's protected status. Only then would the burden of proof shift to the defendant to prove that the decision would have been justified by other, wholly legitimate considerations. See also (WHITE, J., concurring in judgment).

In sum, . . . I would retain but supplement the framework we established in *McDonnell Douglas* and subsequent cases. The structure of the presentation of evidence in an individual treatment case should conform to the general outlines we established in *McDonnell Douglas* and *Burdine*. First, the plaintiff must establish the *McDonnell Douglas* prima facie case by showing membership in a protected group, qualification for the job, rejection for the position, and that after rejection the employer continued to seek applicants of complainant's general qualifications. *McDonnell Douglas*. The plaintiff should also present any direct evidence of discriminatory animus in the decisional process. The defendant should then present its case, including its evidence as to legitimate, nondiscriminatory reasons for the employment decision. As the dissent notes, under this framework, the employer "has every incentive to convince the trier of fact that the decision was lawful." Once all the evidence has been received, the court should determine whether the *McDonnell Douglas* or *Price Waterhouse* framework properly applies to the evidence before it. If the plaintiff has failed to satisfy the *Price Waterhouse* threshold, the case should be decided under the princples enunciated in *McDonnell Douglas* and *Burdine*, with the plaintiff bearing the burden of persuasion on the ultimate issue whether the employment action was taken because of discrimination. In my view, such a system is both fair and workable and it calibrates the evidentiary requirements demanded of the parties to the goals behind the statute itself.

I agree with the dissent, that the evidentiary framework I propose should be available to all disparate treatment plaintiffs where an illegitimate consideration played a substantial role in an adverse employment decision. The Court's allocation of the burden of proof in Johnson v. Transportation Agency, 480 U.S. 616, 626-627 (1987), rested squarely on "the analytical framework set forth in *McDonnell Douglas*," which we alter today. It would be odd to say the least if the evidentiary rules applicable to Title VII actions were themselves dependent on the gender or the skin color of the litigants. . . .

Justice KENNEDY, with whom the Chief Justice and Justice SCALIA join, dissenting.

Today the Court manipulates existing and complex rules for employment discrimination cases in a way certain to result in confusion. Continued adherence to the evidentiary scheme established in *McDonnell Douglas* and *Burdine* is a wiser course than creation of more disarray in an area of the law already difficult for the bench and bar, and so I must dissent. . . .

I

The plurality described this as a case about the standard of causation under Title VII, but I respectfully suggest that the description is misleading. Much of the plurality's rhetoric is spent denouncing a "but-for" standard of causation. The theory of Title VII liability the plurality adopts, however, essentially incorporates the but-for standard. The importance of today's decision is not the standard of causation it employs, but its shift to the defendant of the burden of proof. The plurality's causation analysis is misdirected, for it is clear that, whoever bears the burden of proof on the issue, Title VII liability requires a finding of but-for causation. See also (opinion of O'CONNOR, J.); (opinion of WHITE, J.).

The words of Title VII are not obscure. . . . By any normal understanding, the phrase "because of" conveys the idea that the motive in question made a difference to the outcome. We use the words this way in everyday speech. And assuming, as the plurality does, that we ought to consider the interpretive memorandum prepared by the statute's drafters, we find that this is what the words meant to them as well. . . . Congress could not have chosen a clearer way to indicate that proof of liability under Title VII requires a showing that race, color, religion, sex, or national origin caused the decision at issue.

Our decisions confirm that Title VII is not concerned with the mere presence of impermissible motives; it is directed to employment decisions that result from those motives. The verbal formulae we have used in our precedents are synonymous with but-for causation. . . .

What we term "but-for" cause is the least rigorous standard that is consistent with the approach to causation our precedents describe. If a motive is not a but-for cause of an event, then by definition it did not make a difference to the outcome. The event would have occurred just the same without it. Common law approaches to causation often require proof of but-for cause as a starting point toward proof of legal cause. The law may require more than but-for cause, for instance proximate cause, before imposing liability. Any standard less than but-for, however, simply represents a decision to impose liability without causation. As Dean Prosser puts it, "[a]n act or omission is not regarded as a cause of an event if the particular event would have occurred without it." W. Keeton, D. Dobbs, R. Keeton, & D. Owen, Prosser and Keeton on Law of Torts 265 (5th ed. 1984).

One of the principal reasons the plurality decision may sow confusion is that it claims Title VII liability is unrelated to but-for causation, yet it adopts a but-for standard once it has placed the burden of proof as to causation upon the employer. This approach conflates the question whether causation must be shown with the question of how it is to be shown. Because the plurality's theory of Title VII causation is ultimately consistent with a but-for standard, it might be said that my disagreement with the plurality's comments on but-for cause is simply academic. See (opinion of WHITE, J.). But since those comments seem to influence the decision, I turn now to that part of the plurality's analysis.

The plurality begins by noting the quite unremarkable fact that Title VII is written in the present tense. It is unlawful "to fail" or "to refuse" to provide employment benefits on the basis of sex, not "to have failed" or "to have refused" to have done so. The plurality claims that the present tense excludes a but-for inquiry as the relevant standard because but-for causation is necessarily concerned with a hypothetical inquiry into how a past event would have occurred absent the contested motivation. This observation, however, tells us nothing of particular relevance to Title VII or the cause of action it creates. I am unaware of any federal prohibitory statute that is written in the past tense. Every liability determination, including the novel one constructed by the plurality, necessarily is concerned with the examination of a past event.[1] The plurality's analysis of verb tense serves only to divert attention from the causation requirement that is made part of the statute by the "because of" phrase. That phrase, I respectfully submit, embodies a rather simple concept that the plurality labors to ignore.[2]

We are told next that but-for cause is not required, since the words "because of" do not mean "solely because of." No one contends, however, that sex must be the sole cause of a decision before there is a Title VII violation. This is a separate question from whether consideration of sex must be a cause of the decision. Under the accepted approach to causation that I have discussed, sex is a cause for the employment decision whenever, either by itself or in combination with other factors, it made a difference to the decision. . . .

The plurality's reliance on the "bona fide occupational qualification" (BFOQ) provisions of Title VII, 42 U.S.C. §2000e-2(e), is particularly inapt. The BFOQ provisions allow an employer, in certain cases, to make an employment decision of which it is conceded that sex is the cause. That sex may be the legitimate cause of an employment decision where gender is a BFOQ is consistent with the opposite command that a decision caused by sex

---

1. The plurality's description of its own standard is both hypothetical and retrospective. The inquiry seeks to determine whether "if we asked the employer at the moment of decision what its reasons were and if we received a truthful response, one of those reasons would be that the applicant or employee was a woman."

2. The plurality's discussion of overdetermined causes only highlights the error of its insistence that but-for is not the substantive standard of causation under Title VII. The opinion discusses the situation where two physical forces move an object, and either force acting alone would have moved the object. Translated to the context of Title VII, this situation would arise where an employer took an adverse action in reliance both on sex and on legitimate reasons, and either the illegitimate or the legitimate reason standing alone would have produced the action. If this state of affairs is proved to the factfinder, there will be no liability under the plurality's own test, for the same decision would have been made had the illegitimate reason never been considered.

2. Disparate Treatment Discrimination under Title VII

in any other case justifies the imposition of Title VII liability. This principle does not support, however, the novel assertion that a violation has occurred where sex made no difference to the outcome. . . .

The plurality attempts to reconcile its internal inconsistency on the causation issue by describing the employer's showing as an "affirmative defense." This is nothing more than a label, and one not found in the language or legislative history of Title VII. Section 703(a)(1) is the statutory basis of the cause of action, and the Court is obligated to explain how its disparate treatment decisions are consistent with the terms of §703(a)(1), not with general themes of legislative history or with other parts of the statute that are plainly inapposite. . . . Labels aside, the import of today's decision is not that Title VII liability can arise without but-for causation, but that in certain cases it is not the plaintiff who must prove the presence of causation, but the defendant who must prove its absence.

II

We established the order of proof for individual Title VII disparate treatment cases in McDonnell Douglas Corp. v. Green, and reaffirmed this allocation in Texas Dept. of Community Affairs v. Burdine. . . . I would adhere to this established evidentiary framework, which provides the appropriate standard for this and other individual disparate treatment cases. Today's creation of a new set of rules for "mixed-motive" cases is not mandated by the statute itself. The Court's attempt at refinement provides limited practical benefits at the cost of confusion and complexity, with the attendent risk that the trier of fact will misapprehend the controlling legal principles and reach an incorrect decision. . . .

Downplaying the novelty of its opinion, the plurality claims to have followed a "well-worn path" from our prior cases. The path may be well-worn, but it is in the wrong forest. The plurality again relies on Title VII's BFOQ provisions, under which an employer bears the burden of justifying the use of a sex-based employment qualification. See Dothard v. Rawlinson. In the BFOQ context this is a sensible, indeed necessary, allocation of the burden, for there by definition sex is the but-for cause of the employment decision and the only question remaining is how the employer can justify it. . . .

Closer analogies to the plurality's new approach are found in Mt. Healthy Board of Education v. Doyle, and NLRB v. Transportation Management Corp., but these cases were decided in different contexts. . . .

The potential benefits of the new approach, in my view, are overstated. First, the Court makes clear that the *Price Waterhouse* scheme is applicable only in those cases where the plaintiff has produced direct and substantial proof that an impermissible motive was relied upon in making the decision at issue. The burden shift properly will be found to apply in only a limited number of employment discrimination cases. The application of the new scheme, furthermore, will make a difference only in a smaller subset of cases. The practical importance of the burden of proof is the "risk of nonpersuasion," and the new system will make a difference only where the evidence is so evenly balanced that the factfinder cannot say that either side's explanation of the case is "more likely" true. This category will not include cases in which the allocation of the burden of proof will be dispositive because of a complete lack of evidence on the causation issue, cf. Summers v. Tice, 33 Cal. 2d 80, 199 P.2d 1 (1948) (allocation of burden dispositive because no evidence of which of two negligently fired shots hit plaintiff). Rather, *Price Waterhouse* will apply only to cases in which there is substantial evidence of reliance on an impermissible motive, as well as evidence from the employer that legitimate reasons supported its action.

Although the *Price Waterhouse* system is not for every case, almost every plaintiff is certain to ask for a *Price Waterhouse* instruction, perhaps on the basis of "stray remarks" or other evidence of discriminatory animus. Trial and appellate courts will therefore be saddled with the task of developing standards for determining when to apply the burden shift. One of their new tasks will be the generation of a jurisprudence of the meaning of "substantial factor." Courts will also be required to make the often subtle and difficult distinction between "direct" and "indirect" or "circumstantial" evidence. Lower courts long have had difficulty applying *McDonnell Douglas* and *Burdine*. Addition of a second burden-shifting mechanism, the application of which itself depends on assessment of credibility and a determination whether evidence is sufficiently direct and substantial, is not likely to lend clarity to the process. . . .

Confusion in the application of dual burden-shifting mechanisms will be most acute in cases brought under §1981 or the Age Discrimination in Employment Act (ADEA), where courts borrow the Title VII order of proof for the conduct of jury trials. See, e.g., Note, The Age Discrimination in Employment Act of 1967 and Trial by Jury: Proposals for Change, 73 Va. L. Rev. 601 (1987) (noting high reversal rate caused by use of Title VII burden shifting in a jury setting). Perhaps such cases in the future will require a bifurcated trial, with the jury retiring first to make the credibility findings necessary to determine whether the plaintiff has proved that an impermissible factor played a substantial part in the decision, and later hearing evidence on the "same decision" or "pretext" issues. Alternatively, perhaps the trial judge will have the unenviable task of formulating a single instruction for the jury on all of the various burdens potentially involved in the case.

. . . In sum, the *Burdine* framework provides a "sensible, orderly way to evaluate the evidence in light of common experience as it bears on the critical question of discrimination," and it should continue to govern the order of proof in Title VII disparate treatment cases.[4]

III

The ultimate question in every individual disparate treatment case is whether discrimination caused the particular decision at issue. Some of the plurality's comments with respect to the District Court's findings in this case, however, are potentially misleading. As the plurality notes, the District Court based its liability determination on expert evidence that some evaluations of respondent Hopkins were based on unconscious sex stereotypes,[5] and on the fact that Price Waterhouse failed to disclaim reliance on these comments when it conducted the partnership review. The District Court also based liability on Price Waterhouse's failure to "make partners sensitive to the dangers [of stereotyping], to discourage comments tainted by sexism, or to investigate comments to determine whether they are influenced by stereotypes."

Although the District Court's version of Title VII liability is improper under any of today's opinions, I think it important to stress that Title VII creates no independent cause of action for sex stereotyping. Evidence of use by decisionmakers of sex stereotypes is, of course, quite relevant to the question of discriminatory intent. The ultimate question, however, is whether discrimination caused the plaintiff's harm. Our cases do not support the suggestion that failure to "disclaim reliance" on stereotypical comments itself violates Title VII. Neither do they support creation of a "duty to sensitize." As the dissenting

---

4. The plurality states that it disregards the special context of affirmative action. It is not clear that this is possible. Some courts have held that in a suit challenging an affirmative action plan, the question of the plan's validity need not be reached unless the plaintiff shows that the plan was a but-for cause of the adverse decision. See McQuillen v. Wisconsin Education Association Council, 830 F.2d 659, 665 (CA7 1987), *cert. denied*, 485 U.S. 914 (1988). Presumably it will be easier for a plaintiff to show that consideration of race or sex pursuant to an affirmative action plan was a substantial factor in a decision, and the court will need to move on to the question of a plan's validity. Moreover, if the structure of the burdens of proof in Title VII suits is to be consistent, as might be expected given the identical statutory language involved, today's decision suggests that plaintiffs should no longer bear the burden of showing that affirmative action plans are illegal. See Johnson v. Transportation Agency.

5. The plaintiff who engages the services of Dr. Susan Fiske should have no trouble showing that sex discrimination played a part in any decision. Price Waterhouse chose not to object to Fiske's testimony, and at this late stage we are constrained to accept it, but I think the plurality's enthusiasm for Fiske's conclusions unwarranted. Fiske purported to discern stereotyping in comments that were gender neutral—e.g., "overbearing and abrasive"—without any knowledge of the comments' basis in reality and without having met the speaker or subject. "To an expert of Dr. Fiske's qualifications, it seems plain that no woman could be overbearing, arrogant, or abrasive: any observations to that effect would necessarily be discounted as the product of stereotyping. If analysis like this is to prevail in federal courts, no employer can base any adverse action as to a woman on such attributes." 825 F.2d 458, 477 (1987) (Williams, J., dissenting). Today's opinions cannot be read as requiring factfinders to credit testimony based on this type of analysis. See also (opinion of O'CONNOR, J.).

judge in the Court of Appeals observed, acceptance of such theories would turn Title VII "from a prohibition of discriminatory conduct into an engine for rooting out sexist thoughts." (Williams, J., dissenting).

Employment discrimination claims require factfinders to make difficult and sensitive decisions. Sometimes this may mean that no finding of discrimination is justified even though a qualified employee is passed over by a less than admirable employer. In other cases, Title VII's protections properly extend to plaintiffs who are by no means model employees. As Justice BRENNAN notes, courts do not sit to determine whether litigants are nice. In this case, Hopkins plainly presented a strong case both of her own professional qualifications and of the presence of discrimination in Price Waterhouse's partnership process. Had the District Court found on this record that sex discrimination caused the adverse decision, I doubt it would have been reversible error. Cf. *Aikens*. That decision was for the finder of fact, however, and the District Court made plain that sex discrimination was not a but-for cause of the decision to place Hopkins' partnership candidacy on hold. Attempts to evade tough decisions by erecting novel theories of liability or multitiered systems of shifting burdens are misguided. . . .

NOTES

1. Are you convinced by the plurality that its approach is not but-for causation? Suppose a job requires an applicant to be 18 years old and a resident of the state. A 17-year-old nonresident applies and is rejected. Is it sensible to say that being underage "caused" the applicant to be turned down? Would your answer change if the employer testified that, when he reviewed the application, he noted that the first line indicated that the applicant was under 18? Accordingly, he rejected it without looking further and never knew that the applicant was also a nonresident. How would Justice Kennedy describe this situation?

2. Suppose an employer places a sign outside its personnel office saying that "No blacks need apply." Is that a violation of Title VII? Surprisingly, the majority opinion suggests that the answer is, "not necessarily," since the sign might not be a causative factor in any particular decision. Reread footnote 10, rejecting Hopkins' argument that, once she established that her sex entered into the employer's decision, she was entitled to a finding that defendant had discriminated against her, with any proof that she would not have gotten the job anyway being relevant only to the relief awarded. But even if such a sign would not violate §703(a)(1), consider §704(b) prohibiting notices or advertisements indicating a preference or limitation on one of the prohibited grounds. Does §704(b) cast any light on whether actual adverse effects on an individual are necessary for a §703(a)(1) violation?

3. Why isn't the better view that prohibited bases are just that—prohibited? By making the use of such factors a violation, entitling the employee to appropriate relief—an injunction and attorneys' fees—the purposes of Title VII are served without giving the plaintiff a windfall. Further, the employee may have a real interest in such relief: In the promotion context, for example, the employee may not have been entitled to the promotion in question but would like assurances that her sex will not enter into future decisions. In *Price Waterhouse* itself, even assuming that defendant could carry its burden on remand that plaintiff would not have been made partner in any event that year, Hopkins (had she not resigned) would have had a second chance at making partner, an opportunity which should be free of sex discrimination. See Weber, Beyond Price Waterhouse v. Hopkins: A New Approach to Mixed Motive Discrimination, 68 N. Car. L. Rev. 495 (1990).

4. Reread the plurality's footnote 5. The opinion avoids decision on the point, but is Hopkins arguing that "a biased decisionmaking process that 'tended to deprive' her of partnership" is illegal regardless of actual causal connection under §703(a)(2)?

5. Some have defended a causation requirement (of some kind) as being necessary to avoid first amendment concerns of "thought control." See Belton, Causation in Employment Discrimination Law, 34 Wayne L. Rev. 1235 (1988). What do you think of this argument?

6. Does it make any difference how the causation approach is labeled so long as the allocations of burdens of proof are clear? Isn't Justice White correct on this point?

7. The rule is, as the plurality states it, "Once a plaintiff in a Title VII case shows that gender played a motivating part in an employment decision, the defendant may avoid a finding of liability only by proving that it would have made the same decision even if it had not allowed gender to play such a role." The two concurrences, however, do not adopt this view. Both require the plaintiff to show that discrimination was a "substantial" factor. Is "substantial" different from "motivating"? Did the Court fail to put together a majority because of an adjective?

8. Since the common ground to all nine justices was that allocation of burdens of persuasion is important, it is critical to differentiate a *Price Waterhouse* case from a *Burdine* case since different allocations follow. Justice Kennedy is surely right when he states that "almost every plaintiff is certain to ask for a *Price Waterhouse* instruction." What is the line between the two strands of authority?

9. How would the other justices draw the line? The plurality requires the plaintiff to bear the burden of proving that sex played a "motivating" role in a decision adverse to her. Assuming an employer does not admit at trial that sex played a role, what will suffice to carry plaintiff's burden?

10. Justice O'Connor stresses the need for "direct" evidence of intent to

discriminate. Neither Justice White nor the plurality focus on this. What is "direct evidence"? Is it necessary for a *Price Waterhouse* case, or do five justices permit such a case even in the absence of direct evidence? In Gray v. University of Arkansas at Fayetteville, 883 F.2d 1394 (8th Cir. 1989), plaintiff, who had been dismissed as academic coordinator for the Razorbacks, presented tape recordings in which the Associate Academic Director, Dr. Farrell told her that the football coach wanted a man in her position. Farrell explained, "He wanted somebody to go up there [the athletic dormitory] and jack 'em [the players] out of bed, and that's all he said." Id at. 1399. Despite this smoking gun, the Eighth Circuit upheld the district court's refusal to find a *Price Waterhouse* case because the University had established that Farrell was suffering from a mental illness (which eventually led to his suicide), and that he had a tendency to confabulation. Is this a sufficient reason to reject the *Price Waterhouse* rule? Further, the court did not address the question of why Arkansas knowingly kept in its employ a man suffering from a mental illness that the University claimed made his job performance unreliable, while at the same time firing a woman whose supposed deficiencies were far less significant.

11. The dissenter in *Gray*, Judge McMillan, believed that the district court erroneously discounted the recordings because he disapproved of secret taping. The dissent noted that such evidence was admissible under the Federal Rules of Evidence, Fed. R. Evid. 1101-1104, and that taping was "a practical response to the exigencies of the situation" in which plaintiff found herself. "Gray did nothing illegal or immoral." Id. at 1405. As an attorney for a person facing discharge, would you recommend that your client tape conversations? While a few states bar secret taping even by one of the participants to a conversation, most only make secret taping illegal when done by a third party.

12. Is a *Price Waterhouse* case dependent on employer "admissions"? Is that the distinction between this kind of case and a *Burdine* case? Is *Slack v. Havens* a mixed motive case? Absent admissions, how does one prove that certain statements are the result of stereotyping? See generally Radford, Sex Stereotyping and the Promotion of Women to Positions of Power, 41 Hastings L.J. 471 (1990).

13. The plurality notes that it is not necessary that "a case must be correctly labeled as either a 'pretext' case or a 'mixed motives' case from the beginning," but "[a]t some point in the proceedings . . . the District Court must decide whether a particular case involves mixed motives." At *what* point in the trial does this decision take place? Asked another way, when does a defendant know it has more than a burden of production?

14. Suppose the defendant does have a burden of persuasion. Justice White objects to any requirement that the employer submit objective evidence to support its affirmative defense. Further, he notes that "where the

2. Disparate Treatment Discrimination under Title VII

legitimate motive found would have been ample grounds for the action taken, and the employer credibly testifies that the action would have been taken for the legitimate reason alone, this should be ample proof." Is this true? What about his further statement: "This would even more plainly be the case where the employer denies any illegitimate motive in the first place but the court finds that illegitimate, as well as legitimate, factors motivated the adverse action." The plurality characterized as "baffling" the position of Justice White in giving any special credence to the testimony of an employer who has been found to have relied on an illegal reason in its decisionmaking. Do you agree? Does it matter, given that the plurality and O'Connor form a majority apparently rejecting this view?

15. But note that, to the extent that Justice O'Connor's basic view is closer to the plurality approach, "direct evidence" cases will be decided using the plurality rule. Where the case is a circumstantial evidence case, then Justice White's approach is closer to the plurality position. Thus, the majority rule is the plurality rule as modified by Justice White's "baffling" twist that an employer's testimony is especially credible on the affirmative defense, even after the employer has been found to have relied on an illegal factor in making its decision.

16. On remand, the district court held that Price Waterhouse had not carried its burden and ordered that Ann Hopkins be made a partner. 58 U.S. L. W. 2671 (May 22, 1990).

D. DEFENSES TO DISPARATE TREATMENT CASES

2. *Bona Fide Occupational Qualifications*

Page 155. Add at end of Note 2:

See also EEOC v. The Boeing Co., 843 F.2d 1213 (9th Cir.), *cert. denied*, 109 S. Ct. 222 (1988) (FAA age-60-rule for pilots of commercial planes does not automatically validate age-60-rule for noncommercial pilots).

Page 156. Add new Notes:

9. Although not phrased in terms of "customer preference," recent cases have grappled with the question of whether sex or pregnancy can justify a bfoq when these characteristics may affect the ability of employees to interact

with persons with whom they must work. One example is a girls club's discrimination against an unmarried pregnant employee. In Chambers v. Omaha Girls Club, 834 F.2d 697 (8th Cir. 1987), *reh'g denied*, 840 F.2d 583 (1988), a majority of an Eight Circuit panel upheld a finding of bfoq. It focused on the need for a positive role model, since the organization's major constituency was teenage girls and one of the major concerns of that group was unwed pregnancy. Although the circuit denied rehearing, three judges joined in dissent from that denial, disapproving of the deference paid to an employer's subjective belief that an employee's unwed pregnancy rendered her unqualified for the position of arts and crafts teacher that she had held.

10. A related problem also divided the Seventh Circuit. In Torres v. Wisconsin Dept. of Health and Human Services, 859 F.2d 1523 (7th Cir. 1988) (en banc) (8-3), *cert. denied*, 109 S. Ct. 1133, 1537 (1989), the court considered a policy limiting certain employment in a women's prison to females. The original panel rejected the bfoq: after noting that inmate privacy was adequately safeguarded vis-à-vis guards of both sexes, the panel majority then went on to reject the defendant's "rehabilitation" justification. Essentially, the prison contended that, since its inmates had typically suffered from male domination, rehabilitation efforts would be impaired if males continued to be in positions of authority over them in the prison. On rehearing en banc, a majority agreed that the preference for women could not be justified by considerations of inmate privacy, but was more sympathetic to the rehabilitation claim of the employer. It stressed that the situation was unique—a women's maximum security prison—and therefore lacked the "historical and empirical information" applicable to comparable male prisons. The opinion was deferential to the professional judgment of the prison superintendent, rejecting any necessity for "objective" evidence in this setting. It therefore remanded the case for the district court to evaluate the bfoq on the basis of "the totality of the circumstances."

3. Voluntary Affirmative Action

Page 207. Add new Notes:

10. The most recent Supreme Court decision in the affirmative action area is City of Richmond v. J.A. Croson Co., 109 S. Ct. 706 (1989), striking down a municipal minority set-aside program for construction contracts. Although a decade earlier the Court had approved a congressional set-aside program in Fullilove v. Klutznik, 448 U.S. 448 (1980), a majority in *Croson* applied a more stringent review to state or local plans under the Fourteenth Amendment. While this distinction is not totally without foundation, in reality *Croson* is probably better explained as simply reflecting a greater

hostility to "reverse discrimination" than prevailed a decade previously. Although the Court splintered in a manner typical of affirmative action cases, the most significant aspect of the case was the mustering of a majority for the proposition that racial classifications, even benign ones, must be subjected to strict scrutiny: four justices joined in Justice O'Connor's plurality opinion on this point (herself, Chief Justice Rhenquist and Justices White and Kennedy), and Justice Scalia concurred on the appropriate test.

Under this analysis, the plan could be upheld only if there was a showing of a compelling state interest and the plan was narrowly tailored to meet that interest. While the plurality recognized that remedying prior past discrimination by Richmond would be a compelling interest, it held that the city had not established its past discrimination in contracting. The plan also failed the "narrowly tailored" prong of the test, in part because of the rigidity of the 30 percent set-aside and in part because "minorities" were defined to include groups such as "Aleuts" who had never been victimized by the city. Justice Scalia would have taken an even stricter approach to racial classifications.

11. *Croson* has already generated a large literature. E.g., Constitutional Scholars' statement on Affirmative Action After *City of Richmond v. J. A. Croson Co.*, 98 Yale L. J. 1711 (1989); Fried, Affirmative Action After *City of Richmond v. J. A. Croson Co.*, 99 Yale L.J. 155 (1989); Scholars' Reply to Professor Fried, 99 Yale L.J. 103 (1989); Scherer, Affirmative Action Doctrine and the Conflicting Messages of *Croson*, 38 Kan. L. Rev. 281 (1990); Ross, The Richmond Chronicles, 68 Tex. L. Rev. 381 (1989); Devins, Affirmative Action after Reagan, 68 Tex. L. Rev. 353 (1989); Maltz, Affirmative Action and Employer Autonomy: A Comment on *City of Richmond v. Croson*, 68 Ore. L. Rev. 459 (1989).

Chapter 3

The Definition of Systemic Disparate Impact Discrimination Under Title VII

A. THE STRUCTURE OF DISPARATE IMPACT DISCRIMINATION

Page 220. Add the following notes:

9. In Connecticut v. Teal, 457 U.S. 440 (1982), an employer used a test that had a disparate impact on blacks as part of a promotion selection procedure. While the test had an adverse impact in the sense that it filtered out disproportionately more blacks than whites in the first step of the procedure, the remaining steps "corrected" that result so that at "the bottom line" of the entire promotion procedure there was no adverse impact on blacks. The Court held that plaintiff did not have to prove bottom line discriminatory impact as part of her prima facie case and further that the absence of impact "at the bottom line" did not constitute a defense to a disparate impact claim

made out against one component of the selection procedure. Justice Brennan wrote for the Court an opinion suggesting continued broad application of the disparate impact concept of discrimination.

10. In contrast to the broadranging opinion in Connecticut v. Teal, the opinion for the Court by Justice O'Connor in Watson v. Fort Worth Bank and Trust, 108 S. Ct. 2177 (1988), is quite narrowly drawn. Nevertheless, the Court held that disparate impact analysis could be used to attack subjective selection components and not just objective procedures such as standardized tests or high school diploma requirements: "[Subjective or discretionary employment practices may be analyzed under the disparate impact approach in appropriate cases." The remainder of Justice O'Connor's opinion, not joined by a majority of the Court, foreshadowed the diminished future of the disparate impact concept of discrimination.

Page 220. Replace Connecticut v. Teal with the following:

WARDS COVE PACKING COMPANY, INC. v. ATONIO
109 S. Ct. 2115 (1989)

Justice WHITE delivered the opinion of the Court.

Title VII of the Civil Rights Act of 1964 makes it an unfair employment practice for an employer to discriminate against any individual with respect to hiring or the terms and condition of employment because of such individual's race, color, religion, sex, or national origin; or to limit, segregate or classify his employees in ways that would adversely affect any employee because of the employee's race, color, religion, sex, or national origin. Griggs v. Duke Power Co. construed Title VII to proscribe "not only overt discrimination but also practices that are fair in form but discriminatory in practice." Under this basis for liability, which is known as the "disparate impact" theory and which is involved in this case, a facially neutral employment practice may be deemed violative of Title VII without evidence of the employer's subjective intent to discriminate that is required in a "disparate treatment" case.

I

The claims before us are disparate-impact claims, involving the employment practices of petitioners, two companies that operate salmon canneries in remote and widely separated areas of Alaska. The canneries operate only during the salmon runs in the summer months. They are inoperative and vacant for the rest of the year. In May or June of each year, a few weeks before the salmon runs begin, workers arrive and prepare the equipment and

3. Systemic Disparate Impact Discrimination Under Title VII　　　Page 220

facilities for the canning operation. Most of these workers possess a variety of skills. When salmon runs are about to begin, the workers who will operate the cannery lines arrive, remain as long as there are fish to can, and then depart. The canneries are then closed down, winterized, and left vacant until the next spring. During the off season, the companies employ only a small number of individuals at their headquarters in Seattle and Astoria, Oregon, plus some employees at the winter shipyard in Seattle.

The length and size of salmon runs vary from year to year and hence the number of employees needed at each cannery also varies. Estimates are made as early in the winter as possible; the necessary employees are hired, and when the time comes, they are transported to the canneries. Salmon must be processed soon after they are caught, and the work during the canning season is therefore intense. For this reason, and because the canneries are located in remote regions, all workers are housed at the canneries and have their meals in company-owned mess halls.

Jobs at the canneries are of two general types: "cannery jobs" on the cannery line, which are unskilled positions; and "noncannery jobs," which fall into a variety of classifications. Most noncannery jobs are classified as skilled positions.[2] Cannery jobs are filled predominantly by nonwhites, Filipinos and Alaska Natives. The Filipinos are hired through and dispatched by Local 37 of the International Longshoremen Workers Union pursuant to a hiring hall agreement with the Local. The Alaska Natives primarily reside in villages near the remote cannery locations. Noncannery jobs are filled with predominantly white workers, who are hired during the winter months from the companies' offices in Washington and Oregon. Virtually all of the noncannery jobs pay more than cannery positions. The predominantly white noncannery workers and the predominantly nonwhite cannery employees live in separate dormitories and eat in separate mess halls.

In 1974, respondents, a class of nonwhite cannery workers who were (or had been) employed at the canneries, brought this Title VII action against petitioners. Respondents alleged that a variety of petitioners' hiring/promotion practices — e.g., nepotism, a rehire preference, a lack of objective hiring criteria, separate hiring channels, a practice of not promoting from within — were responsible for the racial stratification of the work force, and had denied them and other nonwhites employment as noncannery workers on the basis of race. Respondents also complained of petitioners' racially segregated housing

---

2. The noncannery jobs were described as follows by the Court of Appeals:

> Machinists and engineers are hired to maintain the smooth and continuous operation of the canning equipment. Quality control personnel conduct the FDA-required inspections and recordkeeping. Tenders are staffed with a crew necessary to operate the vessel. A variety of support personnel are employed to operate the entire canner community, including, for example, cooks, carpenters, store-keepers, bookkeepers, beach gangs for dock yard labor and construction, etc.

and dining facilities. All of respondents' claims were advanced under both the disparate-treatment and disparate-impact theories of Title VII liability. . . .[3]

II

In holding that respondents had made out a prima facie case of disparate impact, the court of appeals relied solely on respondents' statistics showing a high percentage of nonwhite workers in the cannery jobs and a low percentage of such workers in the noncannery positions.[5] Although statistical proof can alone make out a prima facie case, see Teamsters v. United States; Hazelwood School Dist. v. United States, the Court of Appeals' ruling here misapprehends our precedents and the purposes of Title VII, and we therefore reverse.

"There can be no doubt," as there was when a similar mistaken analysis had been undertaken by the courts below in *Hazelwood* "that the . . . comparison . . . fundamentally misconceived the role of statistics in employment discrimination cases." The "proper comparison [is] between the racial composition of [the at-issue jobs] and the racial composition of the qualified . . . population in the relevant labor market." It is such a comparison—between the racial composition of the qualified persons in the labor market and the persons holding at-issue jobs—that generally forms the proper basis for the initial inquiry in a disparate impact case. Alternatively, in cases where such

---

3. The fact that neither the District Court, nor the Ninth Circuit en banc, nor the subsequent Court of Appeals panel ruled for respondents on their disparate treatment claims—i.e., their allegations of intentional racial discrimination—warrants particular attention in light of the dissents' comment that the canneries "bear an unsettling resemblance to aspects of a plantation economy." (Stevens, J., dissenting); (Blackmun, J., dissenting).

Whatever the "resemblance," the unanimous view of the lower courts in this litigation has been that respondents did not prove that the canneries practice intentional racial discrimination. Consequently, Justice Blackmun's hyperbolic allegation that our decision in this case indicates that this Court no longer "believes that race discrimination . . . against nonwhites . . . is a problem in our society," is inapt. Of course, it is unfortunately true that race discrimination exists in our country. That does not mean, however, that it exists at the canneries—or more precisely, that it has been proven to exist at the canneries.

Indeed, Justice Stevens concedes that respondents did not press before us the legal theories under which the aspects of cannery life that he finds to most resemble a "plantation economy" might be unlawful.

Thus, the question here is not whether we "approve" of petitioners' employment practices or the society that exists at the canneries, but rather, whether respondents have properly established that these practices violate Title VII.

5. The parties dispute the extent to which there is a discrepancy between the percentage of nonwhites employed as cannery workers, and those employed in noncannery positions. The District Court made no precise numerical findings in this regard, but simply noted that there were "significant disparities between the at-issue jobs [i.e., noncannery jobs] and the total workforce at the canneries" which were explained by the fact that "nearly all employed in the 'cannery worker' department are non-white."

For reasons explained below, the degree of disparity between these groups is not relevant to our decision here.

3. Systemic Disparate Impact Discrimination Under Title VII   Page 220

labor market statistics will be difficult if not impossible to ascertain, we have recognized that certain other statistics—such as measures indicating the racial composition of "otherwise-qualified applicants" for at-issue jobs—are equally probative for this purpose. See, e.g., New York City Transit Authority v. Beazer, 440 U.S. 568, 585 (1979).[6]

It is clear to us that the Court of Appeals' acceptance of the comparison between the racial composition of the cannery work force and that of the noncannery work force, as probative of a prima facie case of disparate impact in the selection of the latter group of workers, was flawed for several reasons. Most obviously, with respect to the skilled noncannery jobs at issue here, the cannery work force in no way reflected "the pool of qualified job applicants" or the "qualified population in the labor force." Measuring alleged discrimination in the selection of accountants, managers, boat captains, electricians, doctors, and engineers—and the long list of other "skilled" noncannery positions found to exist by the District Court—by comparing the number of nonwhites occupying these jobs to the number of nonwhites filling cannery worker positions is nonsensical. If the absence of minorities holding such skilled positions is due to a dearth of qualified nonwhite applicants (for reasons that are not petitioners' fault),[7] petitioners' selection methods or employment practices cannot be said to have had a "disparate impact" on nonwhites.

One example illustrates why this must be so. Respondents' own statistics concerning the noncannery work force at one of the canneries at issue here indicate that approximately 17 percent of the new hires for medical jobs, and 15 percent of the new hires for officer worker positions, were nonwhite. If it were the case that less than 15-17 percent of the applicants for these jobs were nonwhite and that nonwhites made up a lower percentage of the relevant qualified labor market, it is hard to see how respondents, without more, cf. Connecticut v. Teal, would have made out a prima facie case of disparate impact. Yet, under the Court of Appeals' theory, simply because nonwhites comprise 52 percent of the cannery workers at the cannery in question, respondents would be successful in establishing a prima facie case of racial discrimination under Title VII.

Such a result cannot be squared with our cases or with the goals behind the statute. The Court of Appeals' theory, at the very least, would mean that any employer who had a segment of his work force that was—for some reason—

---

6. In fact, where "figures for the general population might . . . accurately reflect the pool of qualified job applicants," cf. Teamsters v. United States, we have even permitted plaintiffs to rest their prima facie cases on such statistics as well. See, e.g., Dothard v. Rawlinson.

7. Obviously, the analysis would be different if it were found that the dearth of qualified nonwhite applicants was due to practices on petitioner's part which—expressly or implicitly—deterred minority group members from applying for noncannery positions. See, e.g., Teamsters v. United States.

racially imbalanced, could be haled into court and forced to engage in the expensive and time-consuming task of defending the "business necessity" of the methods used to select the other members of his work force. The only practicable option for many employers will be to adopt racial quotas, insuring that no portion of his work force deviates in racial composition from the other portions thereof; this is a result that Congress expressly rejected in drafting Title VII. See 42 U.S.C. §2000e-2(j); see also Watson v. Fort Worth Bank & Trust Co., (opinion of O'Connor, J.). The Court of Appeals' theory would "leave the employer little choice . . . but to engage in a subjective quota system of employment selection. This, of course, is far from the intent of Title VII." Albemarle Paper Co. v. Moody (Blackmun, J., concurring in judgment).

The Court of Appeals also erred with respect to the unskilled noncannery positions. Racial imbalance in one segment of an employer's work force does not, without more, establish a prima facie case of disparate impact with respect to the selection of workers for the employer's other positions, even where workers for the different positions may have somewhat fungible skills (as is arguably the case for cannery and unskilled noncannery workers). As long as there are no barriers or practices deterring qualified nonwhites from applying for noncannery positions, if the percentage of selected applicants who are nonwhite is not significantly less than the percentage of qualified applicants who are nonwhite, the employer's selection mechanism probably does not operate with a disparate impact on minorities.[8] Where this is the case, the percentage of nonwhite workers found in other positions in the employer's labor force is irrelevant to the question of a prima facie statistical case of disparate impact. As noted above, a contrary ruling on this point would almost inexorably lead to the use of numerical quotas in the workplace, a result that Congress and this Court have rejected repeatedly in the past.

Moreover, isolating the cannery workers as the potential "labor force" for unskilled noncannery positions is at once both too broad and too narrow in its focus. Too broad because the vast majority of these cannery workers did not seek jobs in unskilled noncannery positions; there is no showing that many of them would have done so even if none of the arguably "deterring" practices existed. Thus, the pool of cannery workers cannot be used as a

---

8. We qualify this conclusion—observing that it is only "probable" that there has been no disparate impact on minorities in such circumstances—because bottom-line racial balance is not a defense under Title VII. See Connecticut v. Teal. Thus, even if petitioners could show that the percentage of selected applicants who are nonwhite is not significantly less than the percentage of qualified applicants who are nonwhite, respondents would still have a case under Title VII, if they could prove that some particular hiring practice has a disparate impact on minorities, notwithstanding the bottom-line racial balance in petitioners' workforce.

3. Systemic Disparate Impact Discrimination Under Title VII

surrogate for the class of qualified job applicants because it contains many persons who have not (and would not) be noncannery job applicants. Conversely, if respondents propose to use the cannery workers for comparison purposes because they represent the "qualified labor population" generally, the group is too narrow because there are obviously many qualified persons in the labor market for noncannery jobs who are not cannery workers.

The peculiar facts of this case further illustrate why a comparison between the percentage of nonwhite cannery workers and nonwhite noncannery workers is an improper basis for making out a claim of disparate impact. Here, the District Court found that nonwhites were "overrepresent[ed]" among cannery workers because petitioners had contracted with a predominantly nonwhite union (Local 37) to fill these positions. As a result, if petitioners (for some permissible reason) ceased using Local 37 as its hiring channel for cannery positions, it appears (according to the District Court's findings) that the racial stratification between the cannery and noncannery workers might diminish to statistical insignificance. Under the Court of Appeals' approach, therefore, it is possible that with no change whatsoever in their hiring practices for noncannery workers—the jobs at-issue in this lawsuit—petitioners could make respondents' prima facie case of disparate impact "disappear." But if there would be no prima facie case of disparate impact in the selection of noncannery workers absent petitioners' use of Local 37 to hire cannery workers, surely the petitioners' reliance on the union to fill the cannery jobs not at-issue here (and its resulting "overrepresentation" of nonwhites in those positions) does not—standing alone—make out a prima facie case of disparate impact. Yet it is precisely such an ironic result that the Court of Appeals reached below.

Consequently, we reverse the Court of Appeals' ruling that a comparison between the percentage of cannery workers who are nonwhite and the percentage of noncannery workers who are nonwhite makes out a prima facie case of disparate impact. Of course, this leaves unresolved whether the record made in the District Court will support a conclusion that a prima facie case of disparate impact has been established on some basis other than the racial disparity between cannery and noncannery workers. This is an issue that the Court of Appeals or the District Court should address in the first instance.

III

Since the statistical disparity relied on by the Court of Appeals did not suffice to make out a prima facie case, any inquiry by us into whether the specific challenged employment practices of petitioners caused that disparity is pretermitted, as is any inquiry into whether the disparate impact that any employment practice may have had was justified by business considerations.[9] Because we remand for further proceedings, however, on whether a prima facie case of disparate impact has been made in defensible fashion in this case, we address two other challenges petitioners have made to the decision of the Court of Appeals.

A

First is the question of causation in a disparate-impact case. The law in this respect was correctly stated by Justice O'Connor's opinion last Term in Watson v. Fort Worth Bank & Trust:

> [W]e note that the plaintiff's burden in establishing a prima facie case goes beyond the need to show that there are statistical disparities in the employer's work force. The plaintiff must begin by identifying the specific employment practice that is challenged. . . . Especially in cases where an employer combines subjective criteria with the use of more rigid standardized rules or tests, the plaintiff is in our view responsible for isolating and identifying the specific employment practices that are allegedly responsible for any observed statistical disparities.

Cf. also Id. (Blackmun, J., concurring in part and concurring in judgment).

Indeed, even the Court of Appeals—whose decision petitioners assault on this score—noted that "it is . . . essential that the practices identified by the cannery workers be linked causally with the demonstrated adverse impact." Notwithstanding the Court of Appeals' apparent adherence to the proper inquiry, petitioners contend that that court erred by permitting respondents to make out their case by offering "only [one] set of cumulative comparative statistics as evidence of the disparate impact of each and all of [petitioners' hiring] practices."

Our disparate-impact cases have always focused on the impact of particular hiring practices on employment opportunities for minorities. Just as an employer cannot escape liability under Title VII by demonstrating that, "at the bottom line," his work force is racially balanced (where particular hiring practices may operate to deprive minorities of employment opportunities), see Connecticut v. Teal, a Title VII plaintiff does not make out a case of

---

9. As we understand the opinions below, the specific employment practices were challenged only insofar as they were claimed to have been responsible for the overall disparity between the number of minority cannery and noncannery workers. The Court of Appeals did not purport to hold that any specified employment practice produced its own disparate impact that was actionable under Title VII. This is not to say that a specific practice, such as nepotism, if it were proved to exist, could not itself be subject to challenge if it had a disparate impact on minorities. Nor is it to say that segregated dormitories and eating facilities in the workplace may not be challenged under 42 U.S.C. §2000e-2(a)(2) without showing a disparate impact on hiring or promotion.

3. Systemic Disparate Impact Discrimination Under Title VII

disparate impact simply by showing that, "at the bottom line," there is racial imbalance in the work force. As a general matter, a plaintiff must demonstrate that it is the application of a specific or particular employment practice that has created the disparate impact under attack. Such a showing is an integral part of the plaintiff's prima facie case in a disparate-impact suit under Title VII.

Here, respondents have alleged that several "objective" employment practices (e.g., nepotism, separate hiring channels, rehire preferences), as well as the use of "subjective decision making" to select noncannery workers, have had a disparate impact on nonwhites. Respondents base this claim on statistics that allegedly show a disproportionately low percentage of non-whites in the at-issue positions. However, even if on remand respondents can show that nonwhites are underrepresented in the at-issue jobs in a manner that is acceptable under the standards set forth in Part II, supra, this alone will not suffice to make out a prima facie case of disparate impact. Respondents will also have to demonstrate that the disparity they complain of is the result of one or more of the employment practices that they are attacking here, specifically showing that each challenged practice has a significantly disparate impact on employment opportunities for whites and nonwhites. To hold otherwise would result in employers being potentially liable for "the myriad of innocent causes that may lead to statistical imbalances in the composition of their work forces." Watson v. Fort Worth Bank & Trust.

Some will complain that this specific causation requirement is unduly burdensome on Title VII plaintiffs. But liberal civil discovery rules give plaintiffs broad access to employers' records in an effort to document their claims. Also, employers falling within the scope of the Uniform Guidelines on Employee Selection Procedures, 29 C.F.R. §1607.1 et seq. (1988), are required to "maintain . . . records or other information which will disclose the impact which its tests and other selection procedures have upon employment opportunities of persons by identifiable race, sex, or ethnic group[s.]" See §1607.4(A). This includes records concerning "the individual components of the selection process" where there is a significant disparity in the selection rates of whites and nonwhites. See §1607.4(C). Plaintiffs as a general matter will have the benefit of these tools to meet their burden of showing a causal link between challenged employment practices and racial imbalances in the work force; respondents presumably took full advantage of these opportunities to build their case before the trial in the District Court was held.[10]

---

10. Of course, petitioners' obligation to collect or retain any of these data may be limited by the Guidelines themselves. See 29 C.F.R. §602.14(b) (1988) (exempting "seasonal" jobs from certain record-keeping requirements).

Consequently, on remand, the courts below are instructed to require, as part of respondents' prima facie case, a demonstration that specific elements of the petitioners' hiring process have a significantly disparate impact on nonwhites.

B

If, on remand, respondents meet the proof burdens outlined above, and establish a prima facie case of disparate impact with respect to any of petitioners' employment practices, the case will shift to any business justification petitioners offer for their use of these practices. This phase of the disparate-impact case contains two components: first, a consideration of the justifications an employer offers for his use of these practices; and second, the availability of alternate practices to achieve the same business ends, with less racial impact. See, e.g., Albemarle Paper Co. v. Moody. We consider these two components in turn.

(1)

Though we have phrased the query differently in different cases, it is generally well-established that at the justification stage of such a disparate impact case, the dispositive issue is whether a challenged practice serves, in a significant way, the legitimate employment goals of the employer. See, e.g., Watson v. Fort Worth Bank & Trust Co.; New York Transit Authority v. Beazer; Griggs v. Duke Power Co. The touchstone of this inquiry is a reasoned review of the employer's justification for his use of the challenged practice. A mere insubstantial justification in this regard will not suffice, because such a low standard of review would permit discrimination to be practiced through the use of spurious, seemingly neutral employment practices. At the same time, though, there is no requirement that the challenged practice be "essential" or "indispensable" to the employer's business for it to pass muster: this degree of scrutiny would be almost impossible for most employers to meet, and would result in a host of evils we have identified above.

In this phase, the employer carries the burden of producing evidence of a business justification for his employment practice. The burden of persuasion, however, remains with the disparate impact plaintiff. To the extent that the Ninth Circuit held otherwise . . . suggesting that the persuasion burden should shift to the petitioners once the respondents established a prima facie case of disparate impact — its decisions were erroneous. "[T]he ultimate burden of proving that discrimination against a protected group has been caused by a specific employment practice remains with the plaintiff *at all times.*" *Watson,* supra, (O'Connor, J.) (emphasis added). This rule conforms with

3. Systemic Disparate Impact Discrimination Under Title VII

the usual method for allocating persuasion and production burdens in the federal courts, see Fed. Rule Evid. 301, and more specifically, it conforms to the rule in disparate-treatment cases that the plaintiff bears the burden of disproving an employer's assertion that the adverse employment action or practice was based solely on a legitimate neutral consideration. See Texas Dept. of Community Affairs v. Burdine. We acknowledge that some of our earlier decisions can be read as suggesting otherwise. See *Watson*, supra, (Blackmun, J., concurring). But to the extent that those cases speak of an employers' "burden of proof" with respect to a legitimate business justification defense, see, e.g., Dothard v. Rawlinson, they should have been understood to mean an employer's production — but not persuasion — burden. Cf., e.g., NLRB v. Transportation Management Corp., 462 U.S. 393, 404, n.7 (1983). The persuasion burden here must remain with the plaintiff, for it is he who must prove that it was "because of such individual's race, color," etc., that he was denied a desired employment opportunity.

(2)

Finally, if on remand the case reaches this point, and respondents cannot persuade the trier of fact on the question of petitioners' business necessity defense, respondents may still be able to prevail. To do so, respondents will have to persuade the factfinder that "other tests or selection devices, without a similarly undesirable racial effect, would also serve the employer's legitimate [hiring] interest[s]"; by so demonstrating, respondents would prove that "[petitioners were] using [their] tests merely as a 'pretext' for discrimination." *Albemarle Paper Co.*, supra; see also *Watson* (O'Connor, J.); Id. (Blackmun, J.). If respondents, having established a prima facie case, come forward with alternatives to petitioners' hiring practices that reduce the racially-disparate impact of practices currently being used, and petitioners refuse to adopt these alternatives, such a refusal would belie a claim by petitioners that their incumbent practices are being employed for nondiscriminatory reasons.

Of course, any alternative practices which respondents offer up in this respect must be equally effective as petitioners' chosen hiring procedures in achieving petitioners' legitimate employment goals. Moreover, "[f]actors such as the cost or other burdens of proposed alternative selection devices are relevant in determining whether they would be equally as effective as the challenged practice in serving the employer's legitimate business goals." *Watson*, supra (O'Connor, J.). "Courts are generally less competent than employers to restructure business practices," Furnco Construction Corp. v. Waters; consequently, the judiciary should proceed with care before mandating that an employer must adopt a plaintiff's alternate selection or hiring practice in response to a Title VII suit. . . .

Justice STEVENS, with whom Justice BRENNAN, Justice MARSHALL, and Justice BLACKMUN join, dissenting.

Fully 18 years ago, this Court unanimously held that Title VII of the Civil Rights Act of 1964 prohibits employment practices that have discriminatory effects as well as those that are intended to discriminate. Griggs v. Duke Power Co. Federal courts and agencies consistently have enforced that interpretation, thus promoting our national goal of eliminating barriers that define economic opportunity not by aptitude and ability but by race, color, national origin, and other traits that are easily identified but utterly irrelevant to one's qualification for a particular job. Regrettably, the Court retreats from these efforts in its review of an interlocutory judgment respecting the "peculiar facts" of this lawsuit. Turning a blind eye to the meaning and purpose of Title VII, the majority's opinion perfunctorily rejects a longstanding rule of law and underestimates the probative value of evidence of a racially stratified work force.[4] I cannot join this latest sojourn into judicial activism.

I . . .

The *Griggs* framework, with its focus on ostensibly neutral qualification standards, proved inapposite for analyzing an individual employee's claim, brought under §703(a)(1), that an employer intentionally discriminated on account of race. The means for determining intent absent direct evidence was outlined in McDonnell Douglas Corp. v. Green, and Texas Dept. of Community Affairs v. Burdine, two opinions written by Justice Powell for unanimous Courts. In such a "disparate treatment" case, see *Teamsters*, the plaintiff's initial burden, which is "not onerous," is to establish "a prima facie case of racial discrimination," that is, to create a presumption of unlawful discrimina-

---

4. Respondents comprise a class of present and former employees of petitioners, two Alaskan salmon canning companies. The class members, described by the parties as "nonwhite," include persons of Samoan, Chinese, Filipino, Japanese, and Alaska Native descent, all but one of whom are United States citizens. Fifteen years ago they commenced this suit, alleging that petitioners engage in hiring, job assignment, housing, and messing practices that segregate nonwhites from whites, in violation of Title VII. Evidence included this response in 1971 by a foreman to a college student's inquiry about cannery employment:

> We are not in a position to take many young fellows to our Bristol Bay canneries as they do not have the background for our type of employees. Our cannery labor is either Eskimo or Filipino and we do not have the facilities to mix others with these groups.

Some characteristics of the Alaska salmon industry described in this litigation — in particular, the segregation of housing and dining facilities and the stratification of jobs along racial and ethnic lines — bear an unsettling resemblance to aspects of a plantation economy. See generally Plantation, Town, and County, Essays on the Local History of American Slave Society 163-334 (E. Miller & E. Genovese eds. 1974). Indeed the maintenance of inferior, segregated facilities for housing and feeding nonwhite employees strikes me as a form of discrimination that, although it does not necessarily fit neatly into a disparate impact or disparate treatment mold, nonetheless violates Title VII. Responds, however, do not press this theory before us.

3. Systemic Disparate Impact Discrimination Under Title VII

tion by "eliminat[ing] the most common nondiscriminatory reasons for the plaintiff's rejection." "The burden then must shift to the employer to articulate some legitimate, nondiscriminatory reason for the employee's rejection." Finally, because "Title VII does not . . . permit [the employer] to use [the employee's] conduct as a pretext for the sort of discrimination prohibited by §703(a)(1)," the employee "must be given a full and fair opportunity to demonstrate by competent evidence that the presumptively valid reasons for his rejection were in fact a coverup for a racially discriminatory decision." While the burdens of producing evidence thus shift, the "ultimate burden of persuading the trier of fact that the defendant intentionally discriminated against the plaintiff remains at all times with the plaintiff."[13]

Decisions of this Court and other federal courts repeatedly have recognized that while the employer's burden in a disparate treatment case is simply one of coming forward with evidence of legitimate business purpose, its burden in a disparate impact case is proof of an affirmative defense of business necessity. Although the majority's opinion blurs that distinction, thoughtful reflection on common-law pleading principles clarifies the fundamental differences between the two types of "burdens of proof."[15] In the ordinary civil trial, the plaintiff bears the burden of persuading the trier of fact that the defendant has harmed her. See, e.g., 2 Restatement (Second) of Torts §§ 328A, 433B (1965) (hereinafter Restatement). The defendant may undercut plaintiff's efforts both by confronting plaintiff's evidence during her case in chief and by submitting countervailing evidence during its own case. But if the plaintiff proves the existence of the harmful act, the defendant can escape liability only by persuading the factfinder that the act was justified or excusable. See, e.g., Restatement §§ 454-461, 463-467. The plaintiff in turn may try to refute this affirmative defense. Although the burdens of producing evidence regarding the existence of harm or excuse thus shift between the plaintiff and the defendant, the burden of proving either proposition remains throughout on the party asserting it.

In a disparate treatment case there is no "discrimination" within the meaning of Title VII unless the employer intentionally treated the employee

---

13. Although disparate impact and disparate treatment are the most prevalent modes of proving discrimination violative of Title VII, they are by no means exclusive. See generally B. Schlei & P. Grossman, Employment Discrimination Law 13-289 (2d ed. 1983) (four chapters discussing "disparate treatment," "present effects of past discrimination," "adverse impact," and "reasonable accommodation" as "categories" of discrimination). Cf. n.4, supra. Moreover, either or both of the primary theories may be applied to a particular set of facts. See Teamsters v. United States.

15. See, e.g., 9 J. Wigmore, Evidence §§ 2485-2498 (J. Chadbourn rev. 1981); D. Louisell & C. Mueller, Federal Evidence §§ 65-70 (1977) (hereinafter Louisell); 21 C. Wright & K. Graham, Federal Practice and Procedures 5122 (1977) (hereinafter Wright); J. Thayer, A Preliminary Treatise on Evidence 353-389 (1898) (hereinafter Thayer); C. Langdell, Equity Pleading 108-115 (2d ed. 1883).

unfairly because of race. Therefore, the employee retains the burden of proving the existence of intent at all times. If there is direct evidence of intent, the employee may have little difficulty persuading the factfinder that discrimination has occurred. But in the likelier event that intent has to be established by inference, the employee may resort to the *McDonnell/Burdine* inquiry. In either instance, the employer may undermine the employee's evidence but has no independent burden of persuasion.

In contrast, intent plays no role in the disparate impact inquiry. The question, rather, is whether an employment practice has a significant, adverse effect on an identifiable class of workers—regardless of the cause or motive for the practice. The employer may attempt to contradict the factual basis for this effect; that is, to prevent the employee from establishing a prima facie case. But when an employer is faced with sufficient proof of disparate impact, its only recourse is to justify the practice by explaining why it is necessary to the operation of business. Such a justification is a classic example of an affirmative defense.[17]

Failing to explore the interplay between these distinct orders of proof, the Court announces that our frequent statements that the employer shoulders the burden of proof respecting business necessity "should have been understood to mean an employer's production—but not persuasion—burden."[18] Our opinions always have emphasized that in a disparate impact case the employer's burden is weighty. "The touchstone," the Court said in *Griggs*, "is business necessity." Later, we held that prison administrators had failed to "rebu[t] the prima facie case of discrimination by showing that the height and weight requirements are . . . essential to effective job performance," *Dothard v. Rawlinson*. I am thus astonished to read that the "touchstone of this inquiry is a reasoned review of the employer's justification for his use of the challenged

---

17. Accord Fed. Rule Civ. Proc. 8(c) ("In pleading to a preceding pleading, a party shall set forth affirmatively . . . any . . . matter constituting an avoidance or affirmative defense"). Cf. Thayer 368-369:

> An admission may, of course, end the controversy; but such an admission may be, and yet not end it; and if that be so, it is because the party making the admission sets up something that avoids the apparent effect of it. . . . When this happens, the party defending becomes, in so far, the actor or plaintiff. In general, he who seeks to move a court in his favor, whether as an original plaintiff whose facts are merely denied, or as a defendant, who, in admitting his adversary's contention and setting up an affirmative defence, takes the role of actor (reus excipiendo fit actor), — must satisfy the court of the truth and adequacy of the grounds of his claim, both in point of fact and law. . . .

18. The majority's only basis for this proposition is the plurality opinion in *Watson v. Fort Worth Bank & Trust*, which in turn cites no authority. As Justice Blackmun explained in *Watson*, (concurring in part and concurring in judgment), and as I have shown here, the assertion profoundly misapprehends the difference between disparate impact and disparate treatment claims.

The Court also makes passing reference to Federal Rule of Evidence 301. That Rule pertains only to shifting of evidentiary burdens upon establishment of a presumption and has no bearing on the substantive burdens of proof. See Louisell §§ 65-70; Wright §5122.

3. Systemic Disparate Impact Discrimination Under Title VII

practice. [T]here is no requirement that the challenged practice be . . . 'essential,' " This casual — almost summary — rejection of the statutory construction that developed in the wake of *Griggs* is most disturbing. I have always believed that the *Griggs* opinion correctly reflected the intent of the Congress that enacted Title VII. . . .

Also troubling is the Court's apparent redefinition of the employees' burden of proof in a disparate impact case. No prima facie case will be made, it declares, unless the employees " 'isolat[e] and identif[y] the specific employment practices that are allegedly responsible for any observed statistical disparities.' " This additional proof requirement is unwarranted. It is elementary that a plaintiff cannot recover upon proof of injury alone; rather, the plaintiff must connect the injury to an act of the defendant in order to establish prima facie that the defendant is liable. E.g., Restatement §430. Although the causal link must have substance, the act need not constitute the sole or primary cause of the harm. §§ 431-433; cf. Price Waterhouse v. Hopkins, 109 S. Ct. 1775 (1989). Thus in a disparate impact case, proof of numerous questionable employment practices ought to fortify an employee's assertion that the practices caused racial disparities.[20] Ordinary principles of fairness require that Title VII actions be tried like "any lawsuit." Cf. USPS Board of Governors v. Aikens, 460 U.S. 711 (1983). The changes the majority makes today, tipping the scales in favor of employers, are not faithful to those principles.

II

Petitioners seek reversal of the Court of Appeals and dismissal of this suit on the ground that respondents' statistical evidence failed to prove a prima facie case of discrimination. The District Court concluded "there were 'significant disparities' " between the racial composition of the cannery workers and the noncannery workers, but it "made no precise numerical findings" on this and other critical points. Given this dearth of findings and the Court's newly articulated preference for individualized proof of causation, it would be manifestly unfair to consider respondents' evidence in the aggregate and deem it insufficient. Thus the Court properly rejects petitioners' request for a final judgment and remands for further determination of the strength of respondents' prima facie case. Even at this juncture, however, I believe that respondents' evidence deserves greater credit than the majority allows.

Statistical evidence of discrimination should compare the racial composi-

---

20. The Court discounts the difficulty its causality requirement presents for employees, reasoning that they may employ "liberal civil discovery rules" to obtain the employer's statistical personnel records. Even assuming that this generally is true, it has no bearing in this litigation, since it is undisputed that petitioners did not preserve such records.

tion of employees in disputed jobs to that " 'of the qualified . . . population in the relevant labor market.' " That statement leaves open the definition of the qualified population and the relevant labor market. Our previous opinions, e.g., New York City Transit Authority v. Beazer; Dothard v. Rawlinson; Albemarle Paper Co. v. Moody; *Griggs*, demonstrate that in reviewing statistical evidence, a court should not strive for numerical exactitude at the expense of the needs of the particular case.

The District Court's findings of fact depict a unique industry. Canneries often are located in remote, sparsely populated areas of Alaska. Most jobs are seasonal, with the season's length and the canneries' personnel needs varying not just year-to-year but day-to-day. To fill their employment requirements, petitioners must recruit and transport many cannery workers and noncannery workers from States in the Pacific Northwest. Most cannery workers come from a union local based outside Alaska or from Native villages near the canneries. Employees in the noncannery positions—the positions that are "at issue"—learn of openings by word of mouth; the jobs seldom are posted or advertised, and there is no promotion to noncannery jobs from within the cannery workers' ranks.

In general, the District Court found the at-issue jobs to require "skills," ranging from English literacy, typing, and "ability to use seam micrometers, gauges, and mechanic's hand tools" to "good health" and a driver's license.[21] All cannery workers' jobs, like a handful of at-issue positions, are unskilled, and the court found that the intensity of the work during canning season precludes on-the-job training for skilled noncannery positions. It made no findings regarding the extent to which the cannery workers already are qualified for at-issue jobs: individual plaintiffs testified persuasively that they were fully qualified for such jobs,[22] but the court neither credited nor discredited this testimony. Although there are no findings concerning wage differentials, the parties seem to agree that wages for cannery workers are lower than those for noncannery workers, skilled or unskilled. The District Court found that "nearly all" cannery workers are nonwhite, while the percentage of nonwhites employed in the entire Alaska salmon canning industry "has stabilized at about 47 percent to 50 percent." The precise stratification of the work force is not described in the findings, but the parties seem to agree that the noncannery jobs are predominantly held by whites.

---

21. The District Court found that of more than 100 at-issue job titles, all were skilled except these 15: kitchen help, waiter/waitress, janitor, oildock crew, night watchman, tallyman, laundry, gasman, roustabout, store help, stockroom help, assistant caretaker (winter watchman and watchman's assistant), machinist helper/trainee, deckhand, and apprentice carpenter/carpenter's helper.

22. Some cannery workers later became architects, an Air Force officer, and a graduate student in public administration. Some had college training at the time they were employed in the canneries.

3. Systemic Disparate Impact Discrimination Under Title VII   Page 220

Petitioners contend that the relevant labor market in this case is the general population of the " 'external' labor market for the jobs at issue." While they would rely on the District Court's findings in this regard, those findings are ambiguous. At one point the District Court specifies "Alaska, the Pacific Northwest, and California" as "the geographical region from which [petitioners] draw their employees," but its next finding refers to "this relevant geographical area for cannery worker, laborer, and other nonskilled jobs." There is no express finding of the relevant labor market for noncannery jobs.

Even assuming that the District Court properly defined the relevant geographical area, its apparent assumption that the population in that area constituted the "available labor supply" is not adequately founded. An undisputed requirement for employment either as a cannery or noncannery worker is availability for seasonal employment in the far reaches of Alaska. Many noncannery workers, furthermore, must be available for preseason work. Yet the record does not identify the portion of the general population in Alaska, California, and the Pacific Northwest that would accept this type of employment.[23] This deficiency respecting a crucial job qualification diminishes the usefulness of petitioners' statistical evidence. In contrast, respondents' evidence, comparing racial compositions within the work force, identifies a pool of workers willing to work during the relevant times and familiar with the workings of the industry. Surely this is more probative than the untailored general population statistics on which petitioners focus. Cf. *Hazelwood*; *Teamsters*.

Evidence that virtually all the employees in the major categories of at-issue jobs were white,[24] whereas about two-thirds of the cannery workers were

---

23. The District Court's justification for use of general population statistics occurs in these findings of fact:

119. Most of the jobs at the canneries entail migrant, seasonal labor. While as a general proposition, most people prefer full-year, fixed location employment near their homes, seasonal employment in the unique salmon industry is not comparable to most other types of migrant work, such as fruit and vegetable harvesting which, for example, may or may not involve a guaranteed wage.
120. Thus, while census data is [sic] dominated by people who prefer full-year, fixed-location employment, such data is [sic] nevertheless appropriate in defining labor supplies for migrant, seasonal work.

The court's rather confusing distinction between work in the cannery industry and other "migrant, seasonal work" does not support its conclusion that the general population composes the relevant labor market.

24. For example, from 1971 to 1980, there were 443 persons hired in the job departments labeled "machinists," "company fishing boat," and "tender" at petitioner Castle & Cooke, Inc.'s Bumble Bee cannery; only three of them were nonwhites. In the same categories at the Red Salmon cannery of petitioner Wards Cove Packing Co., Inc., 488 whites and 42 nonwhites were hired.

61

nonwhite,[25] may not by itself suffice to establish a prima facie case of discrimination.[26] But such evidence of racial stratification puts the specific employment practices challenged by respondents into perspective. Petitioners recruit employees for at-issue jobs from outside the work force rather than from lower-paying, overwhelmingly nonwhite, cannery worker positions. Information about availability of at-issue positions is conducted by word of mouth;[27] therefore, the maintenance of housing and mess halls that separate the largely white noncannery work force from the cannery workers, coupled with the tendency toward nepotistic hiring,[28] are obvious barriers to employment opportunities for nonwhites. Putting to one side the issue of business justifications, it would be quite wrong to conclude that these practices have no discriminatory consequence.[29] Thus I agree with the Court of Appeals that when the District Court makes the additional findings prescribed today, it should treat the evidence of racial stratification in the work force as a significant element of respondents' prima facie case.

---

25. The Court points out that nonwhites are "overrepresented" among the cannery workers. Such an imbalance will be true in any racially stratified work force; its significance becomes apparent only upon examination of the pattern of segregation within the work force. In the cannery industry nonwhites are concentrated in positions offering low wages and little opportunity for promotion. Absent any showing that the "underrepresentation" of whites in this stratum is the result of a barrier to access, the "overrepresentation" of nonwhites does not offend Title VII.

26. The majority suggests that at-issue work demands the skills possessed by "accountants, managers, boat captains, electricians, doctors, and engineers." It is at least theoretically possible that a disproportionate number of white applicants possessed the specialized skills required by some at-issue jobs. In fact, of course, many at-issue jobs involved skills not at all comparable to these selective examples. Even the District Court recognized that in a year-round employment setting, "some of the positions which this court finds to be skilled, e.g., truckdriving on the beach, [would] fit into the category of jobs which require skills that are readily acquirable by persons in the general public."

27. As the Court of Appeals explained in its remand opinion:

Specifically, the companies sought cannery workers in Native villages and through dispatches from ILWU Local 37, thus securing a work force for the lowest paying jobs which was predominantly Alaska Native and Filipino. For other departments the companies relied on informal word-of-mouth recruitment by predominantly white superintendents and foremen, who recruited primarily white employees. That such practices can cause a discriminatory impact is obvious.

28. The District Court found but downplayed the fact that relatives of employees are given preferential consideration. But "of 349 nepotistic hires in four upper-level departments during 1970-75, 332 were of whites, 17 of nonwhites," the Court of Appeals noted. "If nepotism exists, it is by definition a practice of giving preference to relatives, and where those doing the hiring are predominantly white, the practice necessarily has an adverse impact on nonwhites."

29. The Court suggests that the discrepancy in economic opportunities for white and nonwhite workers does not amount to disparate impact within the meaning of Title VII unless respondents show that it is "petitioners' fault." This statement distorts the disparate impact theory, in which the critical injury is whether an employer's practices operate to discriminate. E.g., *Griggs*. Whether the employer intended such discrimination is irrelevant.

III

The majority's opinion begins with recognition of the settled rule that "a facially neutral employment practice may be deemed violative of Title VII without evidence of the employer's subjective intent to discriminate that is required in a 'disparate treatment' case." It then departs from the body of law engendered by this disparate impact theory, reformulating the order of proof and the weight of the parties' burdens. Why the Court undertakes these unwise changes in elementary and eminently fair rules is a mystery to me.

I respectfully dissent.

Justice BLACKMUN, with whom Justice BRENNAN and Justice MARSHALL join, dissenting.

. . . Sadly, this [decision] comes as no surprise. One wonders whether the majority still believes that race discrimination—or, more accurately, race discrimination against nonwhites—is a problem in our society, or even remembers that it ever was. Cf. City of Richmond v. J.A. Croson Co., 109 S. Ct. 706 (1989).

NOTES

1. The lower court's finding of no disparate treatment discrimination was not reviewed by the Supreme Court. How does the statistical proof here compare with that presented in *Teamsters?* There one comparison was city truck drivers versus those who drove over the road. Here it is cannery versus noncannery workers. What is different? Is Justice Stevens right in his dissent that the key similarity was that both groups of workers were interested in the seasonal work of the salmon fishery?

2. What is the significance to a disparate treatment case of the separate eating and sleeping facilities for the two groups of workers? Was this "smoking gun" evidence of intentional race discrimination?

3. In her opinion in Watson v. Fort Worth Bank and Trust, 108 S. Ct. 2177 (1988), Justice O'Connor described the relationship between disparate treatment and disparate impact concepts of discrimination.

> The distinguishing features of the factual issues that typically dominate in disparate impact cases do not imply that the ultimate legal issue is different than in cases where disparate treatment analysis is used. . . . Nor do we think it is appropriate to hold a defendant liable for unintentional discrimination on the basis of less evidence than is required to prove intentional discrimination.

Rather, the necessary premise of the disparate impact approach is that some employment practices, adopted without a deliberately discriminatory motive, may in operation be functionally equivalent to intentional discrimination.

Id. at 2785. If, in *Wards Cove*, the trial court had relied on a comparison of the racial composition of noncannery jobs with the qualified population in the relevant labor market and found the difference significant, would prima facie cases of both disparate treatment and disparate impact have been established?

4. In Agee v. Seidman, 881 F.2d 375 (7th Cir. 1989), the court upheld plaintiffs showing of a prima facie case after *Wards Cove* where 39 percent of black and 84 percent of white bank examiners at GS-9 passed a test to be promoted to be commissioned bank examiners at GS-11. First, the court held that using the single variable of race was sufficient so plaintiff need not use a multiple regression analysis to include other variables such as education. Second, the court found the pool of black and white bank examiners was sufficiently homogeneous to serve as the qualified labor market. But see Mallory v. Booth Refrigeration Service Supply Co., Inc., 882 F.2d 908 (4th Cir. 1989) (promotion pool not a qualified labor market without evidence of qualifications of pool members).

In Hill v. Seaboard Coast Line Railroad Co., 885 F.2d 908 (11th Cir. 1989), the court held there was no prima facie case where the pool of carmen was 12 percent black while only 4 percent of the foremen promoted from that pool were black. Within the agreed upon period of scrutiny, 2.7 percent of the black carmen were offered promotions while only 1.87 percent of the whites were.

5. What element did *Wards Cove* add to a prima facie case of disparate impact discrimination? Why does a showing that "at the bottom line" there is racial imbalance in the employer's workforce not suffice? After *Wards Cove*, would a plaintiff ever rely on the composition of a employer's workforce in a disparate impact case?

6. What happens if plaintiff cannot show the impact of specific or particular employment practices that has produced the racial imbalance in employer's workforce? Justice White downplays the significance of adding this specific identification element to disparate impact analysis by referring to broad discovery rules and the EEOC requirement that employers' maintain records concerning the individual components of the selection process. But what happens if the employer fails to maintain those records? May the factfinder draw the inference that the records, if kept, would support plaintiff's case?

7. What is the synthesis of *Wards Cove* and Connecticut v. Teal? If *Teal* stands for the proposition that plaintiff may attack individual components of a selection process that at bottom line has no adverse impact, does *Wards Cove*

3. Systemic Disparate Impact Discrimination Under Title VII

limit disparate impact analysis to the components, whether or not the result of the whole process has impact?

8. Once plaintiff establishes a prima facie case, what is the burden that *Wards Cove* says shifts to the employer? Does the burden of production differ from the burden of persuasion? In Agee v. Seidman, 881 F.2d 375 (7th Cir. 1989), Judge Posner described the effect of *Wards Cove*:

> To speak precisely the existence of a *"prima facie* case" *in the specialized Title VII sense of a case strong enough to shift the burden of production to the defendant* becomes moot once the lawsuit is tried. Yet in its older sense of evidence sufficient to defeat a defendant's motion for directed verdict, the existence of a *prima facie* case remains an issue—or would if there were jury trials in Title VII cases. Since there are not, it is simpler and clearer just to ask whether at the conclusion of the trial the evidence pro and con liability support a finding of violation.

Id. at 379. Assuming Judge Posner is correct as to motions for directed verdict at trial, what effect does *Wards Cove* have as to summary judgment motions before trial?

9. Do you agree with Justice Stevens' reason for distinguishing the effect of the establishment of a prima facie case in disparate treatment and disparate impact cases?

10. What is the new standard once the burden of production shifts to the employer? Describing it as the "issue of legitimate employer purpose," Judge Posner in *Agee* says the business necessity defense is "now a misnomer, since the 'defense' does not require a showing of necessity and is no longer an affirmative defense." The fourth circuit in Mallory v. Booth Refrigeration Supply Co., Inc., 882 F.2d 908 (1989) described *Wards Cove*. "[I]f the claimants establish a *prima facie* case of disparate impact with respect to the employer's practices, the claimants must prove that the proffered justification does not serve any legitimate employment goals of the employer." Contrast Evans v. City of Evanston, 881 F.2d 382 (7th Cir. 1989), where the court found the challenged physical agility test as "clearly related to the employer's legitimate need for physically strong firefighters" but questioned whether the test served a legitimate employer purpose because the passing score was so weakly supported. "So feeble was the city's effort to justify the cut-off point for the physical agility test that it can be argued that the city did not carry its burden of production." The court remanded for reconsideration in light of *Wards Cove*.

11. Do plaintiffs necessarily lose if the challenged practices serve legitimate employer interests? If plaintiff shows an alternative that equally serves the employer's announced purpose but the employer fails to adopt it, does that mean the challenged practice is a pretext for discrimination? If *Wards Cove* is

moving away from disparate impact discrimination to leave only the disparate treatment theories, why did the Court not use the word "pretext" to describe the less drastic alternative aspect of legitimate employer purpose?

12. In Evans v. City of Evanston, 881 F.2d 382 (7th Cir. 1989), the main focus of an attack on a physical agility test for firefighting jobs was the way the passing score was set. Plaintiff showed that the score used by the employer on the test in two different years had less impact on women but presumably served the city's purpose equally well. Why did Judge Posner fail to address this under the alternative practice notion?

13. Commentaries on the impact of *Wards Cove* are beginning to emerge. Brodin, Reflections on the Supreme Court's 1988 Term: The Employment Discrimination Decisions and the Abandonment of the Second Reconstruction, 31 B.C.L. Rev. 1 (1989); Player, Is *Griggs* Dead? Reflecting (Fearfully) on *Wards Cove Packing Co. v. Atonio*, 17 Fla. St. L. Rev. 1 (1989).

C. STATUTORY EXCEPTIONS

1. *Professionally Developed Tests*

Page 272. Add to end of Note 1:

After Wards Cove Packing Company, Inc. v. Atonio, 109 S. Ct. 2115 (1989), the real question is whether the law of professionally developed tests survives at all. Arguably, an employer need not now validate a test in confirmance with the guidelines because any attempt at validation will suffice to carry its lightened burden. The plaintiff would then have to invalidate the test. Or is this reading *Wards Cove* too broadly? Is it possible that test validation will continue as a separate wing of disparate impact analysis despite the general *Wards Cove* retreat?

For a post-*Wards Cove* test case, see Evans v. City of Evanston, 881 F.2d 382 (7th Cir. 1989). While the court reversed the judgment for plaintiff, Judge Posner said it was a close question whether to affirm because the city produced so little support for the passing score it used for the challenged physical agility test.

Chapter 4

The Interrelation of the Disparate Treatment and Disparate Impact Theories of Discrimination

B. THE RELATIONSHIP BETWEEN DISPARATE IMPACT AND TREATMENT WHERE THE PRIMA FACIE CASE IS BASED ON STATISTICAL SHOWING OF EFFECTS

Page 314. Add before Segar v. Smith:

The Supreme Court, in two recent decisions, has now spoken more clearly on the relationship between the disparate treatment and impact cases. First, in Watson v. Fort Worth Bank and Trust, 108 S. Ct. 2177 (1988), the Court in an opinion by Justice O'Connor held that subjective as well as objective selection procedures were subject to impact analysis. However, the part of her opinion that was only joined by a plurality foreshadowed a substantial restriction in the application of disparate impact theory. The second decision, Wards Cove Packing Company, Inc. v. Atonio, 109 S. Ct. 2115 (1989), effectuated a substantial change in disparate impact law.

Page 322. Replace *NOTES* with the following:

NOTES

1. While the Court in *Watson* upheld the application of disparate impact discrimination to subjective as well as objective selection procedures, Justice O'Connor's opinion set the stage for establishing new roles for disparate treatment and disparate impact concepts of discrimination.

   a. In a portion of her opinion joined by a majority of the Court, Justice O'Connor appeared to adopt the rationale for disparate impact as a way of guaranteeing that intentional discrimination will be corrected. "[T]he necessary premise of the disparate impact approach is that some employment practices, adopted without a deliberately discriminatory motive, may in operation be functionally equivalent to intentional discrimination." Id. at 2785.

   b. The functional equivalent rationale appears to link the two general theories together. Further linkage between disparate impact and disparate treatment language can be found in language suggesting the issues and levels of proof are the same under the two theories.

   > The distinguishing features of the factual issues that typically dominate in disparate impact cases do not imply that the ultimate legal issue is different than in cases where disparate treatment analysis is used. Nor do we think it is appropriate to hold a defendant liable for unintentional discrimination on the basis of less evidence than is required to prove intentional discrimination. [Id.]

2. Justice White's opinion in Wards Cove Packing Company, Inc. v. Atonio, 109 S. Ct. 2115 (1989), in some senses supports the linkage described in *Watson* but in other senses separates the two theories. The similarities are as follows:

   a. The Court imports the qualified labor market pool from the systemic disparate treatment cases of *Teamsters* and *Hazelwood* into disparate impact cases based on "snapshot" statistics of the racial or gender representation in the employer's workforce.

   b. The Court carried into disparate impact cases from the individual disparate treatment cases the limited significance of plaintiff's establishment of a prima facie case. Thus, the plaintiff maintains the burden of persuasion while the employer need merely carry a burden of producing evidence that the challenged practice serves some legitimate employer purpose. If the em-

4. Interrelation of Disparate Treatment and Disparate Impact Page 322

ployer carries that burden, the plaintiff must convince the factfinder that the practice serves no legitimate purpose or that the employer refused to adopt an alternative practice that equally serves its interests but has a less drastic racial or gender impact.

The main difference highlighted in *Wards Cove* is that the plaintiff must identify the particular practices that produce the overall impact in the employer's workforce in order to satisfy a newly articulated causation element in plaintiff's prima facie disparate impact case.

3. If the levels of proof are the same for the two theories and if plaintiff always bears the burden of persuasion under both theories, why would a plaintiff ever bring a disparate impact case, which also carries the added causation element requiring plaintiff to identify the particular practices that have produced the impact?

What happens if plaintiff makes out a prima facie case of systemic disparate treatment discrimination? The burden of production shifts to the employer to introduce evidence dispelling the inference that it acted with intent to discriminate. Would one way to do that be to introduce evidence that specific employer practices produced the impact? Would the employer also be required to carry a burden of producing evidence that the identified practice served some legitimate purpose?

PART II

TITLE VII: SPECIAL PROBLEMS, PROCEDURES, AND REMEDIES

Chapter 5

Special Problems in Applying Title VII

B. COVERAGE OF TITLE VII

Page 341. Add to end of carryover Note 2:

See Caruso v. Peat, Marwick, Mitchell & Co., 664 F. Supp. 144 (S.D.N.Y. 1987) (holding "partner" to be an employee). See generally, Comment, Partners as Employees Under the Federal Employment Discrimination Statutes: Are the Roles of Partner and Employee Mutually Exclusive?, 42 U. Miami L. Rev. 699 (1988).

Page 341. Add to end of Note 4:

But see Mitchell v. Frank R. Howard Memorial Hosp., 853 F.2d 762 (9th Cir. 1988), *cert. denied*, 109 S. Ct. 1123 (1989) (relationship between an individual and his wholly-owned corporation not an employment relationship within Title VII).

Page 343. Add in carryover Note 8 before "See generally" cite:

Accord Zaklama v. Mt. Sinai Medical Center, 842 F.2d 291 (11th Cir. 1988); Pardazi v. Cullman Medical Center, 838 F.2d 1155 (11th Cir. 1988). Cf. Diggs v. Harris Hospital-Methodist, Inc., 847 F.2d 270 (5th Cir.), *cert. denied*, 109 S. Ct. 394 (1988) (assuming *arguendo* that interference with third-person employment constituted a violation of Title VII, nevertheless interference with a physician's opportunities to care for private patients did not constitute interference with an *employment* relationship).

Page 343. Add in Note 9, before cite to Roberts v. United States Jaycees:

New York State Club Assn. v. City of New York, 487 U.S.1 (1988) (upholding constitutionality of amendment to New York City Human Rights Law substantially narrowing its "private club" exemption);

Page 343. Add at end of Note 10:

The most important authority on this question, since *Sumitomo Shoji*, came from the Third Circuit and dealt with a treaty between the United States and Korea containing language identical to that at issue before the Supreme Court. MacNamara v. Korean Air Lines, 863 F.2d 1135 (3d Cir. 1988), *cert. denied*, 110 S. Ct. 349 (1989), first held that the treaty applied to the plaintiff's case since the position at issue was an "executive" one within its meaning. It also rejected the plaintiff's argument that the treaty was inapplicable to his *discharge* because it authorized foreign companies only to "engage" certain individuals. For the court, the critical question was not the work plaintiff was doing nor the fact that he was discharged; the question, rather, was whether the defendant was employing, at least partly in plaintiff's stead, a Korean citizen who functioned at a sufficiently high level to come within the treaty's exemption.

Turning, then, to the interaction of the treaty with Title VII, the *McNamara* court used an ingenious analysis to avoid most areas of conflict between the two. Finding that "The target of [the treaty] was legislation that forced foreign employers to hire host country personnel," id. at 1144, it concluded that the treaty simply barred the use of citizenship as a criterion for employment. So read, it found no direct conflict with Title VII which does not prohibit the use of citizenship. This interpretation subjected a foreign employer to the same local laws as a domestic employer, thus establishing parity rather than a preferred position. The effect is to prohibit a beneficiary

5. Special Problems in Applying Title VII

of the treaty from discriminating, even in its executive positions, on bases such as age, sex, or race. The only discrimination allowed would be on the basis of "the nationality of its executive labor pool." Id. at 1146.

The *McNamara* court did note that certain of the broader reaches of Title VII might have to be curbed in order to avoid conflict with the treaty. A company of a country like Korea, with a racially and nationally homogeneous population, would tend to discriminate on racial grounds under the disparate impact theory if it employed Korean citizens since the effect would be to exclude members of other races. Although Title VII normally bars practices with such a disparate impact, that theory must give way to the extent that it interferes with a treaty beneficiary's right to choose "the nationality of its executive labor pool."

Page 343. Add a new Note 11:

11. An exemption, perhaps more compelling for what it implicitly brings within Title VII than for what it excludes, is the provision exempts "the employment of aliens *outside any state*," 42 U.S.C.A. §2000e-(1), §702 (emphasis added) (1981). This strongly suggests that aliens within the country are protected from discrimination on prohibited bases. See page 464. But the exemption of alien employment "*outside any state*" also strongly implies that, as to citizens, Title VII has at least some extraterritorial application. That is, the negative inference from the necessity for such an exemption is that Title VII otherwise prohibits discrimination outside the United States. The extraterritorial application of United States law, however, poses international law questions, especially when the host country's law compels such discrimination. The courts have in fact tended to recognize that Title VII reaches beyond the United States when the employer is a domestic corporation, e.g., Seville v. Martin Marietta Corp., 638 F. Supp. 590 (D. Md. 1986); Bryant v. International School Services, Inc., 502 F. Supp. 472 (D.N.J. 1980), *rev'd on other grounds*, 675 F.2d 562 (3d Cir. 1982). See also Lavrov v. NCR Corp., 591 F. Supp. 102 (S.D. Ohio 1984). But see Mas Maques v. Digital Equipment Corp., 637 F.2d 24 (1st Cir. 1980). See generally, Note, Equal Employment Opportunity for Americans Abroad, 62 N.Y.U.L. Rev. 1289 (1987); Note, Title VII of the Civil Rights Act of 1964 and the Multinational Enterprise, 73 Geo. L.J. 1465 (1985). The most important contrary authority rejecting extraterritorial effect is a recent en banc decision by the Fifth Circuit in Boureslan v. Aramco, 892 F.2d 1271 (5th Cir. 1990) (9-5). The majority relied heavily on a presumption against extraterritoriality. The dissent found the presumption adequately rebutted by the negative inference from §702. Even assuming that Title VII has extraterritorial effects when American companies discriminate against Americans abroad, an important question will be

Page 343   5. Special Problems in Applying Title VII

who counts as an American company. Legislation under the ADEA has addressed this question, 29 U.S.C.A. §623(f) and (g), and the courts may tend to look to that legislation for guidance in cases arising under Title VII.

C. GENDER DISCRIMINATION

1. Pregnancy

Page 354. Add at end of Note 6:

See Chambers v. Omaha Girls Club, 834 F.2d 697 (8th Cir. 1987), *reh'g denied*, 840 F.2d 583 (1988) (upholding the disqualification of an unmarried pregnant woman as a teacher in a teenage girls club),

Page 368. Add a new Note 9:

9. In Harness v. Hartz Mountain Corp., 877 F.2d 1307 (6th Cir. 1989) (2-1), *cert. denied*, 110 S. Ct. 728 (1990), the Sixth Circuit, applying Kentucky law, rejected a male employee's attack on a company's leave policy, which facially discriminated in favor of pregnancy as against all other disabilities. Pregnancy leave could extend to one year, while leave for other disabilities was limited to 90 days. Although the court sustained the policy under its reading of the Kentucky fair employment practices law, it seemed to believe that the same analysis would govern under Title VII. The court found no violation of Title VII, but, unlike *Guerra* where the employers could have accorded equal treatment, did not the employer in this case clearly discriminate against males? Does *Guerra* require the result reached by the Sixth Circuit?

Page 371. Delete Hayes v. Shelby Memorial Hospital and accompanying Notes; replace with the following:

UNITED AUTOMOBILE WORKERS OF AMERICA v. JOHNSON CONTROLS, INC.
886 F.2d 871 (7th Cir. 1989) (en banc)
cert. granted, **108 L. Ed. 2d 762 (1990)**

Before BAUER, Chief Judge, CUMMINGS, WOOD, Jr., CUDAHY, POSNER, COFFEY, FLAUM, EASTERBROOK, RIPPLE, MANION and KANNE, Circuit Judges.

5. Special Problems in Applying Title VII　　　　　　　　　　Page 371

COFFEY, Circuit Judge.

Since 1982 Johnson Controls, Inc. . . . has maintained a fetal protection policy designed to prevent unborn children and their mothers from suffering the adverse effects of lead exposure. International Union, United Automobile, Aerospace and Agricultural Implement Workers of America, UAW (hereinafter "UAW"), several UAW local unions and a group of individual employees brought suit alleging that this policy violated Title VII, 42 U.S.C. §2000e, et seq. The district court granted summary judgment in favor of Johnson Controls and the plaintiffs appealed. . . .

I

The Battery Division of Johnson Controls, Inc., was created upon Johnson Controls' 1978 purchase of Globe Union, Inc. [which] was formed through the consolidation of two battery companies and had been in the battery business for almost fifty years before Johnson's purchase. Globe Union and Johnson Controls have maintained ongoing efforts to improve industrial safety through measures designed to minimize the risk lead poses to those directly involved in the manufacturing of batteries.

The steps that Globe Union and Johnson Controls have taken to regulate lead exposure have not been focused merely on complying with governmental safety regulations, but originate from their longstanding corporate concern for the danger lead poses to the health and welfare of their employees, their employees' families and the general public. During the period of the 1970's when OSHA's regulation of employee exposure to lead was virtually non-existent, Johnson Controls' predecessor, Globe Union, initiated a large number of innovative programs in an attempt to control and regulate industrial lead exposure. For example, in 1969, Dr. Charles Fishburn, M.D., who later became one of the primary proponents of Johnson Controls' fetal protection policy, instituted programs for monitoring employee blood lead levels. In an attempt to manage lead exposure, other safety programs were initiated at Globe and Johnson including a lead hygiene program, respirator program, biological monitoring program, medical surveillance program and a program regulating the type, use and disposal of employee work clothing and footwear to minimize lead exposure. Globe Union also transferred employees out of high lead environments whenever a physician's medical evaluation report established that the individual had a high blood lead level. In the case of such transfers, medical removal benefits were provided to the employee before OSHA required such compensation.[6] Globe Union and Johnson Controls have continued to address their serious concern for industrial safety through efforts to design and regulate lead manufacturing areas to

---

6. These benefits provide compensation for transfer from a position for medical reasons.

reduce employee lead exposure. For example, laminar flow pumps constantly supply a down draft of low velocity clean air to improve the environment workstations where employees deal with lead. Central vacuum systems and powered floor scrubbers and sweepers are used to keep the manufacturing area as clear of lead dust as possible. Since Johnson Controls' purchase of Globe Union in 1978, it has spent approximately $15 million on environmental engineering controls at its battery division plants.

Globe Union, Johnson Controls' predecessor, established its first policy regarding fetal protection from lead exposure in 1977 as part of its comprehensive efforts to protect its employees from exposure to lead. Globe Union's announcement of the policy in a memorandum to battery plant and personnel managers stated:

> This change [the announced policy] has come about slowly as more and more medical opinion and evidence is persuasive of the risk to the unborn, developing child.
>
> We have stopped short of excluding women capable of bearing children from lead exposure, but do feel strongly that those women who are working in lead exposure . . . and those women who wish to be considered for employment be advised that there is a risk, that we recommend *not* working in lead if they are considering a family, and further that we ask them to sign a statement that they have been advised of this risk.

(Emphasis in original). . . .

Johnson adopted its current fetal protection program in 1982 following its determination, based upon scientific research, that it was medically necessary to bar women from working in high lead exposure positions in the battery manufacturing division. The fetal protection policy applies to work environments in which any current employee has recorded a blood lead level exceeding 30 μg/dl during the preceding year or in which the work site has yielded an air sample during the past year containing a lead level in excess of 30 μg per cubic meter.[7] The policy recites that women with childbearing capacity will neither be hired for nor allowed to transfer into those jobs in which lead levels are defined as excessive.[8] A grandfather clause in Johnson's fetal protec-

---

7. These lead levels coincided with the Centers for Disease Control's standard in effect at the time which concluded that blood lead levels in excess of 30 μg/dl were excessive for children. (As will be noted later in this opinion, the Centers for Disease Control have since revised downward the acceptable blood lead levels for children.) We note that, because of Johnson's concern for the mother and the unborn baby, the lead levels Johnson established in its fetal protection policy are below the 50 μ/m3 airborne lead levels and 50 μg/100g blood lead levels permitted under OSHA's lead exposure regulations for all employees. 29 C.F.R. §1910.1025(c)(1) and (k)(1)(i)(D). . . .

8. The fetal protection policy defines women of childbearing capacity as:

All women except those whose inability to bear children is medically documented.

5. Special Problems in Applying Title VII

tion policy permits fertile women who were assigned to high lead exposure positions at the time of the adoption of the policy to remain in those job assignments if they are able to maintain blood lead levels below 30 $\mu g/dl$.[9] Those employees who are removed from positions because of excessive lead levels are transferred to another job in Johnson's employ without suffering either a loss of pay or benefits.

The major reason Johnson adopted its current fetal protection policy was the inability of the previous voluntary policy to achieve the desired purpose: protecting pregnant women and their unborn children from dangerous blood lead levels. Between 1979 and 1983, at least six Johnson Controls employees in high lead exposure positions became pregnant while maintaining blood levels in excess of 30 micrograms. In addition, at least one of the babies born to this group of employees later recorded an elevated blood lead level. Moreover, Johnson Controls' medical consultant, Dr. Fishburn, testified . . . concerning a specific lead-related incident [at the Globe plant in Owosso, Michigan that the bloodlead level of the mother while she was pregnant affected the fetus and, therefore, her child]

Q. In just simple terms, what was the nature of the problem?
A. The nature of the problem was hyperactivity and control of the child. And the child had elevated blood-leads and protoporphyrinis.
Q. In your medical judgment was the problem of the child affected in any way by the exposure of the mother during pregnancy?
A. In my opinion the history of the hyperactivity and the difficulty she was having with him could very well and probably was due to the lead that he had.

In announcing its new, more defined policy, Johnson Controls emphasized its continuing interest in the protection of employees and their families from occupational health hazards and was responding to the increased understanding of the risk of lead exposure that had developed in the five years since it established its former voluntary policy. . . .

Prior to adopting its updated fetal protection policy, Johnson seriously considered alternatives to the exclusion of women with childbearing capacity from high lead exposure positions, but after research and consultation with medical and scientific experts found itself unable to structure and implement any alternatives which would adequately protect the unborn child from the risks associated with excessive lead exposure. Johnson's experience demon-

---

9. Under the fetal protection policy an incumbent female employee with a blood lead level reading above 30 $\mu g/dl$ is permitted a period of time to reduce her blood lead level to 30 $\mu g/dl$. If the blood level of a fertile female employee is in excess of 40 $\mu g/dl$, she is transferred at the earliest possible date. The record does not disclose the number, if any, of female employees who remain in high lead exposure positions or who were transferred as a result of the fetal protection policy.

strated that the voluntary exclusion program was ineffective. To date neither Johnson nor any other battery manufacturer has been able to produce a lead free battery, or to utilize engineering research and technology to implement a system or procedure capable of reducing the lead exposure of its employees to acceptable levels for fertile women. Limitation of the fetal protection policy to women actually pregnant was found ineffective because there is the very definite possibility that lead exposure will occur between conception and the time the woman discovers her pregnancy.[11] Such a limitation is further inadequate because reduction of blood lead levels following removal from a lead exposure area requires a significant length of time that frequently extends well into the pregnancy term. Limitation of the policy to women planning pregnancy also was not found to be a suitable alternative because of one of the exigencies of life, the frequency of unplanned or undetected pregnancies. Permitting fertile female employees to attempt to maintain a blood lead level below 30 μg/dl or utilizing the mean or median blood lead levels of current workers as a measure of whether a woman should be permitted in a position would also not effectively protect the unborn child. The reason these actions would be inadequate is that an employee's risk of high lead levels is usually greatest immediately after commencement of work in a high lead environment.

Dr. Fishburn, Johnson Controls' medical consultant, noted that Johnson and other corporations manufacturing batteries accept and routinely follow these medical policies. . . . [Fishburn was familiar with "a good many companies" in the foundry industry, including General Motors, Dow Chemical, Ford Motor Company, and Owens-Corning as well as other large and small companies. He testified:]

> . . . any doctor that has worked with lead, either in the mines as I did with [Dr.] Bellmap, or smelters, primary smelter we did not, and—and I

---

11. There will normally be some delay in diagnosis of pregnancy:

 The first sign of pregnancy and the first reason most pregnant women see a physician is absence of an expected menstrual period. If a patient's periods are usually regular, absence of menses for 1 wk or more is presumptive evidence of pregnancy. Pregnancies are usually dated in weeks, starting from the first day of the last menstrual period. Thus, if the patient's menses were regular and if ovulation did occur on day 14 of the cycle, obstetric dates are about 2 wk longer than embryologic dates. If the patient's periods are irregular, the difference will be greater or less than 2 wk. Usually, 2 wk after missing a period the patient is considered to be six wk pregnant and the uterus is correspondingly enlarged.

 R. Berkow, The Merck Manual of Diagnosis and Therapy, 1744-45 (14th ed. 1987). Thus, even in ideal cases, there is normally some time lag between pregnancy's onset and diagnosis. In other cases, a mother's failure to perceive a pregnancy or a delay in receiving prompt medical care can result in a pregnancy diagnosis later in pregnancy. Under a policy requiring removal only on discovery of pregnancy, the unborn child would be subject to lead exposure throughout the period prior to diagnosis of pregnancy.

5. Special Problems in Applying Title VII

was never taught to place a reproductive female in the average work exposure of lead. And furthermore, before the 60s, to my knowledge, no women were working in lead exposures. It was [Dr.] Kehoe's opinion at the time that any doctor that would allow this to happen was committing malpractice.

Q. Now this was—now my question was: Are you familiar with what other companies are doing now?

A. Yes.

Q. What are they doing?

A. They are restricting women from lead exposure who can have children.

In altering its fetal protection policy to more effectively protect the unborn child and its mother, Johnson responded to the most recent medical evidence which established that lead exposure in utero presents a substantial health risk to the unborn child, as well as its female employees, and believed that Title VII would allow it to address this risk.

II

Proper analysis of the Title VII issues this case presents requires a thorough understanding of the following fundamental question: Does lead pose a health risk to the offspring of Johnson's female employees? In considering the evidence in the record on this subject it is important to note that both the UAW and Johnson Controls agree on appeal that a substantial health hazard to the unborn child in the womb has been established. . . .

The record very clearly establishes that once lead is deposited in a mother's blood, it crosses the placenta and affects her unborn child. Because the fetus' blood system is nourished by the mother, the unborn child possesses approximately the same blood lead level as the mother. It is similarly undisputed that the unborn child "is medically judged to be at least as sensitive, and, indeed, is probably even more sensitive to lead than the young child." . . . The Centers for Disease Control summarized these basic facts in a document questioning the efficacy of current OSHA standards in protecting the unborn child and implying that an unborn child is adversely affected by lead levels lower than the 30 μg/dl reflected in Johnson Controls' fetal protection policy. . . .[19]

---

19. Centers for Disease Control, U.S. Department of Health and Human Services, Preventing Lead Poisoning in Young Children 7, 20, 21 (1985) (emphasis added). In this same document the Centers for Disease Control announced that based upon "current knowledge concerning screening, diagnosis, treatment, followup, and environmental intervention for children with elevated blood lead levels," it was lowering its definition of an elevated blood lead level from 30 to 25 μg/dl. Elevated blood level, according to the CDC, "reflects excessive absorption of lead."

The chief reason why an unborn child's lead exposure is of such great concern is that it has been medically established that lead attacks the fetus' central nervous system and retards cognitive development. . . .

Unlike physical birth defects, such as those associated with thalidomide,[21] lead's sometimes subtle damaging effects may not fully manifest themselves until the child is diagnosed as having learning problems in a school setting some five to six years after birth:

> What we are worried about are very subtle things, the ability to really affect learning ability. And so far as impairing the child's progress, they really aren't evident until he gets into school. He discovers that he can't remember, that his brain cannot pay attention, what our psychologists here called deficits in auditory processing, which is a fancy way of saying they can't understand what they hear, can't process it, and use it effectively. And those things will impair a child perhaps toward the end of the first grade, particularly in the second grade.

Probably the worst aspect of lead's influence upon an unborn child's future intellectual development is that its effects have frequently been found to be irreversible. Further, the most recent research suggests that the unborn child may be affected at lead levels previously believed safe. See J.M. Davis & D. Svendsgaard, Lead and Child Development, 329 Nature 297 (1987) (Collecting results of recent studies in this area).

Lead exposure can also pose other physical threats to the unborn child such as reduction of the infant's birth weight, premature delivery, and stillbirth. Lead may also affect the other vital fetal organs including, but not limited to, the liver and kidneys.

The danger resulting from lead exposure cannot simply be avoided through removing a pregnant woman from lead exposure promptly after the discovery of pregnancy. Dr. Chisholm, a recognized expert in the research field of treatment and prevention of lead poisoning in young children, observed that "excluding only women who are actually pregnant from work areas where there are elevated blood lead levels would not sufficiently protect the health and safety of the unborn child." This is true because lead continues to exert an effect upon the mother and her unborn child for a significant period of time after she has been removed from lead exposure. Dr. Chisholm's uncontroverted affidavit explained:

> [S]ubstantial medical evidence . . . establishes that lead remains in the body for a significant period of time after removal from a high lead environment.

---

21. Thalidomide is "[a] sedative and hypnotic [drug] commonly used in Europe in the late 1950's and early 1960's. Its use was discontinued because it was discovered to cause serious congenital anomalies in the fetus, notably amelia [absence of limbs] and phocomelia [absence of the proximal portion of a limb], when taken by a woman during early pregnancy." Dorland's Illustrated Medical Dictionary 1353 (26th ed. 1981).

5. Special Problems in Applying Title VII

Lead builds up not only in the blood and soft tissues, but is also stored in the bones. Following removal from the high lead environment, as the lead built up in the blood and soft tissues leaves the body, the lead in the bone begins to turnover, thus maintaining high blood lead levels even long after removal. As a general rule of thumb, it takes approximately two or three times as long for the blood leads to decrease as it did for such blood levels to increase. Therefore, if a woman is exposed to blood lead levels in excess of 25 or 30 micrograms for any length of time, such levels will not decrease sufficiently to avoid damage to the fetus, even if she is removed when the pregnancy is discovered.

. . . These conclusions are consistent with research that OSHA relied upon and quoted in establishing its 1978 lead standard:

> The placenta also has considerable storage capacity, and during the first few months of pregnancy, it grows tremendously in size while the fetus remains relatively small. Calcium along with other substances is stored in the placenta to be used in the later months of pregnancy for growth by the fetus. It could be expected that lead would be similarly stored.

Occupational Health and Safety Administration, U.S. Department of Labor, Final Standard for Occupational Exposure to Lead: Attachments to Preamble, 43 Fed. Reg. 54,395 (1978).[24]

The overwhelming evidence in this record establishes that an unborn child's exposure to lead creates a substantial health risk involving a danger of permanent harm. This evidence clearly approaches a "general consensus within the scientific community," and certainly "suffices to show that within that community there is [a] considerable body of opinion that significant risk exists to the unborn child from exposure to lead." Wright v. Olin Corp., 697 F.2d 1172 (4th Cir.1982). Next we consider the proper legal standards to be applied when employees bring a Title VII sex discrimination action challenging an employer's response to this serious health risk.

---

24. OSHA went on to observe that

> Dr. Hunt would not exclude the potential for lead-induced effects on the initial trimester of pregnancy. She maintains that the presence of lead in fetal tissue does not necessarily indicate that the observed effects occurred during the second and third trimester; they may, in fact, be the result of earlier accumulations of lead in the first trimester of pregnancy. [T]he fetus [can be] directly affected by lead which is absorbed during the first trimester of pregnancy. As the placenta is maturing, and the placental barrier is thinning, it is storing calcium necessary for later fetal skeletal production. Concomitant with the first evidence of fetal skeletal calcification, lead is observed present in the fetus. Like calcium, lead may be stored in the placenta during the early stages of pregnancy to be released when the placenta becomes functional.

(citations omitted).

III

. . . Two other federal courts of appeals and the Equal Employment Opportunity Commission have addressed the question of the defenses available to an employer under Title VII in a case challenging a fetal protection program. The first court of appeals to address this question was the Fourth Circuit in Wright v. Olin Corp. That case involved a fetal protection program very similar to the one Johnson instituted, in that it forbade any fertile woman from working in a job which " 'may require contact with and exposure to known or suspected abortifacient or teratogenic agents.' " In considering which of several possible theories of claim and defense should apply in a Title VII analysis of a fetal protection policy, the Fourth Circuit observed:

> We must start by conceding that the fact situation [the fetal protection policy] present does not fit with absolute precision into any of the developed theories. It differs in some respects—either in its claim or defense elements—from each of the paradigmatic fact situations with which the different theories have been centrally concerned. This of course accounts for the conflict on the point between the parties.
>
> That there would be such fact situations in Title VII litigation has always been recognized by the Supreme Court as it has developed and applied the different theories. *The Court has continually admonished, and indeed demonstrated in its own decisions, that these theories were not expected nor intended to operate with rigid precision with respect to the infinite variety of factual patterns that would emerge in Title VII litigation.* So has this court.

(emphasis added, footnotes omitted).

The court applied the disparate impact/business necessity theory of claim and defense that normally is applied only in cases in which an employer's policy is "facially neutral." Even though the court recognized that the facial neutrality of a fetal protection policy "might be subject to logical dispute, the dispute would involve mere semantic quibbling having no relevance to the underlying principle that gave rise to this theory." Because a fetal protection policy involves motivations and consequences most closely resembling a disparate impact case, the Fourth Circuit felt it should be analyzed under the disparate impact/business necessity theory. The Fourth Circuit defined the business necessity defense in the context of a fetal protection policy as requiring a demonstration that "significant risks of harm to the unborn children of women workers from their exposure during pregnancy to toxic hazards in the workplace make necessary, for the safety of the unborn children, that fertile women workers, though not men workers, be appropriately restricted from exposure to those hazards. . . ." However, the Fourth Circuit permitted this evidentiary demonstration to be rebutted with proof that "there are 'acceptable alternative policies or practices which would better accomplish the

5. Special Problems in Applying Title VII

business purpose . . . [or protect against the risk of harm], or accomplish it equally well with a lesser differential . . . impact [between women and men workers].' "[25]

The Eleventh Circuit utilized a similar analysis in Hayes v. Shelby Memorial Hospital, 726 F.2d 1543 (11th Cir. 1984) (Tuttle, J.). In *Hayes* a hospital terminated a pregnant woman's employment upon discovering her pregnancy. In *Hayes* the Court utilized the elements of the business necessity defense found in *Olin* to establish that the involved policy was not "facially discriminatory." The Eleventh Circuit stated: "In other words, the employer must show (1) that there is a substantial risk of harm to the fetus or potential offspring of women employees from the women's exposure, either during pregnancy or while fertile, to toxic hazards in the workplace and (2) that the hazard applies to fertile or pregnant women, but not to men." The theory underlying the facial neutrality analysis utilized in *Hayes* is that a policy meeting the above criteria "is neutral in the sense that it effectively and equally protects the offspring of all employees." If facial neutrality is established, the court proceeds to a disparate impact/business necessity analysis. Under the Eleventh Circuit's analysis, if facial neutrality is not established, the employer must present a bona fide occupational qualification defense to justify its fetal protection policy.

The Eleventh Circuit went on to set out the disparate impact/business necessity analysis it would apply in cases where facial neutrality was established. The court recognized that a fetal protection policy, even if "facially neutral," "clearly has a disproportionate impact on women since only they are affected by it." However "the employer's business necessity defense applies automatically, just as the employee's prima facie case of disparate impact applies automatically. That is because to reach the disparate impact stage of analysis in a fetal protection case, the employer has already proved — to overcome the presumption of facial discrimination — that its policy is justified on a scientific basis and addresses a harm that does not affect men." . . .

---

25. Johnson Controls' primary interest in this case is protecting the development and health of female employees and their unborn children. In construing the business necessity defense the Fourth Circuit in *Olin* cogently observed:

> We do not think that a general basis for the "business necessity" asserted here need be sought in other considerations than the general societal interest — reflected in many national laws imposing legal obligations upon business enterprises — and having those enterprises operate in ways protective of the health of workers and their families, consumers, and environmental neighbors. For this reason it is irrelevant that, as claimants point out, the mere purpose to avoid potential liability and consequent economic loss may not suffice, standing alone, to establish a business necessity defense. See Los Angeles Dept. of Water & Power v. Manhart.
>
> Although costs from tort judgments are merely a secondary consideration, they are still an important and legitimate additional consideration for an employer when lead safety policies may very well affect the development of the child in its most critical stage in the mother's womb.

Although *Olin* and *Hayes* present somewhat different analyses, both cases, in essence, determine that a business necessity defense in a fetal protection policy case requires (1) a demonstration of the existence of a substantial health risk to the unborn child, and (2) establishment that transmission of the hazard to the unborn child occurs only through women. Both cases also allow the employee to present evidence of less discriminatory alternatives equally capable of preventing the health hazard to the unborn.

On October 3, 1988, the Equal Employment Opportunity Commission, the agency responsible for the administration of Title VII, issued a Policy Statement on Reproductive and Fetal Hazards Under Title VII that, in substance, endorsed the approaches that the Fourth and Eleventh Circuits have taken to fetal protection cases (found in Fair Empl. Prac. Manual (BNA) 401:6013). As the Supreme Court has recognized, while such EEOC pronouncements "do not have the force of law, . . . still they ' "constitute a body of experienced and informed judgment to which courts and litigants may resort for guidance." ' " A fair reading of the EEOC's Policy Statement reflects that the EEOC thoroughly considered the various interests under Title VII and followed earlier judicial decisions only after concluding that these decisions properly implemented Title VII policies. The EEOC noted that fetal protection *cases do not fit neatly into the traditional Title VII analytical framework and, therefore, must be regarded as a class unto themselves.*" Policy Statement (emphasis added). The EEOC then candidly recognized that fetal protection policies that "exclude only women constitute *per se* violations of the Act." Id. (footnote omitted). However, the EEOC went on to observe that

> [a]lthough the BFOQ defense is normally the only one available in cases of overt discrimination, *the Commission follows the lead of every court of appeals to have addressed the question [in determining] that the business necessity defense applies to these cases. While business necessity has traditionally been limited to disparate impact cases, there is an argument that in this narrow class of cases the defense should be flexibly applied.*

(emphasis added). . . .

We agree with the Fourth Circuit, the Eleventh Circuit and the EEOC in their conclusion that a business necessity defense may be utilized in a fetal protection policy case. . . .

We are convinced that the components of the business necessity defense the courts of appeals and the EEOC have utilized in fetal protection cases balance the interests of the employer, the employee and the unborn child in a manner consistent with Title VII. The requirement of a substantial health risk to the unborn child effectively distinguishes between the legitimate risk of harm to health and safety which Title VII permits employers to consider and the "[m]yths or purely habitual assumptions" that employers sometimes attempt to impermissibly utilize to support the exclusion of women from employment opportunities. Likewise, the requirement that the risk of harm to offspring be substantially confined to female employees means that a fetal protection policy applying only to women recognizes the basic physical fact of human reproduction, that only women are capable of bearing children. Finally, the employee's option of presenting less discriminatory alternatives to a fetal protection policy assures that these policies are only as restrictive as necessary to prevent the serious risk of harm to the unborn child. . . .

IV

In Wards Cove Packing Co. v. Atonio, the Supreme Court recently described the general policies underlying the business necessity defense that we utilize in considering Johnson Controls' fetal protection policy:

> Though we have phrased the query differently in different cases, it is generally well-established that at the justification stage of . . . a disparate impact case, the dispositive issue is whether a challenged practice serves, in a significant way, the legitimate employment goals of the employer. The touchstone of this inquiry is a reasoned review of the employer's justification for his use of the challenged practice. A mere insubstantial justification in this regard will not suffice, because such a low standard of review would permit discrimination to be practiced through the use of spurious, seemingly neutral employment practices. At the same time, though, there is no requirement that the challenged practice be "essential" or "indispensable" to the employer's business for it to pass muster: this degree of scrutiny would be almost impossible for most employers to meet, and would result in a host of evils. . . .

(citations omitted).

In *Wards Cove* the Court also clarified the proof burdens to be applied in addressing an employer's business necessity defense:

> [T]he employer carries the burden of producing evidence of a business justification for his employment practice. *The burden of persuasion, however, remains with the disparate-impact plaintiff.* "[T]he ultimate burden of proving that discrimination against a protected group has been caused by a specific employment practice remains with the plaintiff *at all times.*" . . .

(emphasis added).

The allocation of the burden of proof under substantive Title VII law outlined in *Wards Cove* plays a significant role in summary judgment proceedings of this nature. [T]he question we must address is whether the UAW, which bears the burden of persuasion, has presented evidence sufficient to permit the district court to conclude that Johnson Controls' business necessity defense cannot be factually supported. . . .

A. SUBSTANTIAL RISK OF HARM TO THE UNBORN CHILD

Both the UAW and Johnson Controls agree on appeal that the significant evidence of risks to the health of the fetus contained in the record establishes a substantial health risk to the unborn child. [Although this agreement disposed of the issue on appeal, the majority went on to state that the record "conclusively supports the accepted medical and scientific finding that lead creates a substantial risk of harm to unborn children" under the *Olin* standard that "within {the scientific} community there is so considerable a body of opinion that significant risk exists . . . that an informed employer could not responsibly fail to act on the assumption that this opinion might be the accurate one."][28]

B. EXPOSURE THROUGH A SINGLE SEX

The UAW's efforts in this case have primarily been devoted toward negating the second element of Johnson's business necessity defense, that the risk of transmission of potentially harmful lead exposure to unborn children is substantially confined to fertile female employees. On this issue, as with the question of substantial risk of harm to the unborn child, "it is not necessary to prove the existence of a general consensus on the [issue] within the qualified scientific community." *Olin*.

In this case Johnson Controls' experts, without exception, testified that a male worker's exposure to lead at levels within the 50 μg/dl maximum set forth in OSHA's current (1978) lead exposure guidelines did not pose a substantial risk of genetically transmitted harm from the male to the unborn child. Moreover, Johnson's experts took the position that because this data dealt exclusively with animals, the results of these studies were not scientifically established as being applicable to humans. In contrast, the UAW witnesses posited that animal studies had demonstrated that there was a possible risk of genetic damage to human offspring as a result of male lead exposure. The UAW witnesses attempt to bridge the wide chasm between the results of animal studies and a conclusion of genetic harm allegedly transmitted through the male human being with human studies merely establishing a

---

28. There might be a suggestion that the unborn child would be harmed if his or her mother were deprived of insurance benefits or wages that could be utilized for prenatal care as a result of the application of Johnson Controls' fetal protection policy. This issue bears no relevance to Johnson Controls' employment practices for any female employees deprived of jobs in high lead environments under Johnson's fetal protection policy, instituted in 1982, are transferred to other positions in Johnson Controls' employ without any loss of either wages or benefits.

5. Special Problems in Applying Title VII

correlation between male lead exposure and changes in sperm shape. It is interesting to note that the UAW has not presented any medical evidence in the record of any human study scientifically documenting genetic defects in human beings resulting from male lead exposure. It is this lack of convincing scientific data that the plaintiffs attempt to gloss over and cast aside in ignoring the differences between the effect of lead on the human and animal reproductive systems.

. . . Unlike the recorded evidence of a substantial risk of harm resulting to an unborn child from exposure to lead through the mother's blood stream and placenta, the evidence of risk to the unborn child resulting from exposure of the father to the lead levels currently present in Johnson Controls' battery manufacturing factories is, at best, speculative and unconvincing. . . . Accordingly, we are convinced that the UAW has failed to present facts sufficient to carry its burden of demonstrating the absence of the second element of Johnson Controls' business necessity defense, application of the risk of transmitting lead exposure to unborn children only through females.

This recognition of the physical differences between the human sexes creates a distinction between men and women that accords with our previous recognition that Title VII permits distinctions based upon the real sex-based differences between men and women, especially those related to child birth. . . .

C. ADEQUATE BUT LESS DISCRIMINATORY ALTERNATIVES

We are cognizant of the fact that Johnson's fetal protection policy might very well not have been sustainable had the UAW presented facts and reasoning sufficient for the trier of fact to conclude that "there are 'acceptable alternative policies or practices which would better accomplish the business purpose . . . [of protecting against the risk of harm], or accomplish equally well with a lesser differential . . . impact [between women and men workers].' "

[The court concluded that the UAW had not preserved this issue for appeal, but even if it had] . . . we would be constrained to hold that the UAW failed to present facts sufficient for a trier of fact to conclude that less discriminatory alternatives would equally effectively achieve an employer's legitimate purpose of protecting unborn children from the substantial risk of harm lead exposure creates. In Wards Cove Packing Co. v. Atonio the Supreme Court recently explained the burden a Title VII plaintiff must carry in order to establish that an employer's policy is invalid on the basis of the availability of less discriminatory alternatives. . . .

. . . *Wards Cove* makes clear (1) that the UAW bears the burden of presenting specific economically and technologically feasible alternatives to Johnson Controls' fetal protection policy; (2) that if the UAW presents such alternatives, the UAW also bears the burden of demonstrating that its proposed alternative policy is *"equally* effective [as Johnson Controls' fetal protection policy] in achieving [Johnson's] legitimate employment goals," (emphasis added); and (3) that this inquiry is to be undertaken with the recognition that " '[f]actors such as the cost or other burdens of proposed alternative selection devices are relevant in determining whether they would be equally as effective as the challenged practices in serving the employer's legitimate business goals,' " and that " '[c]ourts are generally less competent than employers to restructure business practices.' . . ." In our case the inquiry is terminated at the first stage. The UAW, in its briefs and argument, has failed to present even one specific alternative to Johnson's fetal protection policy, much less a demonstration of how any particular economically and technologically feasible alternative would effectively achieve Johnson's purpose of preventing the risk of fetal harm associated with the exposure to lead of fertile female employees.

The record also demonstrates that viable alternatives to the fetal protection program were not presented to the court that would equally effectively further Johnson's legitimate interests. . . . Johnson Controls itself considered various possible less discriminatory alternatives prior to its adoption of the current fetal protection policy in 1982. In considering these alternatives, Johnson realized that lead could not be eliminated as a battery component. Furthermore, technically and economically feasible alternatives in the manufacturing process are incapable of reducing lead exposure to acceptable levels for pregnant women. Limitation of the exclusion from high lead positions to women actually pregnant or planning pregnancy was inadequate because lead exposure frequently takes place during the time period before the woman or her doctor determine her pregnancy. In addition, reduction of blood lead levels following removal of a pregnant female employee from lead exposure requires a significant period of time that can extend well into the pregnancy term. Although the Supreme Court has noted that "there is no requirement that the challenged practice be 'essential' or 'indispensable' to the employer's business for it to pass muster" under the business necessity defense, Johnson's policy could well have met this exacting standard. . . .

V

Having just held that the business necessity defense shields an employer from liability for sex discrimination under Title VII in a fetal protection policy involving the type of facts present herein, we are also convinced that Johnson Controls' fetal protection policy could be upheld under the bona fide occupational qualification defense.

. . . The bona fide occupational qualification defense, like other Title VII defenses, must be construed in a manner which gives meaningful and thoughtful consideration to the *interests of all those affected by a company's policy, in this case the employer, the employee and the unborn child.* Indeed,

5. Special Problems in Applying Title VII

the fact that Johnson's fetal protection policy applies exclusively to the high lead exposure areas of its battery division demonstrates why the policy is drafted with sufficiently definite terminology as to constitute a "narrow exception to the general prohibition of discrimination. . . ."

In the context of the Pregnancy Discrimination Act, application of the bona fide occupational qualification defense requires a court to consider the special concerns which pregnancy poses. A proposed BFOQ relating to capacity for pregnancy (or actual pregnancy) will exclude fewer employees than a BFOQ excluding all women. The court must also consider the physical changes caused by pregnancy, i.e., the presence of the unborn child, in determining whether the employee's continuance in a particular employment assignment will endanger the health of her unborn child. These concerns are in many ways quite similar to those a court should address in a business necessity defense analysis. . . .

Sitting en banc, this court recently considered the bona fide occupational qualification defense in Torres v. Wisconsin Dept. of Health & Social Services, 859 F.2d 1523 (7th Cir. 1988) (en banc). At issue in *Torres* was the question of whether the Wisconsin Department of Health and Social Services could pursue its legitimate goal in furthering prisoner rehabilitation through a policy excluding men from nineteen of twenty-seven guard positions in the living and hygiene areas of an exclusively women's prison institution. We noted with approval the traditional formulations of the business necessity defense. These formulations are that " 'discrimination based on sex is valid only when the *essence* of the business operation would be undermined by not hiring members of one sex exclusively,' " Dothard v. Rawlinson (emphasis in original), and that "an employer [can] rely on the BFOQ exception only by proving 'that he had reason to believe, that is, a factual basis for believing, that all or substantially all women would be unable to perform safely and efficiently the duties of the job involved.' "

We next discussed the need for courts conducting BFOQ analyses to avoid either using traditional stereotypes or falling into the equally unsatisfactory alternative of ignoring the real differences between men and women. We stated:

> It is also well established that a BFOQ may not be based on "stereotyped characterizations of the sexes." Dothard. Nevertheless, while recognizing that sex-based differences may justify a limited number of distinctions between men and women, we must discipline our inquiry to ensure that our tolerance for such distinctions is not widened artificially by—as the district court aptly put it—our "own culturally induced proclivities." Nor, of course, can we tolerate the same preconceptions or predilections on the part of employers. Rather, we must ask whether, given the reasonable objectives of the employer, the very womanhood or very manhood of the employee undermines his or her capacity to perform a job satisfactorily. Dothard

Torres' conclusion that Congress intended the bona fide occupational qualification defense as a recognition of the real differences between men and women accords with Congress' approach in both Title VII and other contexts concerning matters involving distinctions based upon realistic physical differences between men and women. For example, in Rostker v. Goldberg, 453 U.S. 57 (1981), the Supreme Court affirmed the exclusion of women from the military draft based upon a congressional determination that women were not suited for combat. . . . Likewise, in California Federal Savings & Loan Association v. Guerra, 479 U.S. 272 (1987), the Supreme Court recognized that in enacting Title VII Congress did not intend to preclude state pregnancy leave legislation which recognized *"actual physical disability* on account of pregnancy," (emphasis in original), and that did "not reflect archaic or stereotypical notions about pregnancy and the abilities of pregnant workers." Finally, Title IX requirements with respect to equality between men and women in athletic programs have been administratively interpreted to allow separate male and female teams and to permit exclusion of women from contact sports. See 7 C.F.R. §15a.41(b), 10 C.F.R. §1040.44(b), 34 C.F.R. §106.41(b), 45 C.F.R. §86.41(b). The risk of injury to women from contact sports is based upon the recognized innate physical differences between men and women, matters analogous to Johnson's fetal protection policy's concern with the differences between men and women relating to childbearing capacity. . . .

After establishing the general policies underlying the BFOQ defense, *Torres* set forth a method for ascertaining the validity of a BFOQ.

> The validity of a BFOQ can only be ascertained when it is assessed in relationship to the business of the employer. Our first step, therefore, *must be to come to an understanding of the employer's business*—its mission and the methodologies necessary to fulfill that mission. *In accomplishing this task, we cannot deal in generalities. Rather, we must focus on the "particular business" of the employer in which the protected employee worked.* Oftentimes, this task requires that a court recognize factors that make a particular operation of an employer unique or at least substantially different from other operations in the same general business or profession.

(citations omitted, emphasis added). In the context of the administration of a state prison, we considered how a specific definition of a business could permit a bona fide occupational qualification in a case where a general definition of the business might not permit such a qualification:

> Here . . . the broadest description of the "business" of the defendants is to say that they are in the business of governance at the state level. This general description, standing alone, gives them no special license with respect to Title VII. . . . A more precise definition of the "business" of the defendants is to

5. Special Problems in Applying Title VII

recognize that they are in the business of administering a penal institution. Few tasks are more challenging. . . .

This general description of the task of prison administrators is still too general to permit us to assess accurately the claims of the parties. [W]e must . . . refine our focus. The defendants are charged with the administration of a distinct type of penal institution—a women's maximum security facility. [T]he same historical and empirical evidence that might guide the administrator of a similar institution for males simply is not available with respect to this environment. Therefore, *the administrators . . . were obliged, to a greater degree than their counterparts in male institutions, to innovate in achieving one of the tasks mandated by the Wisconsin legislature—rehabilitation.* The defendants' "business" explicitly included—by legislative mandate—the task of rehabilitation.

(emphasis added, citations omitted).

Torres bears particular relevance to our discussion of the description of Johnson Controls' business. At a broad level, Johnson's business, insofar as relevant to this case, is the manufacture of batteries. Johnson's business is "unique" because it requires the use of lead, an extremely toxic substance that has been scientifically established to pose very serious dangers to young children and, in particular, the offspring of female employees. In order to respond to the problems accompanying its unique battery manufacturing operation, Johnson Controls has properly made it part of its business to attempt to manufacture batteries in as safe a manner as possible. This safety interest is every bit as critical to the mission of Johnson's battery manufacturing business as rehabilitation of prisoners is to the mission of the prison facility at issue in *Torres*. Furthermore, like the prison in *Torres*, Johnson has found it necessary to "innovate" to achieve its essential goal of manufacturing batteries through the adoption of a fetal protection policy that would address the health/safety problems related to its female employees significantly more effectively than the alternative policies it had considered.

Having established that industrial safety (preventing hazards to health) is legitimately part of the "essence" of the "business" of a battery manufacturer, as it is of any manufacturing enterprise, the next inquiry under *Torres* is whether Johnson Controls' fetal protection policy is "directly related" to industrial safety. Certainly a policy is directly related to industrial safety when it protects unborn children from a substantial risk of devastating and permanent impairment or loss of intellectual ability or injury to vital organs resulting from exposure to a toxic industrial chemical.

As in *Torres*, "[t]he more difficult question is whether the proposed BFOQ [is] 'reasonably necessary' to furthering the objective of [industrial safety]." In "unique" businesses, like the living areas of the women's prison in *Torres* or Johnson Controls' battery manufacturing operation, where an employer adopts an employment policy designed to address a difficult social problem,

Torres requires that courts reviewing such a determination under Title VII give some deference to the employer's decisions. As we noted in *Torres*:

> We believe . . . that the defendants were required to meet an unrealistic, and therefore unfair burden when they were required to produce "objective evidence, either from empirical studies or otherwise, displaying the validity of their theory." Given the nature of their "business"—administering a prison for female felons—the defendants, of necessity, had to innovate. Therefore, their efforts ought to be evaluated on the basis of the totality of the circumstances as contained in the entire record. In the Title VII context, the decision of penal administrators need not be given as much deference as accorded their decisions in constitutional cases. However, their judgments still are entitled to substantial weight when they are the product of a reasoned decision-making process, based on available information and experience.

[As in *Dothard*], "[m]ore is at stake in this case . . . than an individual woman's decision to weigh and accept the risks of employment." A female's decision to work in a high lead exposure job risks the intellectual and physical development of the baby she may carry. The status of women in America has changed both in the family and in the economic system. Since they have become a force in the workplace as well as in the home because of their desire to better the family's station in life, it would not be improbable that a female employee might somehow rationally discount this clear risk in her hope and belief that her infant would not be adversely affected from lead exposure. The unborn child has no opportunity to avoid this grave danger, but bears the definite risk of suffering permanent consequences. This situation is much like that involved in blood transfusion cases. There courts have held that individuals may choose for themselves whether to refuse to personally acquiesce in a blood transfusion that had been established as medically necessary, but that parents may not always rely upon parental rights or religious liberty rights to similarly refuse to consent to such a medically necessary transfusion for their minor children.[38] The risks to the unborn child from lead are also shared by society in the form of government financed programs to train or maintain a handicapped child in non-institutional or institutional environments and to provide the child with the training necessary to overcome the mental and physical harm attributable to lead exposure.[39] Thus, since "more is at stake" than the individual woman's decision to

---

38. In these cases a court will commonly appoint a guardian ad litem with the authority to consent for the child to the required transfusion and will hold a hearing to determine whether the child has been medically neglected as a result of the denial of the transfusion. See generally In re E.G., 515 N.E.2d 286, 287 (Ill. App. 1987), *appeal allowed*, 520 N.E.2d 385 (Ill. 1988).

39. Cf. State v. Acker, 485 P.2d 1038, 1039 (Utah 1971); Love v. Bell, 465 P.2d 118, 121 (Colo. 1970) (Costs to society from caring for motorcycle victims support mandatory motorcycle helmet laws in states that have these laws). . . .

5. Special Problems in Applying Title VII

risk her own safety, *Dothard* supports, rather than bars, a conclusion that an employer's fetal protection policy constitutes a bona fide occupational qualification. In such circumstances, "given the reasonable objectives of the employer, the very womanhood . . . of the employee undermines . . . her capacity to perform a job satisfactorily."

Against this substantive background, we hold that Johnson has carried its burden of demonstrating that its fetal protection plan is reasonably necessary to further industrial safety, a matter we have determined to be part of the essence of Johnson Controls' business. Initially, there can be no doubt that the exclusion of women who are actually pregnant from positions involving high levels of lead exposure sets forth a bona fide occupational qualification. . . .

We are also of the opinion that Johnson Controls' well reasoned and scientifically documented decision to apply this policy to all fertile women employed in high lead exposure positions constitutes a bona fide occupational qualification. The evidence presented concerning the lingering effects of lead in a woman's body, combined with the magnitude of medical difficulties in detecting and diagnosing early pregnancy, lead us to agree with Johnson Controls that there exists a reasonable basis in fact to conclude that an extension of this policy to all fertile women is proper and reasonably necessary to further the industrial safety concern of preventing the unborn child's exposure to lead.

Based upon the current status of research into lead's hazardous effects, we also agree that Johnson Controls has demonstrated to our satisfaction that exclusion of fertile women from positions in any area of its battery plant in which an employee has reported a blood lead level in excess of 30 μg/dl or where an air lead measurement has been in excess of 30 is reasonably necessary to the industrial safety-based concern of protecting the unborn child from lead exposure. At the time Johnson Controls adopted its policy, the 30 μg/dl lead exposure level coincided with the Centers for Disease Control's determination of acceptable blood lead levels for children. However, it is becoming increasingly clear that the 30 μg/dl lead exposure level once believed to be safe for unborn children is no longer medically accepted as risk free. . . . Medical knowledge is, indeed, a rapidly changing field. . . . Recent advances in scientific knowledge demonstrate that Johnson Controls' cautious approach has been consistent with the emerging knowledge that the unborn child may be adversely affected by lead levels below those permitted by OSHA standards. An example of a similar practice found in everyday experience is the medical and dental professions' extreme care and caution in the use of x-ray procedures on pregnant women. These procedures are generally avoided during pregnancy and, when absolutely necessary, are performed in manners designed to minimize any possible danger to the unborn child.

The analysis that we have conducted under the bona fide occupational qualification standards of Title VII is analogous to the approach the Supreme

Court took in the First Amendment context in *Sable Communications v. F.C.C.*, —U.S.—, 109 S. Ct. 2829, (1989). There the Supreme Court dealt with the question of whether Congress' ban on "dial-a-porn" services was narrowly tailored to serve a compelling governmental interest "in protecting the physical and psychological well-being of minors," very similar to Johnson's interest in protecting the health of the unborn through the female employee. In the constitutional context, as in the bona fide occupational qualification context, when an entity attempts to further this type of interest it must be accomplished with " 'narrowly drawn regulations designed to serve those interests without unnecessarily interfering with First Amendment freedoms,' " or, in this case, Title VII rights. . . . The Court determined that Congress' enactment was improper based upon its conclusion that "the congressional record contains no legislative findings that would justify us in concluding that there is no constitutionally acceptable less restrictive means, short of a total ban, to achieve the Government's interest in protecting minors." . . . In contrast to the government in *Sable*, as noted above, Johnson Controls researched, innovated and spent at least $15 million in lead control policies and has been unable to devise a policy other than the exclusion of fertile women from high lead exposure positions that would be capable of adequately serving Johnson's legitimate interest in protecting the health of the unborn. . . . Accordingly, the absence of economically and technologically feasible alternatives to Johnson Controls' fetal protection policy also supports a bona fide occupational qualification determination.

There is a reasonable basis in fact, grounded in medical and scientific research data, for concluding that Johnson Controls' has met its burden of establishing that the fetal protection policy is reasonably necessary to industrial safety.[43] Thus, the fetal protection policy should be recognized as establishing a bona fide occupational qualification protecting the policy against claims of sex discrimination. . . .

CUDAHY, Circuit Judge, dissenting:

I respectfully dissent from the majority opinion. I would be pleased to join almost all of Judge Easterbrook's eloquent dissent except for its disposition of the case. Here I join Judge Posner's equally cogent statement, which adopts the BFOQ standard but advocates remand for a full trial on that basis. . . .

---

43. Judge Easterbrook suggests that "by one estimate 20 million industrial jobs could be closed to women," if "the majority is right," "for many substances in addition to lead pose fetal risks." . . . This speculative statement, taken at its face value, merely suggests a possibility of reproductive injury from unidentified and undefined toxic substances. Before our decision could be applied to any of these unidentified substances, obviously they would have to be subjected to the myriad tests and research that have conclusively established the grave risk from lead substances. Thus, an employer presenting a business necessity or bona fide occupational qualification defense would have to establish that the substance had undergone the same rigid testing and research. In addition, if ever a lead-free battery were developed, the problems in this case would fall by the wayside. We hope that this is achieved tomorrow.

5. Special Problems in Applying Title VII

It is a matter of some interest that, of the twelve federal judges to have considered this case to date, none has been female. This may be quite significant because this case, like other controversies of great potential consequence, demands, in addition to command of the disembodied rules, some insight into social reality. What is the situation of the pregnant woman, unemployed or working for the minimum wage and unprotected by health insurance, in relation to her pregnant sister, exposed to an indeterminate lead risk but well-fed, housed and doctored? Whose fetus is at greater risk? Whose decision is this to make? We, who are unfortunately all male, must address these and other equally complex questions through the clumsy vehicle of litigation. At least let it be complete litigation focusing on the right standard.

POSNER, Circuit Judge, dissenting.

Johnson Controls refuses to employ any woman to make batteries unless she presents medical evidence of sterility. Today this court holds the refusal lawful under Title VII. A reader of the majority opinion might be excused for thinking that the case had been fully tried — and before this court — rather than decided by a district judge on a motion for summary judgment. I think it is a mistake to suppose that we can decide this case once and for all on so meager a record. . . .

Title VII forbids an employer deliberately to exclude a worker from a particular job because of the worker's sex unless sex is a "bona fide occupational qualification reasonably necessary to the normal operation of that particular business or enterprise." This defense is central to the appeal and we should attend carefully to its scope and meaning. It is written narrowly and has been read narrowly. . . . A broad reading would gut the statute. For it is unlikely that most employment discrimination in the private sector is irrational. Few private employers discriminate without having some reason for doing so; competition tends to drive from the market firms that behave irrationally. See Becker, The Economics of Discrimination (2d ed. 1971). If the defense of bona fide occupational qualification were broadly construed — for example, to excuse all sex discrimination that the employer could show was cost-justified — very little sex discrimination in employment . . . would be forbidden. Title VII's reach would be shortened drastically.

Two courts of appeals faced with challenges under Title VII to fetal protection policies have concluded that such policies can never satisfy the stringent requirements of the occupational qualification defense. See Wright v. Olin Corp., 697 F.2d 1172, 1185 (4th Cir. 1982); Hayes v. Shelby Memorial Hospital, 726 F.2d 1543, 1549 (11th Cir. 1984). But this conclusion, rather than resulting in instant victory for the plaintiffs, led those courts to stitch a new defense expressly for fetal protection cases. I am not myself deeply shocked that courts sometimes rewrite statutes to address problems that the legislators did not foresee. . . .

But we do not need to bite this bullet here, because the wording of the occupational qualification provision is not so cramped that it has to be stretched to bring (some) fetal protection policies within its scope. Nor is it a defensible way of stretching it to recast what is plainly a disparate treatment case—that is, a case of intentional discrimination against a protected group—as a disparate impact case, and then invoke the recent decision in which the Supreme Court expanded the "business necessity" defense. See Wards Cove Packing Co. v. Atonio. This legerdemain is as unnecessary as it is questionable. "[R]easonably necessary," one of the key terms of the occupational qualification defense, means more than just reasonable but less than absolutely necessary. On the way to concluding that the defense is unavailable in fetal protection cases the court in *Wright* misquoted the provision by leaving out the word "reasonably," and the misquotation is faithfully repeated in *Hayes*. The other key words of the defense, "*normal* operation" (emphasis added), should dispel concern that consideration of all interests other than the employer's interest in selling a quality product at the lowest possible price is precluded. It is possible to make batteries without considering the possible consequences for people who might be injured in the manufacturing process, just as it would be possible to make batteries with slave laborers, but neither mode of operation would be normal. To confine the occupational qualification defense to concerns with price and product quality would deny a defense to Johnson Controls even if the company excluded only pregnant women, as distinct from all women who might become pregnant, from making batteries. I do not understand the plaintiffs to be arguing that Title VII requires Johnson Controls to permit women known to be pregnant to continue working in an atmosphere dense with lead. If on the other hand a fetal protection policy that excludes women from a given job classification cannot be said to be reasonably necessary to the employer's normal operation, I do not see why we should want to save it from condemnation under Title VII.

I have described what I conceive to be the scope of the bona fide occupational qualification defense, and its application to sex discrimination, as of the original enactment of Title VII. I must now consider the bearing of the Pregnancy Discrimination Act of 1982 [*sic* — 1978], which amended Title VII by defining sex discrimination to include discrimination on the basis of pregnancy. [T]he amendment shows that the present case really is a disparate treatment case, that is, a case of intentional discrimination that can be excused only if the defendant establishes a bona fide occupational qualification; the amendment makes fertile women, the group that Johnson Controls deliberately excluded from a job classification, a group protected by Title VII. . . .

The defense is applicable to this case and although it is of limited scope it is not the proverbial eye of a needle. In particular, the "normal operation" of a business encompasses ethical, legal, and business concerns about the effects of an employer's activities on third parties. An employer might be validly concerned on a variety of grounds both practical and ethical with the hazards

5. Special Problems in Applying Title VII

of his workplace to the children of his employees. A pregnant employee exposed to heavy concentrations of lead in the air may absorb the lead into her bloodstream and from there transmit it to her fetus through the placenta, causing, years later, mental retardation or other injury to the child. The parties agree that there is a solid medical basis for concern with fetal injury from airborne lead in the concentration found in battery plants, and this concern could in turn cause the employer to worry about being sued by injured children of his employees. Such a suit would not be preempted by workers' compensation law, because the plaintiff would not be the worker. The employer would therefore be exposed to full common law damages, punitive as well as compensatory. The mother's own negligence—for if she had been clearly warned of the hazard, but voluntarily became pregnant anyway and continued to work making batteries, she would be acting negligently with regard to the fetus—would not be imputed to the child and therefore would not reduce the employer's liability. See, e.g., Collins v. Eli Lilly Co., 342 N.W.2d 37, 53 n.14 (Wis. 1984); In re Estate of Infant Fontaine, 519 A.2d 227, 230 (N.H. 1986); Fabianke v. Weaver, 527 So. 2d 1253, 1258 (Ala. 1988). It would merely make the mother a joint tortfeasor with the employer. Moreover, she might not be negligent; the pregnancy might be involuntary, and lead can injure the fetus before the mother knows she is pregnant.

Some courts have said that to create liability, the injury to the fetus must occur after the fetus has become viable (able to survive outside the mother's body). And as I just noted, lead in the mother's bloodstream can enter the fetus very early in the pregnancy—this presumably is the reason that Johnson Controls' fetal protection policy is so strict. But the distinction between injury to the fetus before it becomes viable and injury after makes no sense with regard to tort liability—since the plaintiff is the child, not the fetus—and has generally and correctly been rejected. See, e.g., Renslow v. Mennonite Hospital, 367 N.E.2d 1250 (Ill. 1977); Bergstreser v. Mitchell, 577 F.2d 22 (8th Cir. 1978); Prosser and Keeton on the Law of Torts §55, at pp. 368-69 (5th ed. 1984).

Other questions concerning tort liability remain unanswered—in particular whether the standard of liability is negligence or strict liability and whether compliance with OSHA's rules on safe levels of airborne lead is a defense. As a result it is difficult to estimate Johnson Controls' exposure to tort liability, but it would be premature, in this age of mass-tort suits (which for example drove the asbestos industry into bankruptcy), to dismiss it as trivial. The possibility of tort suits against battery manufacturers for lead injury to the child of a female employee is not merely a theoretical one. . . .

We should not dismiss the concern over tort liability as a narrow, selfish "bottom line" concern irrelevant to the purposes of Title VII. The potential cost of tort liability to Johnson Controls is an approximation of the potential cost to the children who have suffered prenatal injury from the airborne lead absorbed into their mothers' bloodstreams. That is a social cost that Title VII does not require a company to ignore. At some point it may become large enough to affect the company's normal method of operation and supply the ground for a bona fide occupational qualification of infertility.

A related point is that an employer might have moral qualms about endangering children or might fear the effect on his public relations. The ethical concern cannot be wholly dismissed, as could an ethical conviction that a woman's place is in the home. We know from the controversy over abortion that many people are passionately protective of fetal welfare, and they cannot all be expected — perhaps they cannot be required — to park their passions at the company gate. . . . Granted, in Doe v. First National Bank, 865 F.2d 864, 873 (7th Cir. 1989), we assumed that the Pregnancy Discrimination Act forbids an employer to fire a woman for having an abortion, and although the point had not been argued our assumption may well have been correct. See H. Conf. Rep. No. 1786, 95th Cong., 2d Sess. 4 (1978), U.S. Code Cong. & Adm. News 1978, pp. 4749, 4766 ("no employer may, for example, fire or refuse to hire a woman simply because she has exercised her right to have an abortion"). If so, the result is to place a limitation on an employer's effort to protect fetal life. But the Pregnancy Discrimination Act affects only the prima facie case of sex discrimination. The defenses are untouched. No defense of bona fide occupational qualification was pleaded in *Doe*.

If the hazard to the fetus from airborne lead in the mother's workplace is sufficiently great, if the amount of lead in the environment cannot be reduced without discontinuing the production of batteries, and if experience demonstrates that some women will become pregnant even after being clearly warned of the hazards to which the fetus would be exposed (there are many careless pregnancies, as is shown by the frequency of abortion and of illegitimate birth), I can find nothing in the text of the statute, or in its history or purpose, to prevent an employer from defending his refusal to allow fertile women to work in jobs in which they are exposed to dangerous concentrations of airborne lead on the ground that such refusal is reasonably necessary to the normal (civilized, humane, prudent, ethical) operation of his particular business. It is a matter of degree, and this we cannot assess on a summary judgment record. Of course the acceptance of the defense might be a hardship for those women who, though fertile, would not become pregnant. But hardship for the plaintiff is a possibility whenever a defense is sustained. It is no more than a possibility here, as we shall see.

Let us not be deceived by superficial historical analogies or facile invocations of "paternalistic." It is true that laws discriminating against women were once defended on the basis of a compelling social interest in protecting their fitness to bear and raise children, see, e.g., Muller v. Oregon, 208 U.S. 412 (1908), that this ground may have masked a desire to prevent women from

5. Special Problems in Applying Title VII

competing with men for jobs (in any event this may have been the effect, see Landes, The Effect of State Maximum Hours Laws on the Employment of Women in 1920, 88 J. Pol. Econ. 476 (1980)), and that many modern American women resent the suggestion that women have a special responsibility for perpetuating the human race. But we do not have a discriminatory law here. A law that commands all employers in a given line of business to treat women specially cannot be equated to a decision by a firm in a competitive market to treat them specially, if only because in the latter case other firms are free to follow a different course. There is also a difference between protecting women against themselves as well as protecting children, and protecting an employer and his employees' unborn children. A paternalistic measure is one that protects a person against himself, and insofar as Johnson Controls was motivated in adopting its fetal protection policy by concern with tort liability or adverse public relations, it was acting to protect its own interests. A fetus, moreover, is a different person (or proto-person) from its mother, and not all pregnant women fully internalize the welfare of their fetus, infant, or child. There are plenty of selfish and irresponsible parents, not all of whom are male. A fetal protection policy is less paternalistic than a maximum-hours law.

I conclude that Title VII even as amended by the Pregnancy Discrimination Law does not outlaw all fetal protection policies. Whether a particular policy is lawful is a question of fact, and since the burden of proof is on the defendant it will be the rare case where the lawfulness of such a policy can be decided on the defendant's motion for summary judgment. This is not that rare case.

Even if we accept that the amount of airborne lead in Johnson Controls' battery-making operation is dangerous to the fetuses of female employees and that the company cannot reduce the danger further without shutting down the operation, a host of unanswered questions remains. The first concerns the feasibility of warnings as a substitute for a blanket exclusion of all fertile women. Before Johnson Controls adopted the blanket exclusion, eight women employed in the battery operation had become pregnant in three years. But we do not know what fraction of women employed in the operation this was, because — remarkably — the record does not reveal the number of women employed in the operation. And the only warning that was in effect during that period was one more likely to allay than to arouse concern. It compared the fetal hazards of airborne lead to those of cigarette smoking, and many women do not believe that smoking is highly hazardous to the fetus. The plaintiffs believe that a real "scare" warning would have deterred those eight pregnancies; maybe they are right.

We do not know what other manufacturers of batteries do about the hazards of airborne lead to the fetus — whether they are content to rely on warnings, for example, and if so of what kind and with what effect. . . .

The evidence of record concerning the potential hazard to the fetus through a father exposed to airborne lead is fragmentary and stale, yet if that hazard is significant the fact that Johnson Controls does nothing about it undermines the company's argument that its fetal protection policy is motivated by concern for the fetus and reasonably necessary to the operation of the battery business. . . . The record is also blank on the wages and alternative employment opportunities of the women employed in Johnson Controls' battery operation. These data would be pertinent to the plaintiffs' ingenious although speculative argument that by depriving women of high-paying jobs, fetal protection may reduce women's expenditures on fetal and child care. . . .

We also do not know how profitable the business of manufacturing batteries is, and therefore how vulnerable it is to fears, as yet speculative, of litigation arising from fetal damage. (The case at this stage is a tissue of speculation.) [T]he lower the profit margin in making batteries the more plausible a concern with possible litigation becomes. The plaintiffs would have won a Pyrrhic victory if as a result of their winning this suit Johnson Controls shut down its battery operation, or if, as happened with so many products formerly manufactured in this country, production shifted overseas. . . . If Johnson Controls terminated its battery operation as a result of this suit, the plaintiffs would be in the same position as if the occupational qualification defense had prevailed except that they might—which is to say, realistically, that their lawyers might—recover attorney's fees. . . .

Even on the limited record before us, however, it is clear that the defendant's fetal protection policy is excessively cautious in two regards: first in presuming that any woman under the age of 70 is fertile, and second in excluding a presumptively fertile woman from any job from which she might ultimately be promoted into battery making, even if her present job does not expose her to lead. Since these aspects of the policy are severable from the rest of it I do not think their deficiencies need condemn the entire policy, especially since the first is harmless because a woman too old to bear children has only to submit a letter to that effect from her doctor to be permitted to work in the battery plant. But these deficiencies do underscore the precipitancy of deciding this case in the defendant's favor on the basis of the present record. . . .

EASTERBROOK, Circuit Judge, with whom FLAUM, Circuit Judge, joins, dissenting.

Whether employers should restrain adults from engaging in acts hazardous to their children is an ethical, medical, economic, and political problem of great complexity. But this is a statutory case, and we must implement the law rather than give our own answer. Johnson's policy is sex discrimination, forbidden unless sex is a "bona fide occupational qualification"—which it is not.

5. Special Problems in Applying Title VII

I . . .

A

Johnson uses sex as a ground of decision. The fetal protection policy applies to all women and no men. It is not written without reference to gender, having an unwelcome side effect. Cf. Personnel Administrator of Massachusetts v. Feeney. Differences between the sexes are its stated rationale. Only women transmit lead to children during pregnancy. Because a few women become pregnant with elevated levels of lead in the blood (in four years, eight out of an unknown number), Johnson excludes all women from the danger zone. This treats an employee not as an individual but as a woman. A plan using sex as a criterion and justified by arguments referring to sex is "discriminat[ion] . . . because of . . . sex". Los Angeles Department of Water & Power v. Manhart.

General Electric Co. v. Gilbert, 429 U.S. 125 (1976), held that a rule distinguishing on account of pregnancy is not sex discrimination, because women are in both the "pregnant" and "non-pregnant" groups. The Court saw the line as one between pregnant employees and all others, a line based on something other than sex (or at least something in addition to sex). Johnson's line based on ability to become pregnant, however, is assuredly based on sex. That would be ground for distinguishing *Gilbert*, but Congress interred *Gilbert* in 1978 by enacting the Pregnancy Discrimination Act. . . .

This amendment to Title VII makes distinctions based on women's ability to bear children sex discrimination. It also has a built-in BFOQ standard: unless pregnant employees differ from others "in their ability or inability to work", they must be treated "the same" as other employees "for all employment-related purposes." Although located in a definitional provision, the language after the semicolon is substantive and governs Johnson's plan. Wright v. Olin Corp., the only other appellate decision that has dealt with a fetal protection policy similar to Johnson's, took a different view. *Wright* observed that a policy using sex as a ground of decision may cause women no more injury than a policy neutral with regard to sex, yet having a disparate impact. A policy designed to promote the health of offspring of both sexes is neutral in objective. A sex-neutral policy is judged under an approach more lenient than a BFOQ standard. Believing that a fetal protection policy rests on strong justifications, *Wright* treated the policy as sex-neutral so that it could sustain a rule functionally identical to Johnson's.

This makes things turn not on whether the employer uses sex as a ground of decision but on whether the employer uses sex to serve a "good" policy. If the policy is beneficent and the injury to women "tolerable" in light of the interests served, the court changes the standard of inquiry. Yet whether a policy is "good" is a statutory question, governed by the BFOQ test . . . and the supplemental rule of the PDA that women and men who are "similar in their ability or inability to work" must be treated the same. A court's belief that a good end is in view does not justify departure from the statutory framework; it is an occasion for applying the statutory framework. *Wright* ignored the PDA and inverted ordinary rules of statutory interpretation when stating (with echoes in the majority's opinion today): "The inappropriateness of applying the overt discrimination/b.f.o.q. theory of claim and defense . . . is that, properly applied, it would prevent the employer from asserting a justification defense which under developed Title VII [disparate impact] doctrine it is entitled to present." In other words, this must be a disparate impact case because an employer couldn't win it as a disparate treatment case. If the rigors of the BFOQ suggest the need for a fresh approach, that is a job for another branch.

In principle a court could make the legal standard turn on what the authors of a rule are trying to accomplish, rather than on the criteria they use to get there. Whether to do so was the nub of the debate in *Manhart*. Los Angeles adopted a pension plan that collected more per month from women during employment and paid retired women the same per month as men. The city defended the policy by observing that the sums collected matched the actuarial value of the payments over the retired employees' lives, because the average woman lives longer than the average man and so receives more monthly checks. . . . The Court held that the policy was sex discrimination, because the city used sex as the basis of decision. That this criterion produced equal outcomes for groups was irrelevant in the Court's view, because Title VII requires employees to be treated as individuals. To say that sex had been considered in order to achieve equal group averages, the Court believed, was to confess a violation of the law.

Manhart establishes two propositions that together are fatal to Johnson's position. First, Title VII requires equal treatment of employees as persons rather than equal treatment of groups defined by sex (or race, or any other criterion listed in the statute). Observing that the average member of one group does as well as the average member of another does not support the use of any given ground of decision; indeed, resorting to notions of group equality begs the question of how a statute presumptively forbidding the use of these criteria could permit them to be used to justify conduct. Second, that equal treatment of employees as persons will lead to higher costs of employing persons of a given sex is no defense. An obligation to pay men and women equal amounts per month after retirement and deduct from pay the same amount per month during employment means that the employer must contribute greater sums per month during women's working years. That incremental cost of female employees is, as the Court construed the statute, no reason to treat women differently. Again this is part of the idea of an antidiscrimination law. Women may have higher pension costs, or higher medi-

5. Special Problems in Applying Title VII

cal insurance costs (because of pregnancy), or take more days off because of sickness, or have shorter careers (again because of children). Title VII excludes these as reasons for preferring men. The PDA, requiring equal treatment of employees "similar in their ability or inability to work", reinforces this conclusion. . . .

When the employer engages in sex, race, or age discrimination in an effort to protect customers or members of the public, courts regularly see this as disparate treatment, for which a BFOQ is essential. See Johnson v. Mayor and City Council of Baltimore, 472 U.S. 353 (1985); Western Air Lines, Inc. v. Criswell, 472 U.S. 400 (1985). There is no reason why things should be different when fetuses, rather than adult bystanders, are the object of the employer's protection.

. . . When Wisconsin excluded male guards from a women's prison, we saw this as disparate treatment and searched for a BFOQ. Torres v. Wisconsin Department of Health and Social Services (en banc). Here, too, there is disparate treatment. Fetal protection policies therefore may be justified, if at all, as BFOQs.

A word about the enforcement policy of the Equal Employment Opportunity Commission. The Commission told its staff to use *Wright* and the elaboration of its approach in Hayes v. Shelby Memorial Hospital, 726 F.2d 1543 (11th Cir. 1984), when investigating fetal protection policies. Ordinarily the EEOC's views about the meaning of Title VII are entitled to deference. This policy, however, does not so much interpret Title VII as adopt guidelines for prosecution. Prosecutorial guidelines reflect limitations on the agency's resources and existing judicial interpretations; they do not define the meaning of the law. . . .

B

The statute allows an employer to show that consideration of sex is "reasonably necessary to the normal operation of that particular business". Dothard v. Rawlinson; Criswell. The plaintiffs argue that "the sex based practice involved here should . . . be held invalid" because the reasons Johnson offers cannot establish a BFOQ even if factually supported. The Fourth Circuit (unlike the majority of this court) believes that as a matter of law a fetal protection policy does not satisfy the standards for a BFOQ, see *Wright*, and I think it has this much correct for two reasons: Johnson's stated objectives are insufficient, and even if sufficient do not apply to all women.

Johnson defends its fetal protection policy on the basis of concern for the welfare of the next generation, an objective unrelated to its ability to make batteries (§2000e-2(e)(1) speaks of the "operation of the business") or to any woman's "ability or inability to work" (the standard of the PDA). Johnson allowed women to work until 1982, without ill effects on its business; for all we know (the record is silent), other firms in the same business employ women in the kinds of jobs from which Johnson excludes them. The majority does not mention the PDA, which, added to the BFOQ rule, puts out of bounds the justifications Johnson offers.

At oral argument before the panel counsel offered a new defense of Johnson's policy: that it is morally required to protect children from their parents' mistakes. This justification is redolent of Muller v. Oregon, 208 U.S. 412 (1908), which sustained a statute curtailing women's hours of work on the ground that maternal functions unsuited women for long hours. . . . The "abundant testimony of the medical fraternity" [in *Muller*] turned out to be the triumph of imagination over data. Dangers decried in *Muller* are today perceived as chimerical, excuses for blockading women as effective competitors of men in the labor force. Legislation of the sort allowed by *Muller* "protected" women out of their jobs by making women less attractive as employees. An employer that needed flexibility in assigning hours of work had to hire men; women were consigned to jobs with regular hours but lower wages. See Elisabeth M. Landes, The Effect of State Maximum Hours Laws on the Employment of Women in 1920, 88 J. Pol. Econ. 476 (1980) (finding that "protective" legislation reduced women's hours, hourly wages, and annual income). Such laws also treat women in a stereotypical way. State laws requiring or allowing employers to treat women differently, on the assumption that women are less able than men to take the precautions essential for healthy children, are preempted by Title VII — not because of an express preemption clause, but because no state law may require or excuse a violation of federal law. Rosenfeld v. Southern Pacific Co., 444 F.2d 1219, 1225-27 (9th Cir. 1971). Statutes of the sort sustained in *Muller*, supported by the justifications advanced in *Muller*, are museum pieces, reminders of wrong turns in the law. It is not enough to say that Johnson is a private employer while *Muller* dealt with state laws. Title VII is addressed to private employers. The question is whether a justification of a particular kind is an acceptable defense of sex discrimination. This justification is not. No legal or ethical principle compels or allows Johnson to assume that women are less able than men to make intelligent decisions about the welfare of the next generation, that the interests of the next generation always trump the interests of living woman, and that the only acceptable level of risk is zero. "[T]he purpose of Title VII is to allow the individual woman to make that choice for herself." Dothard.

Although some women may become pregnant, and a subset of their children might suffer, Johnson cannot exclude all fertile women from its labor force on their account. Most women in an industrial labor force do not become pregnant;[3] most of these will have blood lead levels under 30 μg/dl

---

3. Although some 9 percent of all fertile women become pregnant each year, the birth rate for blue collar women over 30 is about 2 percent, and of working women 45-49 only 1 in 5,000

5. Special Problems in Applying Title VII   Page 371

(only about ⅓ of the employees exposed to lead at Johnson's plants have higher levels); most of those who become pregnant with levels exceeding 30 μSg/dl will bear normal children (Johnson reports no birth defects or other abnormalities in the eight pregnancies among its employees).[4] Concerns about a tiny minority of women cannot set the standard by which all are judged. An employer establishes a BFOQ only if there is "a factual basis for believing that all or substantially all women would be unable to perform safely and efficiently the duties of the job involved." Fear of prenatal injury (which has not happened in the history of the employer) is a far cry from something that prevents "all or substantially all" women from doing their jobs.

To meet the "all or almost all" requirement, Johnson relies on an elaboration of the BFOQ for age discrimination offered in customer-safety cases: if all persons over a certain age are unsafe pilots (drivers, police officers, etc.), *or* if it is impossible to tell which of the older employees is unsafe, then age may be a BFOQ for employment. E.g., EEOC v. Mississippi State Tax Commission, 873 F.2d 97, 98 (5th Cir. 1989) (en banc). The genesis of the "impossible to tell" branch of the BFOQ in age cases is that an unsafe employee can't do the job the employer demands. It is word play to say that "the job" at Johnson is to make batteries without risk to fetuses in the same way "the job" at Western Air Lines is to fly planes without crashing. . . .

Johnson might be concerned about cost. It could have argued that the only alternative to the fetal protection policy is a much cleaner workplace, so that no employee's blood lead level exceeds 30 μg/dl, which would be prohibitively expensive and lead it to close the business. Johnson does not make that argument, so the majority properly does not decide whether it would be a BFOQ. Another potential cost comes from tort law. Perhaps Johnson anticipated litigation filed by children injured by lead. The firm does not make this argument either, and so far as I know no child has recovered a judgment on account of parents' occupational exposure to lead. Security National Bank v. Chloride, Inc., 602 F. Supp. 294 (D. Kan. 1985), the only reported case, ended in a jury verdict for the employer even though the child argued that the employer violated OSHA's maximum exposure rules. (Johnson says that it complies with OSHA's rules.) Anyway, the prospect of tort judgments means only that female employees' average cost to Johnson exceeds that of male employees. Title VII requires employers to deal with individual employees rather than with group averages. No firm could exclude women from its work

---

becomes pregnant in a given year. The data are collected in Mary E. Becker, From Muller v. Oregon to Fetal Vulnerability Policies, 53 U. Chi. L. Rev. 1219, 1233 (1986). The record does not reveal the birth rate for Johnson's female laborers, but it must be lower given Johnson's strenuous efforts to discourage pregnancy among those exposed to lead.

4. One of the children has an elevated level of lead in the blood, but this has not produced an identifiable problem. It is hard, however, to link outcomes such as learning disabilities to lead, since learning disabilities could have many other causes, and it is therefore hard to show in an individual case (as opposed to statistically) that lead injured the child.

force by saying that higher costs of pensions and health care made them too costly. If these costs do not establish a BFOQ, could not establish it even in principle, how may the prospect of tort judgments do so? Title VII applies even when—*especially* when—discrimination is rational as the employer sees things.

All of this is not to say where wisdom lies. An employer is better situated than its workers to gather and interpret scientific data, for medical studies are hard to evaluate, and the need to earn a living may induce employees to give too little weight to the interests of their offspring. A recent poll showing that more than 20% of American adults do not know that the Earth orbits the Sun does not lend confidence in the ability of the populace to make decisions that depend on scientific or medical data. If any given employer errs, the forces of competition open opportunities elsewhere. No one can treat lightly the possibility of injury to future children, who cannot protect themselves or participate in the decisions that will govern their lives. Trying to find the "right" accommodation would rob many a person of sleep—for rigorous implementation of fetal protection policies could close more than 20 million jobs to women,[7] while failure to do anything causes injury to unknown numbers. Under the PDA neither the employer nor the court is authorized to essay an answer to this social puzzle. The disparate treatment-BFOQ approach governs, and it resolves today's dispute. Title VII gives parents the power to make occupational decisions affecting their families. A legislative forum is available to those who believe that such decisions should be made elsewhere.[8]

II

Having adopted the *Wright-Hayes* approach, we still should not affirm the district court's judgment. *Hayes* opined that a fetal protection policy applicable only to women violates Title VII

> unless the employer shows (1) that a substantial risk of harm exists and (2) that the risk is borne only by members of one sex; and (3) the employee fails to show that there are acceptable alternative policies that would have a lesser impact on the affected sex.

---

7. Fifteen to twenty million jobs is the estimate of the Bureau of National Affairs in Pregnancy and Employment 57 (1987), limited to injury caused by chemicals. Cases such as Hayes and Zuniga show that many additional women are affected by restrictions placed on other jobs, such as x-ray technician jobs that exposed embryos to radiation. Concern about emissions from computers and their terminals has led to proposals that could restrict access even to traditional office jobs.

8. The EPA, which administers the Toxic Substances Control Act, 15 U.S.C. §§ 2601-54, also may have authority over the subject. See Note, Getting Beyond Discrimination: A Regulatory Solution to the Problem of Fetal Hazards in the Workplace, 95 Yale L.J. 577, 592-98 (1986).

5. Special Problems in Applying Title VII   Page 371

At the time *Wright* and *Hayes* were decided, and when EEOC issued its policy statement, courts believed that "business necessity" in a disparate impact case is a defense. "Business necessity" and "BFOQ" were not so distinct. We know from Wards Cove Packing Co. v. Atonio, however, that the plaintiff bears the burden of persuasion on all questions in every disparate impact case, as the majority today emphasizes. So the *Wright-Hayes* standard has been watered down. The court's "adoption" of *Wright*, *Hayes*, and the EEOC's policy statement is thus in practice more favorable to employers than the Fourth and Eleventh Circuits (and the EEOC) anticipated their approach would be. The plaintiff won in *Hayes*; she would lose under the majority's approach.

Even on the majority's undemanding standard, however, there are material disputes. . . .

Substantial Risk. Is there a substantial risk of harm to the offspring of female employees? That lead in the blood is dangerous no one doubts, although experts dispute how much is too much and whether lead is more risky to the fetus and developing infants than to adults.[9] The extent to which lead in a mother's blood, at levels to which Johnson exposes its employees, endangers the fetus is a subject on which there is additional dispute. Showing great injury at 100 μg/dl is one thing; showing risks when no one has levels over 50 μg/dl (and, per OSHA's rules, anyone wanting to get below 30 μg/dl is entitled to a respirator) is another. The record does not quantify the risks at the levels OSHA permits. It also does not reveal the extent to which lead crosses the placenta. Johnson's chief medical consultant, Dr. Fishburn, believes that risk is greatest in the first weeks of pregnancy, before women can withdraw to lead-free environments. Experts take the contrary view that lead does not cross the placenta until late in pregnancy,[10] and that because lead levels in the blood fall substantially within 12 weeks of the last exposure, the danger is reduced if women are removed from contact with lead promptly on becoming pregnant.[11]

---

9. For a review of the evidence see William L. Marcus & C. Richard Cothern, The Characteristics of an Adverse Effect: Using the Example of Developing a Standard for Lead, 16(4) Drug Metabolism Reviews 423 (1985-86). Dr. Michael Silverstein, a board certified specialist in occupational medicine, testified in a deposition that the risks of a given level of lead in the blood are no greater to the fetus and children than to adults. He supported this position with an affidavit to which he attached three scientific studies. . . .

10. Dr. J. Julian Chisolm, Director of the Lead Program at the John F. Kennedy Institute in Baltimore, one of Johnson's witnesses, testified in a deposition that lead does not cross the placenta until late in the pregnancy and that the adverse effect of lead in a mother's blood does not begin until the last half of the third trimester. Dr. Silbergeld took a similar view.

11. According to National Research Council Committee on Lead in the Human Environment 59-60 (1980), almost all lead stored in the body outside of bones is eliminated within four to six weeks of exposure. Dr. Silbergeld used the higher figure of 100 days for the elimination of lead from blood and soft tissues. Lead is released from bones much more slowly, but lead-207, the most common form they contain, is less active biologically. National Research Council on

It is painful to see conflicts of this kind settled by litigation. . . . Yet so long as the substantive rule of law requires a court to resolve scientific disagreements—which the *Wright-Hayes* standard does, though the BFOQ standard avoids the problem—the judge must follow the rules, which means that material disputes must be resolved at trial.

A small risk, even if compellingly documented, is not enough to exclude women from employment. How great is too great? Most women do not become pregnant in any given year, and most female employees do not have blood lead levels exceeding 30 μg/dl, so average risk to the employee population may be small. If a woman becomes pregnant with a blood lead level of 40 μg/dl, is the risk one learning disability in two pregnancies? One in two thousand? One in two million? These figures imply different policies, yet we do not know which is correct. How risky is a blood lead level exceeding 30 μg/dl compared with other hazards? Most comparisons show that smoking and drinking are quite dangerous to fetuses, more so than many contaminants found in the workplace. The hazards created by occupational chemicals span many orders of magnitude: some are safer than the sweeteners we wolf down, some are dangerous indeed. Where does lead fit on that spectrum? I cannot believe that Johnson would be entitled to fire female employees who smoke or drink during pregnancy—let alone fire all female employees because some might smoke or drink—which makes it hard to exclude women to curtail risk from other substances.

How does the risk attributable to lead compare, say, to the risk to the next generation created by driving a taxi? A female bus or taxi driver is exposed to noxious fumes and the risk of accidents, all hazardous to a child she carries. Would it follow that taxi and bus companies can decline to hire women?[15] . . .

The most concerted effort to estimate the risks lead poses to offspring was conducted by OSHA in the course of promulgating its lead rules. OSHA

Biological Effects of Atmospheric Pollutants 68 (1972). Even persons who have no occupational exposure ingest or inhale lead from other sources (paint, leaded gasoline, etc.), so that the actual blood level may drop slowly, but these sources of lead threaten offspring whether or not the mother works in Johnson's plants. It is possible that lead builds up in the placenta during early pregnancy, while the mother's blood lead level is highest, but the extent of this effect is unknown. The net effects of these offsetting processes are not quantified in this record.

15. There is a tradition in public health of resolving doubts by assuming that risks exist until they can be disproved. As the uncertainties are substantial, this process often produces measures of risk that appear to be substantial. Yet whether to assume that the maximum likely hazard will come to pass—a process known as "conservative risk assessment"—is itself a political question. A court would be obliged to try to produce the most accurate, rather than the most conservative, assessment, for resolving doubts in one direction only produces inaccurate comparisons of poorly-understood risks (which will be overstated) against well-understood risks (which would be accurately stated). See Albert L. Nichols & Richard J. Zeckhauser, The Perils of Prudence: How Conservative Risk Assessments Distort Regulation, Regulation 13 (Nov/Dec 1986). Yet in an effort to measure risk accurately a court would get little aid from existing studies, often tailored to fulfill regulatory demands for a "conservative" bias.

5. Special Problems in Applying Title VII

considered and rejected a proposal to exclude women capable of bearing children from jobs in which blood lead levels may exceed 30 μg/100 g. . . . In order to say that the risk to offspring at firms complying with OSHA's rules (as Johnson says it does) is so "substantial" that a woman should not be allowed to work at any job where there is the slightest chance of a blood lead level exceeding 30 μg/dl, a court must disagree with the judgment of OSHA that the 50 μg/100 g limit, plus the availability of respirators to employees seeking to attain a level of 30 μg/dl, is enough. My colleagues essentially take judicial notice that OSHA is wrong, an extraordinary step. The record does not contain evidence sufficient to contradict OSHA's conclusion, let alone evidence so lopsided that summary judgment is appropriate.

One more observation. "Substantial risk" must mean substantial net risk. Excluding women from industrial jobs at Johnson may reduce risk attributable to lead at the cost of increasing other hazards. There is a strong correlation between the health of the infant and prenatal medical care; there is also a powerful link between the parents' income and infants' health, for higher income means better nutrition, among other things. See Aaron Wildavsky, Searching for Safety 59-72 (1988); Victor R. Fuchs, How We Live 31-40 (1983). Removing women from well-paying jobs (and the attendant health insurance), or denying women access to these jobs, may reduce the risk from lead while also reducing levels of medical care and the quality of nutrition. The net effect of lower income and less medical care could be a reduction in infants' prospects.[16] Mary E. Becker, From *Muller v. Oregon* to Fetal Vulnerability Policies, 53 U. Chi. L. Rev. 1219, 1229-31 (1986).

Nothing in the record shows the net risks. . . .

Mediation through a Single Sex. Is the risk to the child transmitted by one sex only? If "the risk" is defined as risk caused by lead entering the fetus's blood via the placenta, it is by definition confined to one sex. But if we ask instead "Does the presence of lead in a parent's blood pose a risk to the fetus?", then the evidence conflicts. The broader perspective is the correct one when aggregate levels of risk are the proper concern.

Three affidavits in the record, and papers in medical journals, maintain that ead in the blood creates risks for offspring of both male and female employees. The American Public Health Association and other medical groups have filed a brief as amici curiae marshaling an impressive array of studies linking lead with injury to the male reproductive system, and thence to offspring.

---

16. The majority says that "[t]his issue bears no relevance to Johnson Controls' employment practices", n.28, because Johnson protected the salary and benefits of women transferred out of jobs in 1982. But Johnson does not offer women excluded from these jobs in 1983 or later the salary and benefits they could have earned in them, and it also does not protect the income and benefits of employees who because of the policy cannot exercise their seniority (bumping) rights to avoid layoffs.

E.g., Christopher Winder, Reproductive Effects of Occupational Exposures to Lead: Policy Considerations, 8 NeuroToxology 411 (1987); Herbert L. Needleman and David Bellinger, Commentary, Environmental Research (1988). Most of the data come from animal studies, but some human studies suggest that the effects occur in our species too. OSHA concluded that lead in men as well as women is hazardous to the unborn. . . . Perhaps OSHA is wrong; its findings do not bind Johnson in this litigation. . . . [But] the district court could not properly reject [OSHA's judgment] without holding a trial. Least of all could a court reject it, as my colleagues do, on the ground that as a matter of law animal studies are not "solid scientific data." . . . The medical profession, like the Food and Drug Administration, will be stunned to discover that animal studies are too "speculative" to be the basis of conclusions about risks. . . .

Less Restrictive Alternatives. An employer cannot close employment opportunities to women in order to protect the next generation if some more modest alternative would do (nearly) as well at protecting the unborn. Johnson's policy has a striking sweep: no fertile woman can be hired for a job in which any employee has had a blood lead level exceeding 30 μg/dl anytime during the last year, or in any job that might lead to a promotion to such a job. As a practical matter, this means every industrial job at Johnson's battery plants. The firm advised its hiring offices to tell women that "we have no openings for women capable of bearing children". To state the policy is to reveal many less stringent options that might be almost as good at protecting the interests of children.

Women over 40 rarely have children. Why are they forbidden to work? (One of the plaintiffs, 50 years old and divorced when the suit was filed, had nonetheless been excluded from jobs covered by the policy.) Covering them reduces the lead risk to zero, but "zero" is not the only acceptable level. Many workers in jobs in which some employee has a level exceeding 30 μg/dl have levels less than that. Only ⅓ of Johnson's industrial employees exceed the 30 μg/dl figure. The levels of lead in the blood depend not only on lead in the air but also on personal hygiene. . . . Johnson replies that lead levels usually are greatest shortly after entering a new job, before the employee learns how to reduce the level; the women might become pregnant during these initial weeks or months. True enough, but again this answer assumes that the only acceptable level of risk is zero.

Some workers who start at entry-level jobs with low exposure to [lead] will be promoted to higher-lead jobs; others will not (or will leave before then). Johnson excludes women even from these safer jobs, although they pose no appreciable risk to offspring. Doubtless Johnson believes that unimpeded lines of progression make its operation more efficient, since it can invest more in training women in skills that are transferrable to new jobs within the firm. Yet this form of savings does not count under Title VII. . . .

5. Special Problems in Applying Title VII

III

... This is the most important sex-discrimination case this circuit has ever decided. It is likely the most important sex-discrimination case in any court since 1964, when Congress enacted Title VII. If the majority is right, then by one estimate 20 million industrial jobs could be closed to women, for many substances in addition to lead pose fetal risks. Whether that would happen is of course a separate question; legal entitlements need not translate to action. But the law would allow employers to consign more women to "women's work" while reserving better-paying but more hazardous jobs for men. Title VII was designed to eliminate rather than perpetuate such matching of sexes to jobs. . . .

. . . Although my colleagues refer to many constitutional cases, such as Rostker v. Goldberg, 453 U.S. 57 (1981), for the proposition that sex discrimination sometimes is permissible, cases showing that Congress *may* authorize sex-based decisions hardly shows that in this instance it *did*. Title VII forbids rather than requires resort to sex as a basis of decision.

Risk to the next generation is incident to all activity, starting with getting out of bed. (Staying in bed all day has its own hazards.) To insist on zero risk, which the court says Johnson may do, is to exclude women from the industrial jobs that have been a male preserve. By all means let society bend its energies to improving the prospects of those who come after us. Demanding zero risk produces not progress but paralysis. Defining tolerable risk, and seeking to reduce that limit, is more useful — but it is a job for Congress or OSHA in conjunction with medical and other sciences. Laudable though its objective be, Johnson may not reach its goal at the expense of women.

NOTES

1. Are you satisfied with the majority's analysis? Isn't it clear, at least after §701(k), that once there is a finding that the employer acted because of the pregnancy of the employee, the appropriate analysis is disparate treatment, which can be justified only under the bfoq test? The majority also tries to cover that base by finding a bfoq established. Are you satisfied that it is in light of what you have learned so far?

2. The *Hayes* case, cited in *Johnson Controls*, was the only appellate decision to strike down an employer's action predicated on a threat to the employee's offspring. In part, the court noted that the employer's policy was ill-tailored to the problem addressed since the greatest danger of harm to the foetus was early in the pregnancy, and the hospital's policy applied only after it learned of Hayes' pregnancy, two months later. Did Johnson Controls read *Hayes* as indicating that it would have been better served with a rule that had

a *greater* impact on the employment opportunities of women? In both *Johnson Controls* and Wright v. Olin, the policy excluded *all* fertile women from jobs involving risk of exposure to lead. Both policies were upheld.

3. Isn't Judge Easterbrook right when he suggests that the courts' struggle with the proper analytic framework in these cases is simply because Title VII, as generally developed, would seem to condemn the discrimination here as disparate treatment for which no bfoq can be established, since that defense focuses on the ability of the worker to do the job? Is it legitimate for courts to manipulate the established doctrine of Title VII to take account of what is perceived as a real problem of toxic exposure in the workplace? If the end is sufficiently compelling, wouldn't it be more straightforward (and less disruptive of the Title VII theories) to simply create a new defense as in *Weber* and *Johnson*? Is that what Judge Posner is doing, or has he bought into the majority's analysis (if not its willingness to dispose of this case on summary judgment)?

4. As between Judge Posner and the majority, who has the better of the argument on the appropriateness of summary judgment? If Judge Cudahy is right, isn't it questionable to dispose of such an important case without a trial?

5. Applying California law, Johnson Controls, Inc. v. California Fair Employment & Housing Commission, 267 Cal. Rptr. 158 (4th Ct. App. 1990), struck down the very policy upheld by the Seventh Circuit. It found discrimination against women of childbearing age to be sex discrimination, and that no bfoq was established by the company. In addition to noting evidence that the offspring of men were also subject to risk from lead exposure, the court stressed that Johnson Controls made a number of unfounded assumptions regarding women:

(1) that all unmarried fertile women are either presently actively involved in sexual relationships with men, or will definitely become so involved;
(2) that fertile women who are actively involved in sexual relationships with men or who may become so involved are or will be involved with a fertile male. . . .
(3) that fertile women who are actively involved in a sexual relationship with a fertile male, or will become so, cannot be trusted to employ reasonable prophylactic measures against an unexpected pregnancy;
(4) that fertile women, even when possessed of sufficient information about the worksite hazard, are incapable of properly weighing the chances of unexpected pregnancy, notwithstanding use of prophylactic measures, against the possibility of fetal hazard should she become pregnant.

Id. at 177.

6. Suppose that "fetal vulnerability" programs are not viewed as formal gender classifications; does §701(k) make it a case for application of disparate

5. Special Problems in Applying Title VII Page 371

impact analysis? What do *Newport News* and *Guerra* say about the application of disparate impact analysis based on adverse impact against pregnant women or fertile women? Does the second clause of §701(k) foreclose application of disparate impact analysis in the pregnancy area? In Abraham v. Graphic Arts International Union, 660 F.2d 811 (D.C. Cir. 1981), the court indicated that a ten-day limit on temporary disability leaves could violate Title VII because of its disparate impact on pregnant women.

7. State "protective" legislation that operated to narrow the employment opportunities of women has been struck down by Title VII. See Note on Protective Laws, *supra*. Why have employers been able to defend their "protective" policies when the states have failed in their efforts to defend theirs? Should private decisionmaking be granted more deference than public policy setting? Professor Becker, in From *Muller v. Oregon* to Fetal Vulnerability Policies, 53 U. Chi. L. Rev. 1219 (1986), traced the arguments of supporters of protective legislation in the heyday of substantive due process and found them to be the same as the arguments employers make today to support their fetal vulnerability programs. She concludes that those arguments are no more compelling now than when they were first made.

> First, supporters of sex-specific labor legislation did not consider the alternatives available to working women and the effects of those alternatives on the workers and their families. Women were seen as uniformly dependent on men, and women's financial contributions to their families as less important than their biologic and domestic contributions. Second, women were not regarded as individuals—who might not have domestic responsibilities for others or even the capacity to reproduce—or as having any autonomous interests apart from their families' interests. Instead, all women were seen only in terms of the biologic and domestic responsibilities associated with motherhood. Third, proponents were willing to place restrictions on women without firm scientific evidence of any need for the restrictions. Fourth, women were excluded only when they were dispensable. No state passed a statute banning all night work for women because of the dangers of walking home at night. Women were too important as hospital workers, for example, to merit such broad "protection." Fifth, supporters dismissed out of hand the possibility that women might be competent decision makers.

Id. at 1224-1225. She concludes that Title VII analysis should not be distorted to uphold fetal vulnerability programs.

> Sex-specific policies, no matter how reasonable, discriminate on the basis of pregnancy or sex, turning a difference between women and men into a disadvantage for women and an advantage for men. Title VII, as amended by the Pregnancy Discrimination Act of 1978, prohibits discrimination on the basis of both pregnancy and sex, unless the BFOQ defense is extended to include

concern for fetal safety. Such an extension would, however, be inconsistent with the language of the Pregnancy Discrimination Act, which mandates that women, whether pregnant or potentially pregnant, are to be treated like others similar in ability to do the job.

8. Special problems also exist for blacks. Thus, the New York Times reported on page 1, February 4, 1980, that "The Du Pont Company, the 13th largest employer in the United States, routinely gives pre-employment blood tests to all blacks who apply for jobs to determine who might be a carrier of the trait for sickle-cell anemia, even though the trait is regarded as largely harmless." There is apparently no evidence that the sickle cell trait makes blacks more vulnerable than whites to workplace hazards. If there were, would the defense suggested in *Johnson Controls* be available, even though there is no statutory bfoq for race?

9. Several more questions are raised by the full terms of the Pregnancy Discrimination Act. For example, may an employer reduce the total fringe benefit package in order to take account of the increased costs associated with including pregnancy-related costs in the benefit scheme? Or would such a reduction violate Title VII? The act amending Title VII, 92 Stat. 2076 1978), included an implementation provision:

> Until the expiration of a period of one year from the date of enactment of this Act . . . no person who, on the date of enactment of this Act, is providing either by direct payment or by making contributions to a fringe benefit fund or insurance program, benefits in violation of this Act shall in order to come into compliance with this Act, reduce the benefits or the compensation provided any employee on the date of enactment of this Act, either directly or by failing to provide sufficient contributions to a fringe benefit fund or insurance program.

Does this provision authorize such a reduction after October 31, 1979, one year from the date of enactment? Compare the no-wage-reduction clause of the Equal Pay Act, Chapter 8, p.733, which requires wage discriminations on the basis of sex to be equalized at the higher rate paid the favored sex.

10. Section 701(k) treats abortion directly:

> This subsection shall not require an employer to pay for health insurance benefits for abortion, except where the life of the mother would be endangered if the fetus were carried to term, or except where medical complications have arisen from an abortion Provided: That nothing herein shall preclude an employer from providing abortion benefits or otherwise effect bargaining agreements in regard to abortion.

Suppose an employee, pursuant to a paid sick leave plan, requested pay for the time she took off work to have an abortion. Would a refusal to pay violate

5. Special Problems in Applying Title VII   Page 371

§701(k)? Under what conditions is the employer required to pay health insurance costs for abortions?

Two constitutional issues are posed by §701(k)'s special treatment of abortion. The first is whether the exclusion of abortions from medical insurance coverage is constitutional. Action in a related context seems to indicate that §701(k) is not unconstitutional for that reason. In passing Medicaid, Congress required the states to fund necessary medical treatment for indigents but in the Hyde Amendment restricted the availability of federal funds for abortions "except where the life of the mother would be endangered if the fetus were carried to term; or except for such medical procedures necessary for the victims of rape or incest when such rape or incest has been reported promptly to a law enforcement agency or public health service." Pub. L. No. 96-123, §109, 93 Stat. 926 (1973). In Maher v. Roe, 423 U.S. 464 (1977), the Supreme Court found that the constitutional right to reproductive freedom (Roe v. Wade, 410 U.S. 113 (1973)) did not include entitlement to Medicaid payment for an abortion that was not medically necessary. In Harris v. McRae, 448 U.S. 297 (1980), the Court held that a state that participates in the Medicaid program is not obligated to fund medically necessary abortions for which federal reimbursement is unavailable under the Hyde Amendment, even though childbirth expenses are reimbursed.

The second constitutional question is whether Congress can impose a requirement on all employers to provide sick leave for all abortions, or whether that requirement creates an unconstitutional burden on the First Amendment free exercise rights of those employers with religious convictions opposed to abortion. In National Conference of Catholic Bishops v. Bell, 490 F. Supp. 734 (D.D.C. 1980), the Bishops' Conference sought as an employer to have §701(k) found unconstitutional. The court described §701(k)'s treatment of abortion as follows:

> The Pregnancy Discrimination Act was enacted as a compromise reached in conference to resolve the differences between the House and Senate versions of §995. As finally enacted, it provided for *paid sick leave benefits* for the pregnancy, childbirth, or related medical conditions and would include elective or optional abortions. On the other hand, it would not require an employer to pay *health insurance costs* for abortions, except when the life of the mother would be endangered if the fetus were carried to term, or where medical complications have arisen from an abortion, elective or otherwise.
> [490 F. Supp. at 736 n.2]

Despite alleging that as an employer the Conference was not complying with §701(k), the court found no case or controversy and dismissed for lack of subject matter jurisdiction.

2. Sexual Harassment

Page 393. Add in carryover Note before "Every pass by a supervisor?":

In Lipsett v. University of Puerto Rico, 864 F.2d 881 (1st Cir. 1988), the court held that whether a particular approach was sexual was a question of fact, but that explicit sexual demands were not necessary to constitute a sexual approach.

Page 393. Add at end of carryover Note:

A number of cases have found harassment sufficiently pervasive to alter the terms and conditions of employment. E.g., Hall v. Gus Construction Co., 842 F.2d 1010 (8th Cir. 1988); Hicks v. Gates Rubber Co., 833 F.2d 1406 (10th Cir. 1987).

Page 393. Add at end of Note 4:

The question has been phrased as to whether a plaintiff can aggregate harassment aimed at her with harassment aimed at other females. One court answered the question clearly in the affirmative, Hicks v. Gates Rubber Co., 833 F.2d 1406 (10th Cir. 1987), while another seemed to believe that the answer was no. Hall v. Gus Construction Co., 842 F.2d 1010 (8th Cir. 1988). But if plaintiff knows of other harassment, isn't that likely to contribute to her fears and insecurities?

Page 393. Add a new Note 4a:

4a. Another issue is how egregious the conduct in question must be for an environment to be "contaminated." In Rabidue v. Osceola Refining Co., 805 F.2d 611 (6th Cir. 1986), *cert. denied*, 481 U.S. 1041 (1987), a panel of the Sixth Circuit, despite a strong dissent, adopted the most restrictive rule possible by announcing both objective and subjective tests:

> . . . a trier of fact, when judging the totality of the circumstances impacting upon the asserted abusive and hostile environment placed in issue by the plaintiff's charges must adopt the perspective of a reasonable person's reactions to a similar environment under like or similar circumstances. Thus, in the absence of conduct which would interfere with that hypothetical reasonable

5. Special Problems in Applying Title VII

individual's work performance and effect seriously the psychological well-being of that reasonable person under like circumstances, a plaintiff may not prevail . . . regardless of whether the plaintiff was actually offended by the defendant's conduct. Assuming that the plaintiff has successfully [carried this burden], the particular plaintiff would nevertheless also be required to demonstrate that she was actually offended by the defendant's conduct and that she suffered some degree of injury.

Id. at 620. The use of an objective test is common to many kinds of tort liability, but does this mean that the mere fact that a plaintiff was truly affected in a serious way is not dispositive since she may be hypersensitive? But should co-workers be legally free to persecute a more-sensitive-than-average person? And, if the appropriate test is objective—the reasonable person test—why must plaintiff also prove that *she* was affected adversely? Is this simply a restatement of the Supreme Court's specification that the conduct be "unwelcome"? *Rabidue* has generated enormous criticism, but its major fault may lie less in the standard the court announces than in its insensitive application of that standard to the facts before the court. The *Rabidue* dissent makes a strong case for condemning the majority's result on the facts before it as tolerating misogyny manifested in a predominantly antifemale environment.

Page 394. Add in Note 11 at end of seventh line:

See Bennett v. Corroon and Black Corp., 845 F.2d 104 (5th Cir. 1988), *cert. denied*, 109 S. Ct. 1140 (1989) (no equitable relief appropriate where the employer continued to pay plaintiff until she found a new job and had removed the chief executive officer who failed to adequately respond to the harassment).

Page 394. Add a new Note 11a:

11a. In the wake of *Meritor*, the courts have frequently imposed liability on the employer. If the harasser (or one of them) is himself in a high enough position to fire plaintiff or to substantially affect her employment status, the courts will hold the employer liable. Opinions taking this position frequently describe this kind of liability as "direct," not merely respondeat superior. E.g., Paroline v. Unisys. Corp., 879 F.2d 100 (4th Cir. 1989), *reh'g granted en banc*, 900 F.2d 27 (1990); Sparks v. Pilot Freight Carriers, 830 F.2d 1554 (11th Cir. 1987). See also Restatement (Second) of Agency, §219(2). When the supervisor is not the harasser, courts have tended to both describe liability as flowing from respondeat superior, e.g., Steele v. Offshore Shipbuilding,

Inc., 867 F.2d 1311 (11th Cir. 1989), and to require some kind of fault on the part of the company. Thus, absent direct management involvement, courts have held in contaminated work environment cases that the company is liable if "management-level employees knew, or in the exercise of reasonable care, should have known about a barrage of offensive conduct." Hall v. Gus Construction Co., 842 F.2d 1010 (8th Cir. 1988); Lipsett v. University of Puerto Rico, 864 F.2d 881 (1st Cir. 1988). See also Davis v. Monsanto Chemical Co., 858 F.2d 345 (6th Cir. 1988), *cert. denied*, 109 S. Ct. 3166 (1989) (employer not liable for alleged lunchroom segregation because supervisors did not have actual or constructive knowledge of it). Given the necessity for "pervasive" harassment to establish a violation in the first place, it would seem that few employers could plausibly claim that their management did not have actual or constructive knowledge under such a view.

Page 394. Add at end of Note 12:

The most effective way to escape liability in such a situation is to act promptly to resolve the problem, since courts have been sympathetic to employers who attempt to deal with the harassment, even if they are not completely successful. For example, in one case an employer painted over offensive graffiti within a day of its being reported. Davis v. Monsanto Chemical Co., 858 F.2d 345 (6th Cir. 1988), *cert. denied*, 109 S. Ct. 3166 (1989). See also Swentik v. USAIR, Inc., 830 F.2d 552 (4th Cir. 1987) (investigation, written reprimand, and order to stay away from plaintiff sufficient). In another decision, the court found adequate the assurances of the employer's president that he would insulate her from the harasser when those assurances were made within 12 hours of the incident complained of. Dornhecker v. Malibu Grand Prix Corp., 828 F.2d 307 (5th Cir. 1987).

By way of comparison, the court found not adequate the failure of a chief executive officer of a company to remove from a company mens' room highly offensive cartoons depicting plaintiff "in crude and deviant sexual activities" for more than a day after seeing them—and not until plaintiff learned of them and complained. Bennett v. Corroon and Black Corp., 845 F.2d 104 (5th Cir. 1988), *cert. denied*, 109 S. Ct. 1140 (1989)

Page 395. Add at end of carryover Note 13:

See also Mitchell v. Hutchings, 116 F.R.D. 481 (D. Utah 1987). But see McLean v. Satellite Technology Serv., 673 F. Supp. 1458 (E.D. Mo. 1987) (evidence of plaintiff's "lusty libido" showed that she was responsible for any sexually suggestive conduct).

The Fourth Circuit, however, has made clear that any sexually-oriented

5. Special Problems in Applying Title VII

conduct on plaintiff's part can be relevant to the "welcome" question only if the harasser knew of that conduct. Swentik v. US AIR, Inc., 830 F.2d 552 (4th Cir. 1987). Accordingly, it found that "plaintiff's use of foul language or sexual innuendo in a consensual setting" does not waive her legal protections. Id. at 557. When a harasser does not know of such actions by plaintiff, he has no reason to believe that his own conduct is "welcome." The court stressed that the question is not whether the victim welcomes in the abstract but whether she welcomes the advances of the harasser. In any event, when the victim indicates that the conduct is unwelcome, it must stop at that point to avoid a violation. See also Lipsett v. University of Puerto Rico, 864 F.2d 881 (1st Cir. 1988) (while the victim has the responsibility for clearly signalling that the conduct is unwelcome, she need not do so directly; "a woman's consistent failure to respond to suggestive comments or gestures may be sufficient to communicate that the man's conduct is unwelcome"). Id. at 898.

May a court order a mental examination of harassment plaintiffs? Some courts have refused to order a mental examination of plaintiff in such cases, Robinson v. Jacksonville Shipyards, Inc., 118 F.R.D. 525 (M.D. Fla. 1988), relying heavily on a California decision, Vinson v. Superior Court, 43 Cal. 3d 833, 740 P.2d 404, 239 Cal. Rptr. 292 (1987). While other courts have ordered such examinations, they are most likely to do so where plaintiff has bought a claim which allows recovery for mental distress; even here, they may establish as a prerequisite to any examination that plaintiff put her mental state in issue by herself introducing psychiatric evidence. E.g., Zabkowicz v. West Bend Co., 585 F. Supp. 635 (E.D. Wis. 1984); Lowe v. Philadelphia Newspapers, Inc., 101 F.R.D. 296 (E.D. Pa. 1983). Not all cases in which mental distress damages are sought, however, have been held adequate to put the sexual harassment plaintiff's mental state in controversy sufficiently to warrant an examination. Cody v. Marriott Corp., 103 F.R.D. 421 (D. Mass. 1984).

Page 395. Add new Notes 19a and 19b:

19a. Sexual harassment is only a subset of sex discrimination. Accordingly, when there is objectionable conduct aimed at person because of her gender, even if not directed at sexual activity, Title VII is violated. In McKinney v. Dole, 765 F.2d 1129 (D.C. Cir. 1985), the court held that physical violence, if directed at a woman because she is a woman, would be a violation of Title VII even if not a sexual advance or having any sexual overtones. Accord Lipsett v. University of Puerto Rico, 864 F.2d 881 (1st Cir. 1988); Hall v. Gus Construction Co., 842 F.2d 1010 (8th Cir. 1988). See also Gilardi v. Schroeder dba Gary Schroeder Trucking, 833 F.2d 1226 (7th Cir. 1987) (plaintiff stated claim of sex discrimination when she alleged that she was discharged after her employer raped her and her employer's wife demanded that she be fired).

19b. Perhaps in response to the sexual harassment cases, there has been a revival of litigation over work environments that have been contaminated by racial or national origin discrimination. These cases have continued to require "more than an episodic pattern of racial antipathy," Ways v. City of Lincoln, 871 F.2d 750 (11th Cir. 1988); Batts v. NLT Corp., 844 F.2d 331 (6th Cir. 1988) (five isolated incidents over six years not sufficient, especially where the incidents were either not brought to management's attention or ceased after having been reported). See also Patterson v. McLean Credit Union, 109 S. Ct. 2363 (1989).

Page 395. Add before "Moire" citation in Note 20:

Lipsett v. University of Puerto Rico, 864 F.2d 881 (1st Cir. 1988)

Page 396. Add before "Bohen" cite in carryover Note 20:

Starrett v. Wadley, 876 F.2d 808 (10th Cir. 1989); Lipsett v. University of Puerto Rico, 864 F.2d 881 (1st Cir. 1988); Volk v. Coler, 845 F.2d 1422 (7th Cir. 1988). Another constitutional cause of action for public employees could be rooted in the right of privacy, insofar as the Supreme Court precedents can be read to establish that the right encompasses freedom of sexual autonomy. Griswold v. Connecticut, 381 U.S. 479 (1965); Eisenstadt v. Baird, 405 U.S. 438 (1973) (1969). Interference with that right by conditioning of some job benefit upon sexual activity with a person not of the victim's free choice should give rise to a cause of action.

Page 399. Add at end of Note 2:

See generally Comment, The Meaning of "Sex" in Title VII: Is Favoring an Employee Lover a Violation of the Act?, 83 Nw. U.L. Rev. 612 (1989).

Page 400. Add at end of Hopkins cite in Note 7:

rev'd on other grounds, 109 S. Ct. 1775 (1989).

3. Affectional Preferences

Page 406. Add a new Note 7:

7. There has been a revival of cases striking down discrimination against homosexuals in the federal sector. Perhaps the most important authority is

5. Special Problems in Applying Title VII

Watkins v. U.S. Army, 875 F.2d 699 (9th Cir. 1989), an en banc decision upholding an injunction ordering the Army to re-enlist a homosexual on the grounds of equitable estoppel when he had originally enlisted and re-enlisted several times although the Army knew of his homosexuality. In one sense the court's decision was narrow because estopping the army from relying on its regulations prohibiting re-enlistment by homosexuals pretermitted a decision on the constitutionality of the regulation. But, on the other hand, judicial intervention in a military personnel decision is highly unusual, and the invocation of estoppel against the government equally rare. Several judges dissented on this ground. But two more judges concurred, finding the Army's sweeping disqualification of reenlistment by homosexuals a denial of equal protection. Contra Ben-Shalom v. Marsh, 881 F.2d 454 (7th Cir. 1989), *cert. denied*, 110 S. Ct. 1296 (1990) (upholding a denial of reenlistment to an acknowledged lesbian against first amendment and equal protection attacks; the court noted that *Watkins'* estoppel holding was "doubtful," but did not reach that issue).

In Dubbs v. Central Intelligence Agency, 866 F.2d 1114 (9th Cir. 1989), the Ninth Circuit reversed summary judgment in favor of the CIA in a case by a lesbian working for a defense contractor who claimed that denial of a security clearance to her was based on a sweeping policy disqualifying gays. After finding a genuine factual issue as to whether the CIA had such a policy, the court questioned the district court's conclusion that such a policy would necessarily be constitutional. In this regard, the opinion is tentative because it intimates, but does not hold, that it is unconstitutional for the CIA to employ a policy denying security clearances to all gays while examining heterosexuals on the basis of such factors as susceptibility to blackmail. Ms. Dubbs was openly gay, and therefore presumably not susceptible to blackmail with respect to her sexual orientation.

D. RELIGIOUS DISCRIMINATION

Page 417. At this point read Blaylock v. Metal Trades, Inc. reprinted on p. 68.

Page 77. Add the following to Note 7:

See Underkuffler, "Discrimination" On the Basis of Religion: An Examination of Attempted Value Neutrality in Employment, 30 Will. & Mary L. Rev. 581 (1989).

2. The Special Duty to Accommodate Employees' Religious Practices

Page 442. Add at end of line 5 in Note 9:

See United States v. Board of Ed. for School Dist. of Philadelphia, 50 EPD ¶39,146 (E.D. Pa. 1989) (unlawful for school district to fail to accommodate Muslim woman's religion which required her to wear a head scarf and a long, loose dress, despite state statute banning dress indicating that a public school teacher "is a member or adherent of any religious order, sect or denomination").

E. NATIONAL ORIGIN AND ALIENAGE DISCRIMINATION

Page 457. Add a new Note 4:

4. The Supreme Court's decision in Employment Division v. Smith, 110 S. Ct. 1595 (1990), may have radically affected free exercise clause analysis in constitutional "accommodation" cases like *Hobbie* and its predecessors. At issue in *Smith* was whether Oregon could validly deny unemployment benefits to persons dismissed from their jobs because of their use of peyote for sacramental purposes as members of the Native American Church. The Court had previously remanded the case to determine whether Oregon law, which proscribed peyote as a controlled substance, recognized an exception for sacramental use. The Oregon Supreme Court held that, despite the recognition of such an exception by the federal government and by a number of states, Oregon law precluded such use of peyote.

When the case reached the United States Supreme Court a second time, five justices held that an otherwise valid state criminal law did not raise free exercise issues when it incidentally impacted religious practices of certain believers. Since the criminal statute was valid as applied to members of the Native American Church, the denial of unemployment benefits to those members who were discharged for conduct in violation of that law was permissible. The result reached was less surprising than the analysis adopted by the majority. Justice O'Connor, for example, concurred because she perceived a sufficiently compelling state interest to justify Oregon's failure to accord an exemption for sacramental use of peyote. The three dissenters, Justices Blackmun, Brennan, and Marshall, favored this mode of analysis, although they would have required an exemption in the circumstances. Under the majority's view, however, no such balancing of religious interests and state interests occurs because free exercise is simply not implicated. For such a law to be attacked, it would presumably have to be aimed at religious practices.

5. Special Problems in Applying Title VII

1. National Origin Discrimination

Page 460. Add at end of Note 2:

Fragrante v. City and County of Honolulu, 888 F.2d 591 (9th Cir. 1989), *cert. denied*, 108 L. Ed. 2d 992 (1990).

Page 462. Add at end of Note 5:

, *vacated as moot*, 109 S. Ct. 1737 (1989); See generally Note, English-only Rules and "Innocent" Employers, Clarifying National Origin Discrimination and Disparate Impact Theory Under Title VII, 74 Minn. L. Rev. 387 (1989).

2. Alienage Discrimination

Page 466. Add at end of last full paragraph:

See Mester Manufacturing Co. v. INS, 879 F.2d 561 (9th Cir. 1989).

F. RETALIATION

Page 469. Add at end of carryover paragraph:

The validity of these precedents, however, is questionable after Patterson v. McLean Credit Union, 109 S. Ct. 2363 (1989), in which a majority of the Supreme Court held that section 1981 "covers only conduct at the initial formation of the contract, and conduct which impairs the right to enforce contract obligations through legal process." Id. at 2374. While *Patterson* involved harassment on the job rather than retaliation, it seems clear that at least the broader lower court retaliation cases will have to be reconsidered. While some acts of retaliation may fit within the *Patterson* formula, most will not. See Overby v. Chevron USA, Inc., 884 F.2d 470 (9th Cir. 1989); Malhotra v. Cotter & Co., 885 F.2d 1305 (7th Cir. 1989).

Where public employment is involved, retaliation may violate an employee's rights under the first amendment to freedom of speech or freedom of petition. Starrett v. Wadley, 876 F.2d 808 (10th Cir. 1989); Johnston v. Harris Cty. Flood Control Dist., 869 F.2d 1565 (5th Cir. 1989), *cert. denied*,

110 S. Ct. 718 (1990). Cf. Yatvin v. Madison Metropolitan School Dist., 840 F.2d 412 (7th Cir. 1988).

Page 471. Add at end of carryover paragraph after "411 F.2d at 1004-1005.":

Cf. Barnes v. Small, 840 F.2d 972 (D.C. Cir. 1988), which involved a retaliation suit by a federal employee who claimed that he was discharged for assisting a co-worker in proceedings alleging race discrimination. Plaintiff had written certain letters alleging serious misconduct on the part of a management representative. Although finding that the letters were sufficiently related to the race discrimination proceedings to be protected, the court upheld the discharge because the letters were both false and malicious. The *Barnes* court, however, did not cite *Pettway*.

Page 472. Delete *Jennings* case; replace with

JENNINGS v. TINLEY PARK COMMUNITY CONSOLIDATED SCHOOL DISTRICT NO. 146
864 F.2d 1368 (7th Cir. 1988)

Before CUMMINGS and CUDAHY, Circuit Judges, and PELL, Senior Judge. CUMMINGS, Circuit Judge. . . .

I. FACTS AND PROCEEDINGS BELOW

Jennings was employed by the Tinley Park (Illinois) Community Consolidated School District No. 146 from November 1973 until June 1979, serving as secretary to the Superintendent of the School District, Robert Procunier. Jennings' employment ended on June 15, 1979, when she was discharged by Procunier due to events and conduct surrounding a protest of alleged unlawful discrimination based upon sex.

The alleged sex discrimination concerned a disparity in pay between the School District's secretaries and custodians. During this period in issue, the School District designated the two groups of employees, secretaries and custodians, as "Class I" employees. Class I employees were full-time, salaried, non-certified employees. All secretaries were female; all custodians were male. Custodians were paid one and one-half times their hourly rate for overtime work as approved by a supervisor. Secretaries were not paid for overtime work. Defendants argued that secretaries were not required to work overtime.

5. Special Problems in Applying Title VII

Beginning in February 1979, the secretaries as a group first voiced concern over the perceived disparity in compensation between themselves and the custodians. . . . [They sent in a letter to the School Board, which was given to Procunier to present; they requested permission from Procunier to meet on a bimonthly basis, and held a meeting, providing Procunier with the minutes. Jennings also spoke to Procunier about the secretaries' concerns. Despite this activity, at their next meeting Procunier's delegate informed them of a salary schedule he proposed to present to the School Board at its next meeting, which was on the following day. The secretaries opposed the schedule, primarily because they perceived that it continued pay disparities between them and the custodians. They formed an ad hoc committee to attend the School Board meeting on the following day, May 24, again giving minutes of their meeting to Procunier. He and Jennings again discussed the secretaries' concerns.]

The following day during the School Board meeting Procunier proposed his salary schedule as planned. The secretaries' ad hoc committee was in attendance and, after Procunier presented his salary schedule, explained the secretaries' opposition thereto. The School Board passed the salary schedule despite the secretaries' opposition.

In response to the School Board action on the salary schedule proposed by Procunier, the secretaries decided to prepare their own salary schedule, one that would contradict Procunier's. Jennings was the principal draftsman. The final draft, entitled "P.S. Salary Study" and consisting of the secretaries' proposed salary schedule and the minutes of their March and May meetings, was set for distribution on June 1, 1979. The P.S. Salary Study was signed collectively by the Committee of Concerned Secretaries, and individually by, among others, Jennings. This action, in contrast to the other meetings and activities, was done without Procunier's knowledge.

Rather than deliver the P.S. Salary Study to Procunier and instruct him to present it to the School Board at the next meeting (apparently scheduled for June 19th), as they had done previously, the secretaries decided to deliver individually the P.S. Salary Study to each Board member on June 1. Jennings was responsible for delivering a copy to Procunier, who heretofore was unaware of the P.S. Salary Study. Although delivery of the P.S. Salary Study to School Board members began at 2:00 P.M., and despite seeing and speaking to Procunier throughout the day—in fact Procunier asked Jennings to arrange a meeting with the secretaries so that Procunier could address their concerns—she did not deliver a copy to Procunier, nor inform him of its existence, until 3:50 P.M. that same day. Because of the timing of the delivery, Procunier was unable to respond to individual School Board members' inquiries, which began that same day.

Following receipt of the P.S. Salary Study, the working relationship between Procunier and Jennings deteriorated. Procunier distanced himself from Jennings. Whereas prior to June 1, the delivery date of the P.S. Salary Study, Procunier had Jennings open the mail and the two would then review it together, after June 1 Procunier instructed her to leave the unopened mail in his office. He also instructed her not to answer phone calls on his personal line, as she had done in the past. A chair was removed from Procunier's office, apparently so that Jennings would have no place to sit.

On June 13, Procunier met with Jennings to discuss the timing and direct delivery of the P.S. Salary Study to Board members. Procunier expressed his displeasure at not being informed of its preparation and especially at not receiving a copy sooner. Jennings responded that some of the secretaries did not trust Procunier to present the P.S. Salary Study to the School Board, and thus the reason for the extraordinary delivery to Board members. Procunier replied that if such was the case, he expected Jennings to stand up and vouch for his trustworthiness, and if Jennings was unable to do this, then he could not in turn trust her.

On June 15, Procunier again met with Jennings and informed her that because she had not been loyal and supportive, he would recommend to the School Board that she be terminated. The reasons for her discharge were set forth in a letter of that same day, reciting in pertinent part:

> It is with considerable reluctance that I terminate your employment as my secretary. Although your technical and professional competence have been outstanding throughout the period of your employment, events of the past 2-3 weeks have generated serious questions relative to your ability to serve me or the Board of Education in an effective manner as required.
>
> The very important element of mutual trust and support which is so essential in the relationship of a personal secretary to the administrator responsible for an operation similar to this school district, has been seriously undermined. As a result of your reluctance to inform me [in advance] of actions which you and other secretaries took relative to communication with the Board of Education, you have created a situation which is antagonistic to the close, confidential working relationship which is necessary in this office.
>
> The deterioration of the level of trust and support leaves no alternative open to me.

The sole rationale for Jennings' termination was her conduct arising out of the preparation and delivery of the P.S. Salary Study as it related to Procunier, her supervisor. No other secretary was terminated or disciplined for participating in the P.S. Salary Study or for delivering it directly to Board members. . . .

In *Jennings I*, this Court affirmed the lower court's holding that any disparate treatment accorded to the secretaries and custodians was based upon reasons other than sex. However, this Court vacated Judge McMillen's hold-

5. Special Problems in Applying Title VII

ing on the retaliatory discharge claim and remanded that issue for factual findings. On remand the case was assigned to Judge Norgle. By agreement of both parties, the case was submitted to him on the transcript of the previous trial; no further evidence was considered. Judge Norgle also held in favor of the defendants, determining that Procunier's reaction to Jennings' conduct was reasonable and as such constituted a legitimate basis for discharge and therefore was not retaliatory in contravention of Title VII.

II. DISCUSSION

As noted in *Jennings I*, this Court remanded to the district court the issue of whether the termination of Jennings was unlawful pursuant to Title VII, which proscribes "discrimination against any . . . employee[s] . . . [who] has opposed any practice made an unlawful employment practice by this subchapter, or because he has made a charge, testified, assisted, or participated in any manner in an investigation, proceeding, or hearing under this subchapter." 42 U.S.C. §2000e-3(a). A claim of retaliatory discharge in contravention of Title VII prompts a three-step analysis as set forth by the Supreme Court in Texas Department of Community Affairs v. Burdine and McDonnell Douglas Corp. v. Green.

First, the plaintiff has the burden of proving a prima facie case of discrimination based upon opposition to an unlawful employment practice. See *Burdine*. The plaintiff meets this burden by establishing that: (1) she was engaged in statutorily protected expression, viz., opposition to a seemingly unlawful employment practice; (2) she suffered an adverse employment action; and, (3) there was a causal connection between the statutorily protected expression and the adverse employment action. See Equal Employment Opportunity Commn. v. Crown Zellerbach Corp., 720 F.2d 1008, 1012 (9th Cir. 1983); Payne v. McLemore's Wholesale and Retail Stores, 654 F.2d 1130, 1136 (5th Cir. 1981), *certiorari denied*, 455 U.S. 1000. The plaintiff need not establish that the action she was protesting was actually an unlawful employment practice; but rather only that she had a reasonable belief that the action was unlawful. Berg v. La Crosse Cooler Co., 612 F.2d 1041, 1045-1046 (7th Cir. 1980).

Second, assuming the plaintiff is able to establish a prima facie case, the burden shifts to the defendant to "articulate some legitimate nondiscriminatory reason" for the adverse employment action. See *Burdine; Crown Zellerbach*. Disciplining an employee for protesting apparently unlawful employment discrimination is, of course, not a legitimate, nondiscriminatory reason. However, courts have held that a decision to discipline an employee whose conduct is unreasonable, even though borne out of legitimate protest, does not violate Title VII. *McDonnell Douglas* (illegal acts held unreasonable form of protest); Hochstadt v. Worcester Foundation for Experimental

Biology, 545 F.2d 222, 229-234 (1st Cir. 1976) (hostile, disruptive conduct held unreasonable form of protest).

Finally, if the defendant is able to carry its burden of articulating some legitimate, nondiscriminatory reason for the adverse action, the burden then shifts to the plaintiff to show that the defendant's articulated reason was truly pretextual for the defendant's actual discriminatory motive. *McDonnell Douglas; Burdine.*

1. THE DISTRICT COURT'S DECISION

On remand the district court was to resolve the issue of whether the defendants had articulated a legitimate reason for the discharge. The original district judge did "not make clear exactly what reason the court thought defendant had proven." Therefore the second district judge was to determine factually whether the reason for Jennings' discharge was a legitimate business reason.

On remand Judge Norgle, by agreement of both parties, did not hold evidentiary proceedings; rather he decided the case based upon the trial record developed previously. In his written order, Judge Norgle lists as findings of fact several significant items. The essential ones are: mutual trust and confidence between Procunier and Jennings were essential to the proper functioning of the workplace; Jennings told Procunier she did not trust him to deliver the salary study to the School Board; Jennings' belief that Procunier would not deliver the salary study to the School Board was unreasonable; the salary study was not presented to Procunier prior to being delivered to members of the School Board in order to enhance its effectiveness; Procunier discharged Jennings because of the form of her protest, i.e., not informing Procunier of the salary study or giving him a copy before it was delivered to the School Board; Jennings' discharge was based upon a loss of trust and confidence by Procunier, which was reasonable under the circumstances.

2. ANALYSIS ON APPEAL

Jennings appeals the district court's findings, essentially challenging its factual determinations. Federal Rule of Civil Procedure 52(a) provides that "[f]indings of fact . . . shall not be set aside unless clearly erroneous." . . .

Although unable freely to set aside factual determinations of the district court, we are not precluded from reviewing errors of law that are based upon factual findings. Rule 52(a) does not prevent a reviewing court from correcting "errors of law, including those that may infect a so-called mixed finding of law and fact, or a finding of fact that is predicated on a rule of law." Bose Corp. v. Consumers Union of United States, Inc., 466 U.S. 485, 501 (1984) (citation omitted). Accordingly, respect and deference are owed to the district

5. Special Problems in Applying Title VII

court's purely factual determinations, but less so to those determinations that depend upon or incorporate a rule of law. This distinction is especially crucial in this case where the legal conclusions rest so heavily on the particular factual findings.

In *Jennings I*, this Court expressed some doubt as to whether mere "disloyalty" can ever be the sole legitimate nondiscriminatory reason for discharging an employee protesting unlawful employment practices. Noting the Ninth Circuit's opinion in *Crown Zellerbach*, the panel majority observed that almost every form of opposition to an employment practice is in some sense disloyal.

In *Crown Zellerbach*, a group of minority employees, seeking to remedy what they perceived to be unlawful employment discrimination, filed complaints with the Equal Employment Opportunity Commission and engaged in other forms of protest activity. In particular, the group wrote letters not only to the employer's corporate parent requesting an open meeting to discuss the situation, but also to local officials, protesting the failure of public officials to investigate. The group picketed the office of the Mayor of Los Angeles. The group also lodged an administrative complaint with the Office of Federal Contract Compliance, charging that the employer's practices did not conform to Executive Order 11246, and this was later borne out by a General Services Administration investigation. All of this activity apparently was readily known by the employer. Finally, the group discovered through the company newspaper that the employer was to receive an award from the Los Angeles School District, a significant customer, for sponsorship of a program designed to provide career guidance to students at a predominantly Hispanic school. The group, believing that the employer did not merit an award for undertaking affirmative action, then wrote a letter to the School Board, composed of elected officials, to inform it of the "bigoted position of racism" and of various discrimination charges that had been filed against the company.

As a consequence, the employer fired the group of employees for "disloyalty." The Ninth Circuit applied a reasonableness test to determine whether the conduct could provide a legitimate nondiscriminatory basis for the discharge. Holding for the employees, the court determined that disloyalty alone would not suffice as reason for discharge, remarking that otherwise virtually any opposition, no matter how reasonable, could be chilled in that opposition by definition connotes overtures of disloyalty. Rather, the court determined that the letter to the School Board was an appropriate response to a decision by a body of elected officials to bestow an affirmative action award upon the employer.

The Ninth Circuit carefully distinguished cases in which an employee's opposition to perceived unlawful employment practices was determined to be unreasonable. In particular, the court distinguished Hochstadt v. Worcester Foundation for Experimental Biology, where the manner of opposition by an employee was held unreasonable. Although the First Circuit in *Hochstadt* expressly determined that the employee's conduct was "disloyal," it was also clear that the employee's conduct resulted in her poor work performance and also in fellow employees' diminished performance and reduced morale. The employee in *Hochstadt* would have been fired based on her employment performance alone without reference to the crux of her opposition.

The standard adopted in *Crown Zellerbach* remains applicable in this case. The issue before us is whether Jennings' conduct gave rise to a legitimate nondiscriminatory reason for her discharge, despite the fact that the substance of her protest was protected. Although the district court held that "objection to the form of the protest cannot be easily divorced from an objection to the protest itself," that is exactly the result compelled by *Crown Zellerbach*. The substance of the secretaries' protest, unlawful sex discrimination, is of course protected. But the outcome here depends on whether in pursuing her protest, Jennings exceeded the cloak of statutory protection by engaging in unreasonable conduct.

The district court found, and we do not question, that in order to enhance its effectiveness Procunier was not informed of the P.S. Salary Study, nor given an advance copy. Despite seeing and speaking to Procunier throughout the day, Jennings deliberately chose to keep him in the dark instead of following past practice of letting him present such a study to the Board. Accordingly Procunier, the proponent of the competing salary schedule, was not given an opportunity to respond promptly to the School Board members' inquiries. Judge Norgle determined that the decision to withhold notice from Procunier and then surprise him with the P.S. Salary Study after the School Board members had been receiving their own copies, was unreasonable. Judge Norgle's findings compel the conclusion that Jennings' decision was a conscious effort to hamper a superintendent's ability to respond to his superiors for the purpose of accomplishing her own ends.

With Federal Rule of Civil Procedure 52(a) in mind, it would be improper to conclude that Judge Norgle's determinations are clearly erroneous. Moreover, despite Jennings' contentions, his determinations were purely factual. Jennings' motivations and the reasonableness of her actions do not by themselves invoke questions of law. As a consequence of the crucial findings below, it follows as a matter of law that the cloak of statutory protection does not extend to deliberate attempts to undermine a superior's ability to perform his job. As in *Hochstadt*, when an employee engaged in opposition to a perceived unlawful employment practice participates in conduct which does not further the protest, but rather merely hinders another person's ability to perform his job, that employee relinquishes statutory protection. Here Jennings relinquished Title VII statutory protection. The substance of her protest was protected; she could not have been disciplined for her opposition to a reasonably perceived unlawful employment practice. Her decision to sandbag Procunier, however, was not entitled to protection. Perhaps if she had shown that Procunier was initially unresponsive, hostile or adversarial, such action might have been reasonable. But such was not the case. The facts indicate that Procunier was responsive, albeit his responses were not what the secretaries wanted to hear. The work environment was not disturbed because Procunier lessened Jennings' responsibilities; rather the environment was disturbed due to her decision to hinder her supervisor's ability to do his job. The record before Judge Norgle supports his conclusion that an adversarial relationship developed because of Jennings' unreasonable conduct.

An employee need not always inform a supervisor of her plans to, and substance of, protest. There are doubtless times where such a requirement would chill the rights of employees to engage in reasonable protest. Rather, we hold only that an employee may not use legitimate opposition to perceived unlawful employment discrimination as a gratuitous opportunity to embarrass a supervisor or thwart his ability to perform his job. Jennings' actions to hinder Procunier's ability to perform his job were purely gratuitous. If Procunier had been likely to disrupt or prevent legitimate opposition, contrary to what the district court found, the outcome of this litigation might be different.

Today's decision is not an affirmation of the "loyalty" defense that was questioned in *Jennings I*. It is doubtful whether loyalty alone can be a legitimate, nondiscriminatory reason for disciplining an employee engaged in opposition to an unlawful employment practice. The issue here is not simply loyalty; it is whether a supervisor can discipline an employee who deliberately interferes with the supervisor's efficacy in relationship to his superiors, particularly when the employee is in a position to repeat the interference. This decision recognizes that it is not unreasonable for a supervisor who has been thwarted once vis a vis his superiors to expect a repetition and to take action to avoid another attempt. An employer may in such circumstances discipline the employee, not because of her opposition, not because of a sense of disloyalty, but rather because of the employee's deliberate decision to disrupt the work environment, including her superior's standing with his own superiors. . . .

NOTES

1. In *McDonnell Douglas*, the defendant admitted the retaliation, that is, that it had refused to rehire plaintiff because of his civil rights activities. The only issue was whether Green's conduct was protected within the meaning of §704(a). In other cases, however, the basis for the employer's decision will be unknown because there will be no employer admissions. In such instances the threshold question is whether the employer acted because of conduct that

may fit within either the free access or the opposition clause. Only if it is determined that the employer was so motivated will the question of whether the conduct is in fact protected arise.

2. *Jennings* follows the approach unanimously adopted by the circuit courts in analyzing the threshold question of employer motivation when there is no direct evidence. That is, the *McDonnell Douglas* method of drawing inference is used. This includes the three stages of prima facie case, employer articulation of a non-discriminatory reason for its actions, and plaintiff's rebuttal by proving pretext.

3. As for the prima facie case, the *Jennings* court's statement of three elements is generally recognized: (1) plaintiff engaged in protected conduct; (2) she suffered an adverse employment action; and (3) there was a causal link between the former and the latter.

4. As for engaging in protected conduct, *Jennings* joins the other circuits in holding that opposition is protected regardless of whether, in fact, the challenged conduct is a "practice made an unlawful employment practice by this title." In other words, plaintiff does not have to be correct that the defendant is violating Title VII in order to be protected, e.g., Sias v. City Demonstration Agency, 588 F.2d 692 (9th Cir. 1978). But what should be the test for protection? Is it enough that the employee believe in good faith that there is a violation, or must she also be reasonable in that belief?

5. The *Jennings* court had little problem with the plaintiff's prima facie case. But the defendant's "legitimate, nondiscriminatory reason" caused difficulties. The appellate court stressed that not any reason satisfies the employer's burden of production: Some reasons may not be "legitimate." Put another way, some reasons may amount to an admission of retaliation. Isn't it clear that Procunier lost "trust" in plaintiff precisely because of her protected conduct? Why was there any need for a remand?

6. Is the point that Procunier did act against plaintiff because of plaintiff's protected conduct but that his response was justified? Isn't that precisely what the defendant did in *McDonnell Douglas*? Of course, in *McDonnell Douglas*, the employer basically claimed that the manner of opposition was beyond the statute's protection because it was illegal. In *Jennings*, the employer did not seem to contend that there was anything inappropriate in the preparation of the study; rather, he criticized the plaintiff's failure to notify him about it. Can it possibly be that failures of tact or politeness deprive an employee of §704(a)'s protections?

7. Or might one argue that the question is not what the employee did but whether Procunier in fact lost confidence in her? Should a superior be forced to work with a subordinate he doesn't trust? In the prior appeal one judge suggested that trust and confidence are "bona fide occupational qualifications," at least for certain employees. But the bfoq does not reach to race or retaliation discrimination as far as the language of the statute is concerned.

5. Special Problems in Applying Title VII Page 472

More importantly, wouldn't Title VII be rendered nugatory if it were a defense to discrimination charges that employees shouldn't have to work with persons they disliked?

8. *McDonnell Douglas* may establish that some conduct is too disloyal to be protected. But *Crown Zellerbach* indicates that the mere fact that an employer perceives conduct to be disloyal does not deprive it of protection. When is conduct disloyal enough to be unprotected? Does *Jennings* answer that question? Are the courts really establishing a balancing test? If so, what goes on the scales? Is the validity of the charge a factor, or the extent to which the employer reacts to complaints? What about the extent of the disruption? Could even substantial disruption be outweighed by employer provocation? Should the court inquire into whether the plaintiff's conduct was more disruptive than necessary to achieve his ends, or whether the employee had ulterior motivations?

9. In *Jennings*, was any disruption more the result of Procunier's reaction than of the plaintiff's conduct? Won't that always be true? Might Procunier have overreacted in the sense that a reasonable employer wouldn't have lost confidence in Jennings over such behavior?

10. If the defendant's reason in *Jennings* were to count as a legitimate nonretaliatory reason, how would the plaintiff have proven pretext?

11. Suppose the court finds that an employer is influenced by retaliatory motives. Is that the end of the case, or may defendant escape (or limit) liability by proving that its action would have been taken even without the prohibited motivation? See Price Waterhouse v. Hopkins, reproduced at p. 68. As applied to the retaliation context, the *Price Waterhouse* decision essentially suggests that, if a plaintiff can establish that a retaliatory motive was present in an adverse employment decision, the burden of persuasion shifts to the employer to demonstrate that the same decision would have been made in any event. However, that burden is carried out the normal preponderance of evidence standard rather than the more demanding "clear and convincing" test used by some courts.

12. The other side of the coin is that even the employer who has good reason to discharge an employee cannot necessarily escape a finding of unlawful retaliation. This makes pretext critical in many cases. Note that if good cause exists with respect to several employees but only the employee who engaged in protected activity is discharged, pretext is probable. Francis v. American Telephone & Telegraph Co., 55 F.R.D. 202 (D.D.C. 1972). Note also that if the employer discovers the good cause by a program of surveillance that is instituted in response to the exercise of §704 rights, the discharge is not justified. Id. at 207.

13. Some cases take a broader view of the ability of an employer to discharge an employee for opposition when the employee is an equal opportunity officer. See Pendleton v. Rumsfeld, 628 F.2d 102 (D.C. Cir. 1980).

The rationale appears to be a conflict of interest, since an EEOC officer's duty is to minimize the employer's vulnerability. Does this rationale reflect a proper conception of such an officer's role?

14. Pettway v. American Cast Iron Pipe Co., 411 F.2d 998 (5th Cir. 1968), suggested that an employer defamation suit under state law against an employee based on the charging process might be possible. Should such a suit be allowed? See Linn v. United Plant Guard Workers, 383 U.S. 53 (1966). The EEOC has decided in the negative. EEOC Dec. No. 74-77, 2 Empl. Prac. Guide ¶6417 (Jan. 18, 1974). Even if such suits were allowed, might Title VII require a liability standard similar to the one in New York Times Co. v. Sullivan, 376 U.S. 254 (1964)? See also Conrad v. Robinson, 871 F.2d 612 (6th Cir. 1989) (permitting defendant's removal of defamation suit to federal court where defendant could more effectively assert his claim that the suit was in retaliation for conduct protected under Title VII).

15. In defending a discrimination case on the merits, the employer must be careful to avoid infringing the anti-retaliation provision. See EEOC v. Plumbers Local 189, 311 F. Supp. 464 (S.D. Ohio 1970), where the court found a defense attorney's interrogation of various employees to be coercive.

16. The courts have addressed the question of whether federal antidiscrimination statutes bar the employer's withholding of certain benefits where the employee has agreed not to engage in otherwise protected conduct in return for receiving those benefits. For example, in EEOC v. Cosmair, 821 F.2d 1085 (5th Cir. 1987), the employer agreed to provide severance pay to a departing employee in exchange for his releasing the employer from, inter alia, discrimination claims. When the employee nevertheless filed a charge of age discrimination with the EEOC, the employer refused to continue the severance payments. In the Commission's suit alleging retaliation against the employee, the *Cosmair* court held not only that the underlying agreement did not explicitly bar a charge filing, but also that an employee could not waive a right to file a charge. Thus, the employer was not justified in terminating severance pay. In reaching this decision, the court stressed that charges served a public interest in calling the EEOC's attention to discrimination that might affect others in addition to the charging party. Therefore, while an employee might, in return for benefits such as severance, waive any right to recover for discrimination, she could not waive her right to file a charge. See also EEOC v. US Steel Corp., 44 EPD ¶37,312 (W.D. Pa. 1987) (injunction issued against employer's use of a waiver form as a condition of early retirement that included promises not to file charges or assist the EEOC). Suppose the employee did validly waive a right that was waivable (e.g., the right to sue for discrimination). Would it be impermissible retaliation for an employer to withhold the bargained for benefits? Obviously, an employer in such a situation could move to dismiss the suit on the grounds of a valid release. But do the anti-retaliation provisions bar more direct action?

5. Special Problems in Applying Title VII   Page 472

From a contract perspective, an employer could otherwise elect one of two remedies: (1) affirming the contract and asserting the release as a defense to the employee's action or (2) rescinding the agreement for a material breach, withholding any unpaid benefits, and suing for recovery of benefits already paid.

17. Section 704(a) has been held to bar not only retaliation against applicants and present employees but against past employees, as by giving bad references to new prospective employers. Bailey v. USX Corp., 850 F.2d 1506 (11th Cir. 1988); EEOC v. Cosmair, Inc., 821 F.2d 1085 (5th Cir. 1987) (ADEA).

18. Sources discussing retaliation questions include Walterscheid, A Question of Retaliation: Opposition Conduct as Protected Expression Under Title VII of the Civil Rights Act of 1964, 29 B.C.L. Rev. 391 (1988); Lopatka, Protection under the National Labor Relations Act and Title VII of the Civil Rights Act for Employees Who Protest Discrimination in Private Employment, 50 N.Y.U.L. Rev. 1179 (1975); Spurlock, Proscribing Retaliation under Title VII, 8 Ind. L. Rev. 453 (1975); Kattan, Employee Opposition to Discriminatory Employment Practices: Protection from Retaliation under Title VII, 19 Wm. & Mary L. Rev. 217 (1977).

Chapter 6

Procedures for Enforcing Title VII

A. INTRODUCTION

Page 493. Add after "first to attempt conciliation" in third line from bottom:

(see generally, Silver, The Uses and Abuses of Informal Procedures in Federal Civil Rights Enforcement, 55 Geo. Wash. L. Rev. 482 (1987))

B. PRIVATE ENFORCEMENT OF TITLE VII: THE ADMINISTRATIVE PHASE

2. *Filing a Timely Charge*

c. Continuing Violations

Page 517. Add a new Note 6:

6. Prior to *Bazemore*, most lower courts had held that, in compensation cases, each paycheck constituted a violation rather than merely the initial

setting of the discriminatory salary. E.g., Perez v. Laredo Junior College, 706 F.2d 731 (5th Cir. 1983), *cert. denied*, 464 U.S. 1047 (1984); Bartelt v. Berlitz School, 698 F.2d 1003 (9th Cir.), *cert. denied*, 464 U.S. 915 (1983). In the wake of *Bazemore*, one would think these cases surely correct. But one court in a sex discrimination case brought under both Title VII and the EPA held that, at least absent a "longstanding and demonstrable policy of discrimination, such as an established and repeated policy of paying men more than women," an isolated case of wage discrimination exists only so long as the employer continues to pay at least one male more than the disfavored females. EEOC v. Penton Industrial Publishing Co., 851 F.2d 835, (6th Cir. 1988). Is this correct?

Page 517. Add at end of Notes:

LORANCE v. AT & T TECHNOLOGIES, INC.
109 S. Ct. 2261 (1989)

Justice SCALIA delivered the opinion of the Court.

Respondent AT & T Technologies, Inc. (AT & T) manufactures electronics products at its Montgomery Works plant. The three petitioners, all of whom are women, have worked as hourly wage employees in that facility since the early 1970's, and have been represented by respondent Local 1942, International Brotherhood of Electrical Workers, AFL-CIO. Until 1979 all hourly wage earners accrued competitive seniority exclusively on the basis of years spent in the plant, and a worker promoted to the more highly skilled and better paid "tester" positions retained this plantwide seniority. A collective-bargaining agreement executed by respondents on July 23, 1979, altered the manner of calculating tester seniority. Thenceforth a tester's seniority was to be determined not by length of plantwide service, but by time actually spent as a tester (though it was possible to regain full plantwide seniority after spending 5 years as a tester and completing a prescribed training program). The present action arises from that contractual modification.

Petitioners became testers between 1978 and 1980. During a 1982 economic downturn their low seniority under the 1979 collective-bargaining agreement caused them to be selected for demotion; they would not have been demoted had the former plantwide seniority system remained in place. Claiming that the present seniority system was the product of an intent to discriminate on the basis of sex, petitioners . . . filed the present lawsuit in the District Court for the Northern District of Illinois, and sought certification as class representatives for women employees of AT & T's Montgomery Works plant who had lost plantwide seniority or whom the new system had

6. Procedures for Enforcing Title VII

deterred from seeking promotions to tester positions. Their complaint alleged that among hourly wage earners the tester positions had traditionally been held almost exclusively by men, and nontester positions principally by women, but that in the 1970's an increasing number of women took the steps necessary to qualify for tester positions and exercised their seniority rights to become testers. They claimed that the 1979 alteration of the rules governing tester seniority was the product of a "conspir[acy] to change the seniority rules, in order to protect incumbent male testers and to discourage women from promoting into the traditionally-male tester jobs," and that "[t]he purpose and the effect of this manipulation of seniority rules has been to protect male testers from the effects of the female testers' greater plant seniority, and to discourage women from entering the traditionally-male tester jobs."

. . . Section 706(e) of Title VII . . . provides that "[a] charge . . . shall be filed [with the EEOC] within [the applicable period] after the alleged unlawful practice occurred." 42 U.S.C. §2000e-5(e). Assessing timeliness therefore "requires us to identify precisely the 'unlawful employment practice' of which [petitioners] complai[n]." Delaware State College v. Ricks. . . .

Petitioners' allegation of a disparate impact on men and women would ordinarily suffice to state a claim under §703(a)(2), since that provision reaches "practices that are fair in form, but discriminatory in operation," Griggs v. Duke Power Co.. "[S]eniority systems," however, "are afforded special treatment under Title VII," by reason of §703(h). . . . We have construed this provision to mean that "absent a discriminatory purpose, the operation of a seniority system cannot be an unlawful employment practice even if the system has some discriminatory consequences." Thus, for liability to be incurred "there must be a finding of actual intent to discriminate on [statutorily proscribed] grounds on the part of those who negotiated or maintained the [seniority] system." Pullman-Standard v. Swint, 456 U.S. 273, 289 (1982).

Petitioners do not allege that the seniority system treats similarly situated employees differently or that it has been operated in an intentionally discriminatory manner. Rather, they claim that its differential impact on the sexes is unlawful because the system "ha[d] its genesis in [sex] discrimination." Teamsters v. United States. Specifically, the complaint alleges that respondents "conspired to *change* the seniority rules, in order to protect incumbent male testers," and that the resulting agreement effected a "*manipulation of* seniority rules" for that "purpose." (emphasis added). This is in essence a claim of intentionally discriminatory *alteration* of their contractual rights. Seniority is a contractual right, Aaron, Reflections on the Legal Nature and Enforceability of Seniority Rights, 75 Harv. L. Rev. 1532, 1533 (1962), and a competitive seniority system establishes a "hierarchy [of such rights] . . . according to which . . . various employment benefits are distributed." Under the collective-bargaining agreements in effect prior to 1979, each petitioner had earned the right to receive a favorable position in the hierarchy of seniority among testers (if and when she became a tester), and respondents eliminated those rights for reasons alleged to be discriminatory. Because this diminution in employment status occurred in 1979—well outside the period of limitations for a complaint filed with the EEOC in 1983—the Seventh Circuit was correct to find petitioners' claims time-barred under §706(e).

We recognize, of course, that it is possible to establish a different theoretical construct: to regard the employer as having been guilty of a continuing violation which "occurred," for purposes of §706(e), not only when the contractual right was eliminated but also when each of the concrete effects of that elimination were felt. Or it would be possible to interpret §703 in such fashion that when the proviso of §703(h) is not met ("provided that such differences are not the result of an intention to discriminate because of race, color, religion, sex, or national origin") and that subsection's protection becomes unavailable, nothing prevents suits against the later effects of the system on disparate impact grounds under §703(a)(2). The answer to these alternative approaches is that our cases have rejected them.

The continuing violation theory is contradicted most clearly by two decisions, Delaware State College v. Ricks and United Air Lines, Inc. v. Evans. In *Ricks*, we treated an allegedly discriminatory denial of tenure—rather than the resulting nondiscriminatory termination of employment one year later—as the act triggering the limitations period under §706(e). Because Ricks did not claim "that the manner in which his employment was terminated differed discriminatorily from the manner in which the College terminated other professors who also had been denied tenure," we held that "the only alleged discrimination occurred—and the filing limitations periods therefore commenced—at the time the tenure decision was made and communicated to Ricks." "That is so," we found, "even though one of the *effects* of the denial of tenure—the eventual loss of a teaching position—did not occur until later." (emphasis in original) We concluded that "'[t]he proper focus is upon the time of the *discriminatory acts*, not upon the time at which the *consequences* of the acts became most painful.'"[3]

---

[3]. The dissent attempts to distinguish Delaware State College v. Ricks on the ground that there "[t]he allegedly discriminatory denial of tenure . . . served notice to the plaintiff that his termination a year later would come as a 'delayed, *but inevitable*, consequence.'" (emphasis in original) (citation omitted). This builds on its earlier criticism that "[o]n the day AT & T's seniority system was adopted, there was no reason to believe that a woman who exercised her plantwide seniority to become a tester would *ever* be demoted as a result of the new system," so that at that point the prospect of petitioners' suffering "concret[e] harm" was "speculative." (emphasis in original). Of course the benefits of a seniority system, like those of an insurance policy payable upon the occurrence of a noninevitable event, are by their nature speculative—if only because they depend upon the employee's continuing desire to work for the particular employer. But it makes no more sense to say that no "concrete harm" occurs when an employer provides a patently less desirable seniority guarantee than what the law requires, than it does to say that no concrete harm occurs when an insurance company delivers an accident insurance policy with a face value of $10,000, when what has been paid for is a face value of $25,000. It is

6. Procedures for Enforcing Title VII

(emphasis in original); accord, Chardon v. Fernandez, 454 U.S. 6, 8 (1981) (per curiam).

In *Evans*, United Air Lines had discriminatorily dismissed the plaintiff after she had worked several years as a flight attendant, and when it rehired her some years later, gave her no seniority credit for her earlier service. Evans conceded that the discriminatory dismissal was time-barred, but claimed that the seniority system impermissibly gave "present effect to a past act of discrimination." While agreeing with that assessment, we concluded under §703(h) that "a challenge to a neutral system may not be predicated on the mere fact that a past event which has no present legal significance has affected the calculation of seniority credit, even if the past event might at one time have justified a valid claim against the employer." Like Evans, petitioners in the present case have asserted a claim that is wholly dependent on discriminatory conduct occurring well outside the period of limitations, and cannot complain of a continuing violation.

The second alternative theory mentioned above would view §703(h) as merely providing an affirmative defense to a cause of action brought under §703(a)(2), rather than as making intentional discrimination an element of any Title VII action challenging a seniority system. The availability of this affirmative defense would not alter the fact that the claim asserted is one of discriminatory impact under §703(a)(2), causing the statute of limitations to run from the time that impact is felt. As an original matter this is a plausible, and perhaps even the most natural, reading of §703(h). (We have construed §703(e), 42 U.S.C. §2000e-2(e) — which deals with bona fide occupational qualifications — in this fashion. See Dothard v. Rawlinson). But such an interpretation of §703(h) is foreclosed by our cases, which treat the proof of discriminatory intent as a necessary element of Title VII actions challenging seniority systems. At least as concerns seniority plans, we have regarded subsection (h) not as a defense to the illegality described in subsection (a)(2), but as a provision that itself "delineates which employment practices are illegal and thereby prohibited and which are not." Thus, petitioners' claim depends on proof of intentionally discriminatory adoption of the system, which occurred outside the limitations period.

That being the case, Machinists v. NLRB, 362 U.S. 411 (1960), establishes that the limitations period will run from the date the system was adopted (at least where the adoption occurred after the effective date of Title VII, and a cause of action against it was available). *Machinists* was a decision under the National Labor Relations Act (NLRA), but we have often observed

---

true that the injury to the employee becomes substantially more concrete when the less desirable seniority system causes his demotion, just as the injury to the policy-holder becomes substantially more concrete when the accident occurs and the payment is $15,000 less than it should be. But that is irrelevant to whether there was any concrete injury at the outset. What the dissent means by "concrete harm" is what *Ricks, supra* referred to as the point at which the injury becomes "most painful" — and that case rejected it as the point of reference for liability.

that the NLRA was the model for Title VII's remedial provisions, and have found cases interpreting the former persuasive in construing the latter. Such reliance is particularly appropriate in the context presented here, since the highly unusual feature of requiring an administrative complaint before a civil action can be filed against a private party is common to the two statutes. The NLRA's statute of limitations—which provides that "no complaint shall issue based upon any unfair labor practice occurring more than six months prior to the filing of the charge with the Board," 29 U.S.C. §160(b)—is even substantively similar to §706(e). . . . In Zipes v. Trans World Airlines, Inc., 455 U.S. 385 (1982), we specifically relied on cases construing the NLRA's timely filing requirement in determining whether §706(e)—the very provision we construe here—constituted a waivable statute of limitations or rather a jurisdictional prerequisite to a Title VII action. . . .

Machinists considered and rejected an approach to the limitations period identical to that advanced here. The suit involved the timeliness of an unfair labor practice complaint directed at a so-called "union security clause," which required all employees to join the union within 45 days of the contract's execution. Under the NLRB's precedents, agreeing to such a clause when the union lacked majority status constituted an unfair labor practice, as did continued enforcement of the clause. The agreement at issue in *Machinists* had been *adopted* more than 6 months before the complaint issued (outside the limitations period), but had been *enforced* well within the period of limitations. "Conceding that a complaint predicated on the *execution* of the agreement here challenged was barred by limitations," the NLRB contended that "its complaint was nonetheless timely since it was 'based upon' the parties' continued *enforcement*, within the period of limitations, of the union security clause." (emphasis in original). We found, however, that "the entire foundation of the unfair labor practice charged was the Union's time-barred lack of majority status when the original collective-bargaining agreement was signed," and that "[i]n the absence of that fact enforcement of this otherwise valid union security clause was wholly benign." "[W]here a complaint based upon that earlier event is time-barred," we reasoned, "to permit the event itself" "to cloak with illegality that which was otherwise lawful" "in effect results in reviving a legally defunct unfair labor practice."[4] This analy-

---

4. Like *Ricks* and United Air Lines, Inc. v. Evans, our decision in Machinists v. NLRB also rejected an attempt to cure untimeliness by asserting a continuing violation:

> The applicability of these principles cannot be avoided here by invoking the doctrine of continuing violation. It may be conceded that the continued enforcement, as well as the execution, of this collective bargaining agreement constitutes an unfair labor practice, and that these are two logically separate violations, independent in the sense that they can be described in discrete terms. Nevertheless, the vice in the enforcement of this agreement is manifestly not independent of the legality of its execution, as would be the case, for example, with an agreement invalid on its face or with one validly executed, but unlawfully administered.

6. Procedures for Enforcing Title VII

sis is squarely in point here. Because the claimed invalidity of the facially nondiscriminatory and neutrally applied tester seniority system is wholly dependent on the alleged illegality of signing the underlying agreement, it is the date of that signing which governs the limitations period.

In holding that, when a seniority system is nondiscriminatory in form and application, it is the allegedly discriminatory adoption which triggers the limitations period, we respect not only §706(e)'s general " 'value judgment concerning the point at which the interests in favor of protecting valid claims are outweighed by the interests in prohibiting the prosecution of stale [claims],' " (citation omitted), but also the considerations underlying the "special treatment" accorded to seniority systems under §703(h). This "special treatment" strikes a balance between the interests of those protected against discrimination by Title VII and those who work—perhaps for many years—in reliance upon the validity of a facially lawful seniority system. There is no doubt, of course, that a facially discriminatory seniority system (one that treats similarly situated employees differently) can be challenged at any time,[5] and that even a facially neutral system, if it is adopted with unlawful discriminatory motive, can be challenged within the prescribed period after adoption. But allowing a facially neutral system to be challenged, and entitlements under it to be altered, many years after its adoption would disrupt those valid reliance interests that §703(h) was meant to protect. In the context of the present case, a female tester could defeat the settled (and worked-for) expectations of her co-workers whenever she is demoted or not promoted under the new system, be that in 1983, 1993, 2003, or beyond. Indeed, a given plaintiff could in theory sue successively for not being promoted, for being demoted, for being laid off, and for not being awarded a sufficiently favorable pension, so long as these acts—even if nondiscriminatory in themselves—could be attributed to the 1979 change in seniority. Our past cases, to which we adhere today, have declined to follow an approach that has such disruptive implications. . . .

[Justice O'CONNOR did not participate, and Justice STEVENS, concurred on the grounds of state decisis.]

---

5. The dissent is mistaken to equate the application of a facially neutral but discriminatorily adopted system with the application of a system that is facially discriminatory. With a facially neutral system the discriminatory act occurs only at the time of adoption, for each application is nondiscriminatory (seniority accrues for men and women on an identical basis). But a facially discriminatory system (e.g., one that assigns men twice the seniority that women receive for the same amount of time served) by definition discriminates each time it is applied. This is a material difference for purposes of the analysis we employed in *Evans* and *Ricks*—which focuses on the timing of the discriminatory acts for purposes of the statute of limitations. It is also why the dissent's citation of Bazemore v. Friday, 478 U.S. 385 (1986)— in which "[e]ach week's paycheck . . . deliver[ed] less to a black than to a similarly situated white,"—is misplaced.

Justice MARSHALL, with whom Justice BRENNAN and Justice BLACKMUN join, dissenting.

The majority holds today that, when it is alleged that an employer and a union have negotiated and adopted a new seniority system with the intention of discriminating against women in violation of Title VII, the limitations period set forth in §706(e) begins to run immediately upon the adoption of that system. This is so even if the employee who subsequently challenges that system could not reasonably have expected to be demoted or otherwise concretely harmed by the new system at the time of its adoption, and, indeed, even if the employee was not working in the affected division of the company at the time of the system's adoption. This severe interpretation of §706(e) will come as a surprise to Congress, whose goals in enacting Title VII surely never included conferring absolute immunity on discriminatorily adopted seniority systems that survive their first 300 days. Because the harsh reality of today's decision, requiring employees to sue anticipatorily or forever hold their peace, is so glaringly at odds with the purposes of Title VII, and because it is compelled neither by the text of the statute nor our precedents interpreting it, I respectfully dissent.

The facts of this case illustrate the austere practical consequences of the majority's holding. On the day AT & T's seniority system was adopted, there was no reason to believe that a woman who exercised her plantwide seniority to become a tester would ever be demoted as a result of the new system. Indeed, under the new system, after five years a woman tester would regain her plantwide seniority; only in the intervening five years was she potentially endangered. Patricia Lorance, who was already a tester when the new system was adopted, almost made it; only after four years as a tester was she demoted under the terms of the new system. That the new system would concretely harm petitioners Janice King and Carol Bueschen was even more speculative. They became testers several months after the seniority system was modified, and like Lorance, they were not adversely affected by the restructured seniority system until 1982. (Indeed, absent the nationwide recession in the early 1980's, the petitioners might never have been affected.) Today, however, the majority concludes that these women are barred from bringing this suit because they failed to anticipate, within 300 days of the new system's adoption, that these contingencies would one day place them among the new system's casualties.

Nothing in the text of Title VII compels this result. On the contrary, even the majority concedes that a plausible reading of Title VII would regard the employer as having violated §703(a)(1), the disparate treatment wing of the statute, not only at the time of the system's adoption, but also when each concrete effect of that system is felt. Under this continuing violation theory, each time a discriminatory seniority system is applied, like each time a discriminatory salary structure is applied, an independent "unlawful employment practice" under §703(a)(1) takes place, triggering the limitations period anew. See Bazemore v. Friday; cf. Havens Realty Corp. v. Coleman. Viewing each application of a discriminatory system as a new violation serves the equal opportunity goals of Title VII by ensuring that victims of discrimination are not prevented from having their day in court.

. . . The majority contends that the result it reaches today is dictated by [the] ill-advised precedents involving seniority systems, but in my view, today's decision compounds the Court's prior decisional errors by giving them unnecessarily broad scope. This extension is particularly inappropriate because it forces the Court to reach such a bizarre and impractical result. Never have we held or even intimated that, in the context of a statute of limitations inquiry, one must evaluate challenges to a seniority system born of discriminatory intent as of the moment of its adoption. Indeed, had we so held, the majority's concession that a worker may at any time challenge a facially discriminatory seniority plan under §703(a)(1) would be flatly contradicted by precedent. The discriminatory intent that goes into the creation of even a facially flawed seniority plan is, after all, no different than the discriminatory intent that informs the creation of a facially neutral one. To impute ongoing intent in the former situation but not in the latter is untenable. The distinction the majority erects today serves only to reward those employers ingenious enough to cloak their acts of discrimination in a facially neutral guise, identical though the effects of this system may be to those of a facially discriminatory one.

Neither United Air Lines Inc. v. Evans nor Delaware State College v. Ricks on which the majority premises its rejection of the continuing violation theory, compel today's result. In *Evans*, unlike the instant case, the plaintiff never alleged that the seniority system itself was set up in order to discriminate. . . . The sole discrimination alleged in *Evans* was in the plaintiff's prior discharge, the impact of which, she alleged, had been enhanced upon her return to work by the failure of the seniority system to accord her credit for time she would have served had she not been discharged. In denying her challenge to that system, we held that "a challenge to a neutral system may not be predicated on the mere fact that a past event [Evan's prior discharge] which has no present legal significance has affected the calculation of seniority credit." That holding is plainly inapposite here, where the very essence of petitioners' claim is that AT & T's discriminatorily adopted seniority system is not neutral. Thus, the majority's conclusion that the "past event" cited in this case—the discriminatory adoption of the very seniority system under legal challenge—has " 'no present legal significance,' " is ipse dixit.

Ricks is likewise inapposite. The allegedly discriminatory denial of tenure in that case served notice to the plaintiff that his termination a year later would come as a "delayed, *but inevitable* consequence" (emphasis added). It was thus appropriate, as in so many areas involving statutes of limitations doctrine, to set the limitations clock running upon the plaintiff's discovery of harm to herself. Petitioners Lorance, King, and Bueschen, however, were given no such advance warning. For them, the majority holds, the limitations clock began running, and ran out, long before it was apparent that they would be demoted by AT & T's discriminatory system. Like *Evans*, *Ricks* stands for the proposition that neutral employment practices that passively perpetuate the consequences of prior time-barred discrimination but are not themselves bred of discriminatory intent do not constitute actionable wrongs under Title VII. Neither case suggests that the operation of a seniority system set up in order to discriminate should be treated the same way as a legitimate seniority (or tenure) system, born of nondiscriminatory motives, which in a particular case may have the effect of passively reinforcing prior time-barred acts of discrimination.

Nor, finally, is it correct to say that Machinists v. NLRB, "establishes that the limitations period will run from the date the system was adopted," and therefore controls this case. Initially, it bears mention that *Machinists* arose under a different statute, the Labor Management Relations Act (NLRA), 29 U.S.C. §§ 151-169, and that *Machinists* did not involve a seniority system, but instead a union security clause which, it was alleged, had been defectively adopted. Significant though the role of the NLRA was as a model for Title VII's remedial provisions, these are hardly the indicia of a controlling precedent. Moreover, sound reasons support the finding of a time-bar in *Machinists*, but no time-bar here. In *Machinists*, as in *Ricks*, the enforcement of the challenged security clause was the inevitable consequence of its execution. The clause affected all nonunion employees alike, and from its very inception there was no mystery about which employees would be affected and about the impact it would have on them. By contrast, in this case, the very essence of petitioners' claim is that AT & T's new seniority system was designed to have a long-range discriminatory impact, hurting women employees as a group but, as of the time of its inception, only theoretically hurting particular woman employees. Unlike *Machinists*, there is no indication that anyone employed at AT & T was, during the limitations period chosen by the majority, so tangibly affected by the new plan as to create any incentive to sue.[3] . . .

---

3. Tellingly, none of the Courts of Appeals presented with a claim of a continuing violation has reached the result the majority today reaches. Indeed, two of the Courts of Appeals have interpreted our precedents to permit claims of continuing violation. Cook v. Pan American World Airways, Inc., 771 F.2d 635, 646 (CA2 1985); cf. Johnson v. General Electric, 840 F.2d 132, 135 (CA1 1988). . . . Even the Seventh Circuit, finding petitioners' claim time-barred in the judgment under review, adopted a far narrower interpretation than the majority, under which the limitations period begins to run on the date when the employee first becomes subject to the seniority system.

NOTES

1. Consider Cook v. Pan American World Airways, Inc., cited in the dissent's footnote 3, in which the court found a continuing violation where an arbitration award establishing seniority rights was published more than 300 days before the charge, but the charge was timely filed as measured from the point at which the employer implemented that award by making assignments from the seniority list. Is it clear that *Lorance* overrules *Cook*? What if the employer did not accede to the arbitration award, but challenged it in court?

2. Does *Lorance* implicitly disapprove cases like Johnson v. General Electric, also cited by the dissent, which held that a discriminatory subjective evaluation, while it might be viewed as a violation itself, does not ripen until the victim suffers adverse consequences, such as denial of a promotion or of other benefits. The *Johnson* court rejected the "continuing violation" analysis that other courts had used to analyze similar situations, believing the "time of accrual" approach more appropriate. While the *Lorance* majority did not cite *Johnson*, it did reject the argument that the changes in the seniority system should not trigger the limitations period, since at the time of adoption they had only speculative effects on individuals. *Johnson* had stressed precisely this point with respect to evaluations. On the other hand, the *Lorance* Court stated that, while the effects of the change in seniority were uncertain at the time they were adopted, the changes made constituted a "concrete injury at the outset." Arguably, an unfavorable evaluation, by itself, does not constitute a "concrete injury." Cf. Price Waterhouse v. Hopkins, reproduced at p. 9.

3. At first glance, *Lorance* seems to be another blow to the continuing violation theory. It is, of course, in line with both *Ricks* and *Evans*, cases which held EEOC filings time barred. Although *Evans* is unlike *Lorance*, in that the latter case challenged a seniority system on the ground of intent to discriminate, not merely on disparate impact, the two cases both view the "violation" as no later than the creation of the system. Similarly, *Lorance* parallels *Ricks* in that the later adverse consequences were simply the result of the earlier violation. The fact that those results were inevitable in *Ricks* and contingent in *Lorance* was viewed as not important by the Court.

4. But doesn't *Lorance* clearly affirm the essence of the continuing violation theory? "There is no doubt, of course, that a facially discriminatory seniority system (one that treats similarly situated employees differently) can be challenged at any time." Is the distinction between "facial" and "non-facial" discrimination?

5. Did this distinction arise because of the majority's efforts to reconcile *Lorance* with *Bazemore*, which had used the continuing violation theory? The *Lorance* Court stressed that the system's claimed invalidity "is wholly dependent on the alleged illegality of signing the underlying agreement." For that reason, the date of signing governs the limitations period. On this basis the Court could distinguish the dissent's citation of *Bazemore* as "misplaced."

149

But is *Bazemore* so easily dismissed? The prior case could be viewed as an example of facial discrimination, since a central issue was whether salary differentials originating in pre-Title VII discrimination would constitute present violations. But wasn't a major issue in *Bazemore* whether those discrepancies had been erased, that is, whether there was in fact any continuing discrimination in compensation?

6. Is *Lorance* "only" a seniority decision? That is, can the case be viewed as limiting the continuing violation concept only when the "special treatment" that §703(h) affords seniority systems is implicated?

7. That would explain the majority's failure to deal with *Havens Realty*, an omission that is all the more surprising since the majority departed from discrimination law precedents to look to the National Labor Relations Act to bulwark its decision, citing Machinists v. NLRB. But the dissent stresses that *Machinists* was not a seniority case.

8. To test these possibilities, reconsider a variation of Dothard v. Rawlinson in light of *Lorance*. A woman applies for a contact position in a men's prison in 1978 and is denied it on the grounds of her inability to satisfy the employer's height and weight minima and the rule against female guards in such positions. She waits until 1988 to file a charge with the EEOC, but during the entire decade the defendant continues to use the same requirements. With respect to the formal gender exclusion, doesn't *Lorance* permit the charge at any time? What about the height and weight criteria?

There are two possibilities here. First, that the requirements were adopted precisely because they would exclude women, and, second, that they have an unintended gender impact. If *Lorance* is limited to seniority systems, the case says nothing about these requirements. If, on the other hand, *Lorance* reaches all disparate treatment cases, save those where the treatment is facial, disparate treatment suit may be time barred. What about disparate impact? Is it relevant that there may be no way to determine if they have a disparate impact until they are applied in fact?

9. Does *Lorance* implicitly bar a "discovery" rule? Suppose the plaintiffs proved that they had no reason to believe there was a discriminatory purpose in the changes in the seniority system until a union leader "blew the whistle" years after the change but within 300 days of the plaintiffs' EEOC charge?

3. Filing a Timely Charge: Deferral States

Page 520. Delete last paragraph, beginning "Further. . . ."; replace with new text:

While *Oscar Mayer* had held that a timely state filing was not necessary for purposes of the ADEA, it was not until EEOC v. Commercial Office

6. Procedures for Enforcing Title VII

Products Co., 486 U.S. 107 (1988), that the Supreme Court confirmed unanimous circuit court authority, which held that a timely state filing was also unnecessary under Title VII. Even more significantly, *Commercial Office Products* also held that the 300 day period for filing with the EEOC, which applies in deferral states, controls in Title VII suits regardless of whether there has been a filing that is timely under state law with the state agency.

Page 521. Add new text before "Note on the Interrelationship . . .":

Subsequent appellate cases have read *Commercial Office Products* to allow such agreements to expand filing parties' rights. For example, in McKelvy v. Metal Container Corp., 854 F.2d 448 (11th Cir. 1988) (ADEA), the court held that "waiver" of the state agency's jurisdiction pursuant to a worksharing agreement with the EEOC constituted "termination" of state proceedings for Title VII purposes, thereby permitting the EEOC to immediately begin processing the charge. At the same time, this "waiver" is not held to disqualify the state agency as a deferral agency, which would re-institute the 180 day period. The result is highly favorable to charging parties in jurisdictions with such worksharing agreements: they may file with the EEOC within 300 days of the violation, rather than having to file within the 180 days (where no agency exists) or 240 days (which would be necessary in the absence of a worksharing agreement in order to accord the state agency the otherwise-requisite 60 days for charge processing).

b. Coordination of State and Federal Remedies

Page 524. Add at end of carryover paragraph:

Gardner-Denver has generally been followed and even extended. See Swenson v. Management Recruiters Intl., Inc., 858 F.2d 1304 (8th Cir. 1988), *reh'g denied*, 872 F.2d 264 (1989), *cert. denied*, 110 S. Ct. 143 (1989), reversing a district court's stay of a state law employment discrimination action pending arbitration. The Eighth Circuit refused to enforce an agreement the plaintiff had signed requiring all controversies between the parties to be resolved according to the Commercial Arbitration Rules of the American Arbitration Association. It concluded that the Federal Arbitration Act did not apply where Title VII was concerned, and that state antidiscrimination remedies were so intertwined with Title VII enforcement that they, too, could not be subordinated to arbitration agreements. Accord Utley v. Goldman, Sacks & Co., 883 F.2d 184 (1st Cir. 1989), *cert. denied*, 110 S.

Ct. 842 (1990); Nicholson v. CPI, Intl., Inc., 877 F.2d 221 (3d Cir. 1989) (ADEA). These decisions generally reject the argument that subsequent Supreme Court decisions had undermined the *Gardner-Denver* rationale. Contra Gilmer v. Interstate/Johnson Lane Corp., 895 F.2d 195 (4th Cir. 1990).

Page 524. Add at end of page:

The effect of *Kremer* and *Elliott* on ADEA cases is unclear. See generally Comment, Res Judicata and the Age Discrimination in Employment Act, 89 Colum. L. Rev. 1111 (1989).

Page 525. Delete second from last paragraph; replace with:

Whether claim preclusion applies depends in large part on whether state courts have concurrent jurisdiction with federal courts over Title VII suits. If they do not, it would obviously be unfair to bar a subsequent Title VII action in federal court because the plaintiff had failed to assert that claim in a prior state proceeding. Although the issue of state court jurisdiction was for a long time unsettled, the Supreme Court has recently unanimously held that state courts have concurrent jurisdiction of such claims. Yellow Freight System v. Donnelly, 110 S. Ct. 1566 (1990). At least prospectively, this decision should make it much more probable that claim preclusion will apply when a plaintiff first proceeds in the state courts. It should be noted, however, that there may be residual problems of claim preclusion where the prior proceeding was brought in a state court of limited jurisdiction, or where the state court involvement was only at the appellate level by review of an administrative action. In both these settings, claim preclusion may still be inappropriate because the state forum lacked jurisdiction to hear a Title VII claim.

C. PRIVATE ENFORCEMENT OF TITLE VII: FILING SUIT

Page 527. Add after first sentence in first full paragraph:

Cleveland Newspaper Guild, Local No. 1. v. Plain Dealer Publishing Co., 839 F.2d 1147 (6th Cir. 1988) (en banc), *cert. denied*, 109 S. Ct. 245 (1988), firmly rejected en banc the view, earlier espoused by a panel, that there is an unqualified right to rely on the EEOC's processing of charges of discrimination. Accord Rushton v. Nebraska Public Power Dist., 844 F.2d 562 (8th Cir. 1988). See generally Comment, Title VII—The Doctrine of Laches as a Defense To Private Plaintiff Title VII Employment Discrimination Claims, 11 W.N. Eng. L. Rev. 235 (1989).

D. PRIVATE ENFORCEMENT OF TITLE VII: RELATION OF THE EEOC CHARGE TO PRIVATE SUIT

1. Proper Plaintiffs

Page 530. Add after "See generally" in 11th line from bottom:

Torrey, Indirect Discrimination Under Title VII: Expanding Male Standing to Sue for Injuries Received as a Result of Employer Discrimination Against Females, 64 Wash. L. Rev. 365 (1989);

Page 531. Add at end of carryover paragraph:

See Larkin v. Pullman, Inc, Pullman Standard Div., 854 F.2d 1549 (11th Cir. 1988) (Commissioner charge may be predicate for later class suit); Wu v. Thomas, 863 F.2d 1543 (11th Cir. 1989) (husband did not have to file separate charge where wife's charge alleged that their employer had retaliated for her protected conduct by acting against her husband).

K. TITLE VII SUIT AGAINST STATE AND LOCAL GOVERNMENTS

Page 583. Add immediately before Part L:

While Title VII can be used in tandem with §§ 1981 and 1983, the Supreme Court has recently held that, where state or local governments are concerned, §1981 rights are no broader than those under §1983, thus essentially collapsing those two causes of action into one. Jett v. Dallas Ind.

School Dist., 109 S. Ct. 2702 (1989). One major implication of this decision is that, as with §1983, such entities can not be liable merely on the basis of respondeat superior in suits under §1981.

L. TITLE VII ENFORCEMENT AGAINST FEDERAL EMPLOYERS

Page 586. Add new text after carryover paragraph:

The disposition of some courts to treat the filing period as jurisdictional is exacerbated by two other aspects of the §717 suit-filing provision, the short 30-day limitation, and the requirement of the statute that "the head of the department, agency, or unit, as appropriate" be named as defendant. Indeed, the confluence of these latter requirements, even in circuits not treating the filing period as jurisdictional, has created what is fair to describe as a scandal—federal employees making trivial mistakes in naming defendants are permanently barred from suing under §717. The problem typically arises when a plaintiff files suit within 30 days of notice, naming as defendant the agency itself or some official in the chain of command. After the 30 days have expired, the agency moves to dismiss the suit for failure to name the agency head.

In addressing this question, courts have taken a strict, but not always consistent view, of the proper defendant. The agency itself is not the correct defendant, and, while a literal reading of the statute suggests a number of possible proper defendants, depending upon how far up the chain of command the plaintiff wishes to proceed, the courts have generally thought there is only one correct individual. See Honeycutt v. Long, 861 F.2d 1346 (5th Cir. 1988), where plaintiff named Major General Long, the head of the agency in which he worked, the Army & Air Force Exchange Service. The court concluded that the AAFES was not a "department, agency, or unit," so that plaintiff should have named the Secretary of Defense. This stringency is especially ironic since the courts frequently cannot agree among themselves who the correct party is. See Paulk v. Dept of the Air Force, 830 F.2d 79 (7th Cir. 1987).

Such a misnomer problem would be of little moment if the mistake could be corrected by refiling suit or amending the complaint. But in those circuits which have held the provisions in §717 "jurisdictional," suit is forever barred. Even in the circuits which do not view compliance with the 30-day time limit as jurisdictional, some cases have found that merely naming the wrong defendant is no basis for relief: the plaintiff must show something more than a

6. Procedures for Enforcing Title VII   Page 592

unilateral mistake. E.g., Johnson v. United States Postal Service, 861 F.2d 1475 (10th Cir. 1988), *cert. denied*, 110 S. Ct. 54 (1989); Williams v. Army & Air Force Exchange Service, 830 F.2d 27 (3d Cir. 1987). See also Harris v. Brock, 835 F.2d 1190 (7th Cir. 1987).

An alternative method of avoiding the harsh result of dismissal is the doctrine of amendments "relating back" to the time of the original complaint under Rule 15 of the Federal Rules of Civil Procedure, theoretically available in both "jurisdictional" and "nonjurisdictional" circuits. Unfortunately, this doctrine has been held inapplicable in a number of section 717 cases because of its own technical requirements. As interpreted by the lower courts in the §717 context, the Supreme Court's decision in Schiavone v. Fortune, 477 U.S. 21 (1986), requires either that the plaintiff effect service on the proper defendant within 30 days or that plaintiff's service on the misnamed defendant have somehow reached the proper party within that time. E.g., Harris v. United States Dept. of Transportation, 843 F.2d 219 (5th Cir. 1988); Gonzalez v. Secretary of the Air Force, 824 F.2d 392 (5th Cir. 1987), *cert. denied*, 485 U.S. 969 (1988). The one salvation for plaintiffs who are aware of this problem before the 30-day period has expired is the provision in Rule 15(c) that service on the relevant United States Attorney or on the Attorney General will satisfy the requirement of notice. Bates v. Tennessee Valley Authority, 851 F.2d 1366 (11th Cir. 1988), *cert. denied*, 109 S. Ct. 3157 (1989); Jordan v. Clark, 847 F.2d 1368 (7th Cir. 1988), *cert. denied*, 109 S. Ct. 786 (1989); Paulk v. Department of the Air Force, 830 F.2d 79 (7th Cir. 1987).

M. SETTLEMENT OF TITLE VII SUITS

Page 592. Delete from first full paragraph until end of chapter; replace with:

MARTIN v. WILKS
109 S. Ct. 2180 (1989)

Chief Justice REHNQUIST delivered the opinion of the court.

A group of white firefighters sued the City of Birmingham, Alabama (City) and the Jefferson County Personnel Board (Board) alleging that they were being denied promotions in favor of less qualified black firefighters. They claimed that the City and the Board were making promotion decisions on the basis of race in reliance on certain consent decrees, and that these decisions constituted impermissible racial discrimination in violation of the Constitution and federal statute. The District Court held that the white firefighters were precluded from challenging employment decisions taken pursuant to the decrees, even though these firefighters had not been parties to the proceedings in which the decrees were entered. We think this holding contravenes the general rule that a person cannot be deprived of his legal rights in a proceeding to which he is not a party.

The litigation in which the consent decrees were entered began in 1974, when the Ensley Branch of the NAACP and seven black individuals filed separate class-action complaints against the City and the Board. They alleged that both had engaged in racially discriminatory hiring and promotion practices in various public service jobs in violation of Title VII. . . . After a bench trial on some issues, but before judgment, the parties entered into two consent decrees, one between the black individuals and the City and the other between them and the Board. These proposed decrees set forth an extensive remedial scheme, including long-term and interim annual goals for the hiring of blacks as firefighters. The decrees also provided for goals for promotion of blacks within the department.

The District Court entered an order provisionally approving the decrees and directing publication of notice of the upcoming fairness hearings. Notice of the hearings, with a reference to the general nature of the decrees, was published in two local newspapers. At that hearing, the Birmingham Firefighters Association (BFA) appeared and filed objections as amicus curiae. After the hearing, but before final approval of the decrees, the BFA and two of its members also moved to intervene on the ground that the decrees would adversely affect their rights. The District Court denied the motions as untimely and approved the decrees. Seven white firefighters, all members of the BFA, then filed a complaint against the City and the Board seeking injunctive relief against enforcement of the decrees. The seven argued that the decrees would operate to illegally discriminate against them; the District Court denied relief.

Both the denial of intervention and the denial of injunctive relief were affirmed on appeal. The District Court had not abused its discretion in refusing to let the BFA intervene, thought the Eleventh Circuit, in part because the firefighters could "institut[e] an independent Title VII suit, asserting specific violations of their rights." And, for the same reason, petitioners had not adequately shown the potential for irreparable harm from the operation of the decrees necessary to obtain injunctive relief.

A new group of white firefighters, the *Wilks* respondents, then brought suit against the City and the Board in district court. They too alleged that, because of their race, they were being denied promotions in favor of less qualified blacks in violation of federal law. The Board and the City admitted to making race conscious employment decisions, but argued the decisions were unassailable because they were made pursuant to the consent decrees. A

6. Procedures for Enforcing Title VII

group of black individuals, the *Martin* petitioners, were allowed to intervene in their individual capacities to defend the decrees.

The defendants moved to dismiss the reverse discrimination cases as impermissible collateral attacks on the consent decrees. The District Court denied the motions, ruling that the decrees would provide a defense to claims of discrimination for employment decisions "mandated" by the decrees, leaving the principal issue for trial whether the challenged promotions were indeed required by the decrees. After trial the District Court granted the motion to dismiss. The court concluded that "if in fact the City was required to [make promotions of blacks] by the consent decree, then they would not be guilty of [illegal] racial discrimination" and that the defendants had "establish[ed] that the promotions of the black individuals . . . were in fact required by the terms of the consent decree."

On appeal, the Eleventh Circuit reversed. It held that "[b]ecause . . . [the *Wilks* respondents] were neither parties nor privies to the consent decree, . . . their independent claims of unlawful discrimination are not precluded."

We . . . affirm the Eleventh Circuit's judgment. All agree that "[i]t is a principle of general application in Anglo-American jurisprudence that one is not bound by a judgment in personam in a litigation in which he is not designated as a party or to which he has not been made a party by service of process." Hansberry v. Lee, 311 U.S. 32, 40 (1940). This rule is part of our "deep-rooted historic tradition that everyone should have his own day in court." 18 C. Wright, A. Miller, & E. Cooper, Federal Practice and Procedure §4449, p.417 (1981) (18 Wright). A judgment or decree among parties to a lawsuit resolves issues as among them, but it does not conclude the rights of strangers to those proceedings.[2]

Petitioners argue that, because respondents failed to timely intervene in the initial proceedings, their current challenge to actions taken under the consent decree constitutes an impermissible "collateral attack." They argue that respondents were aware that the underlying suit might affect them and if they chose to pass up an opportunity to intervene, they should not be permitted to later litigate the issues in a new action. The position has sufficient appeal to

---

[2]. We have recognized an exception to the general rule when, in certain limited circumstances, a person, although not a party, has his interests adequately represented by someone with the same interests who is a party. See Hansberry v. Lee ("class" or "representative" suits); Fed. Rule Civ. Proc. 23 (same); Montana v. United States, 440 U.S. 147, 154-155 (1979) (control of litigation on behalf of one of the parties in the litigation). Additionally, where a special remedial scheme exists expressly foreclosing successive litigation by nonlitigants, as for example in bankruptcy or probate, legal proceedings may terminate preexisting rights if the scheme is otherwise consistent with due process. See NLRB v. Bildisco & Bildisco, 465 U.S. 513, 529-530, n.10 (1984) ("proof of claim must be presented to the Bankruptcy Court . . . or be lost"); Tulsa Professional Collection Services, Inc. v. Pope 108 S. Ct. 1340 (1988) (nonclaim statute terminating unsubmitted claims against the estate). Neither of these exceptions, however, applies in this case.

have commanded the approval of the great majority of the federal courts of appeals, but we agree with the contrary view. . . .

We begin with the words of Justice Brandeis in Chase National Bank v. Norwalk, 291 U.S. 431 (1934):

> The law does not impose upon any person absolutely entitled to a hearing the burden of voluntary intervention in a suit to which he is a stranger. . . . Unless duly summoned to appear in a legal proceeding, a person not a privy may rest assured that a judgment recovered therein will not affect his legal rights.

While these words were written before the adoption of the Federal Rules of Civil Procedure, we think the Rules incorporate the same principle; a party seeking a judgment binding on another cannot obligate that person to intervene; he must be joined. See Zenith Radio Corp. v. Hazeltine Research, Inc. 395 U.S. 100, 110 (1969) (judgment against Hazeltine vacated because it was not named as a party or served, even though as the parent corporation of one of the parties it clearly knew of the claim against it and had made a special appearance to contest jurisdiction). Against the background of permissive intervention set forth in *Chase National Bank*, the drafters cast Rule 24, governing intervention, in permissive terms. See Fed. Rule Civ. Proc. 24(a) (intervention as of right) ("[u]pon timely application anyone shall be permitted to intervene"); Fed. Rule Civ. Proc. 24(b) (permissive intervention) ("[u]pon timely application anyone may be permitted to intervene"). They determined that the concern for finality and completeness of judgments would be "better [served] by mandatory joinder procedures." 18 Wright §4452, p.453. Accordingly, Rule 19(a) provides for mandatory joinder in circumstances where a judgment rendered in the absence of a person may "leave . . . persons already parties subject to a substantial risk of incurring . . . inconsistent obligations. . . ."[4] Rule 19(b) sets forth the factors to

---

4. Rule 19(a) provides (emphasis added):

A person who is subject to service of process and whose joinder will not deprive the court of jurisdiction . . . shall be joined as a party in the action if (1) in the person's absence complete relief cannot be accorded among those already parties, or (2) the person claims an interest relating to the subject of the action and is so situated that the disposition of the action in the person's absence may (i) *as a practical matter impair or impede the person's ability to protect that interest or* (ii) *leave any of the persons already parties subject to a substantial risk of incurring double, multiple, or otherwise inconsistent obligations by reason of the claimed interest.* If the person has not been so joined, the court shall order that the person be made a party. If the person should join as a plaintiff but refuses to do so, the person may be made a defendant, or, in a proper case, an involuntary plaintiff. If the joined party objects to venue and joinder of that party would render the venue of the action improper, that party shall be dismissed from the action.

6. Procedures for Enforcing Title VII   Page 592

be considered by a court in deciding whether to allow an action to proceed in the absence of an interested party.[5]

Joinder as a party, rather than knowledge of a lawsuit and an opportunity to intervene, is the method by which potential parties are subjected to the jurisdiction of the court and bound by a judgment or decree.[6] The parties to a lawsuit presumably know better than anyone else the nature and scope of relief sought in the action, and at whose expense such relief might be granted. It makes sense, therefore, to place on them a burden of bringing in additional parties where such a step is indicated, rather than placing on potential additional parties a duty to intervene when they acquire knowledge of the lawsuit. The linchpin of the "impermissible collateral attack" doctrine — the attribution of preclusive effect to a failure to intervene — is therefore quite inconsistent with Rule 19 and Rule 24.

Petitioners argue that our decisions in Penn-Central Merger and N & W Inclusion Cases, 389 U.S. 486 (1968) . . . suggest[s] an opposite result. The *Penn-Central* litigation took place in a special statutory framework enacted by Congress to allow reorganization of a huge railway system. . . . We do not think that this holding in *Penn-Central*, based as it was upon the extraordinary nature of the proceedings challenging the merger of giant railroads and not even mentioning Rule 19 or Rule 24, affords a guide to the interpretation of the rules relating to joinder and intervention in ordinary civil actions in a district court. . . .

Petitioners contend that a different result should be reached because the need to join affected parties will be burdensome and ultimately discouraging to civil rights litigation. Potential adverse claimants may be numerous and difficult to identify; if they are not joined, the possibility for inconsistent

---

5. Rule 19(b) provides that:

> If a person . . . cannot be made a party, the court shall determine whether in equity and good conscience the action should proceed among the parties before it, or should be dismissed, the absent person being thus regarded as indispensable. The factors to be considered by the court include: first, to what extent a judgment rendered in the person's absence might be prejudicial to the person or to those already parties; second, the extent to which, by protective provisions in the judgment, by the shaping of relief, or other measures, the prejudice can be lessened or avoided; third, whether a judgment rendered in the person's absence will be adequate; fourth, whether the plaintiff will have an adequate remedy if the action is dismissed for nonjoinder.

6. The dissent argues on the one hand that respondents have not been "bound" by the decree but rather, that they are only suffering practical adverse affects from the consent decree. On the other hand, the dissent characterizes respondents' suit not as an assertion of their own independent rights, but as a collateral attack on the consent decree which, it is said, can only proceed on very limited grounds. Respondents in their suit have alleged that they are being racially discriminated against by their employer in violation of Title VII: either the fact that the disputed employment decisions are being made pursuant to a consent decree is a defense to respondents' Title VII claims or it is not. If it is a defense to challenges to employment practices which would otherwise violate Title VII, it is very difficult to see why respondents are not being "bound" by the decree.

judgments exists. Judicial resources will be needlessly consumed in relitigation of the same question.

Even if we were wholly persuaded by these arguments as a matter of policy, acceptance of them would require a rewriting rather than an interpretation of the relevant Rules. But we are not persuaded that their acceptance would lead to a more satisfactory method of handling cases like this one. It must be remembered that the alternatives are a duty to intervene based on knowledge, on the one hand, and some form of joinder, as the Rules presently provide, on the other. No one can seriously contend that an employer might successfully defend against a Title VII claim by one group of employees on the ground that its actions were required by an earlier decree entered in a suit brought against it by another, if the later group did not have adequate notice or knowledge of the earlier suit.

The difficulties petitioners foresee in identifying those who could be adversely affected by a decree granting broad remedial relief are undoubtedly present, but they arise from the nature of the relief sought and not because of any choice between mandatory intervention and joinder. Rule 19's provisions for joining interested parties are designed to accommodate the sort of complexities that may arise from a decree affecting numerous people in various ways. We doubt that a mandatory intervention rule would be any less awkward. As mentioned, plaintiffs who seek the aid of the courts to alter existing employment policies, or the employer who might be subject to conflicting decrees, are best able to bear the burden of designating those who would be adversely affected if plaintiffs prevail; these parties will generally have a better understanding of the scope of likely relief than employees who are not named but might be affected. Petitioners' alternative does not eliminate the need for, or difficulty of, identifying persons who, because of their interests, should be included in a lawsuit. It merely shifts that responsibility to less able shoulders.

Nor do we think that the system of joinder called for by the Rules is likely to produce more relitigation of issues than the converse rule. The breadth of a lawsuit and a concomitant relief may be at least partially shaped in advance through Rule 19 to avoid needless clashes with future litigation. And even under a regime of mandatory intervention, parties who did not have adequate knowledge of the suit would relitigate issues. Additional questions about the adequacy and timeliness of knowledge would inevitably crop up. We think that the system of joinder presently contemplated by the Rules best serves the many interests involved in the run of litigated cases, including cases like the present one.

Petitioners also urge that the congressional policy favoring voluntary settlement of employment discrimination claims, referred to in cases such as Carson v. American Brands, Inc., 450 U.S. 79 (1981), also supports the "impermissible collateral attack" doctrine. But once again it is essential to

6. Procedures for Enforcing Title VII

note just what is meant by "voluntary settlement." A voluntary settlement in the form of a consent decree between one group of employees and their employer cannot possibly "settle," voluntarily or otherwise, the conflicting claims of another group of employees who do not join in the agreement. This is true even if the second group of employees is a party to the litigation:

> [P]arties who choose to resolve litigation through settlement may not dispose of the claims of a third party . . . without that party's agreement. A court's approval of a consent decree between some of the parties therefore cannot dispose of the valid claims of nonconsenting intervenors.

Firefighters v. Cleveland, 478 U.S. 501, 529 (1986).

Insofar as the argument is bottomed on the idea that it may be easier to settle claims among a disparate group of affected persons if they are all before the Court, joinder bids fair to accomplish that result as well as a regime of mandatory intervention.

For the foregoing reasons we affirm the decision of the Court of Appeals for the Eleventh Circuit. That court remanded the case for trial of the reverse discrimination claims. Petitioners point to language in the District Court's findings of fact and conclusions of law which suggests that respondents will not prevail on the merits. We agree with the view of the Court of Appeals, however, that the proceedings in the District Court may have been affected by the mistaken view that respondents' claims on the merits were barred to the extent they were inconsistent with the consent decree.

Justice STEVENS, with whom Justice BRENNAN, Justice MARSHALL, and Justice BLACKMUN join, dissenting.

As a matter of law there is a vast difference between persons who are actual parties to litigation and persons who merely have the kind of interest that may as a practical matter be impaired by the outcome of a case. Persons in the first category have a right to participate in a trial and to appeal from an adverse judgment; depending on whether they win or lose, their legal rights may be enhanced or impaired. Persons in the latter category have a right to intervene in the action in a timely fashion,[1] or they may be joined as parties against their will [under Rule 19]. But if they remain on the sidelines, they may be harmed as a practical matter even though their legal rights are unaffected.

---

1. Federal Rule Civ. Proc. 24(a) provides, in part:

   Upon timely application everyone shall be permitted to intervene in an action: . . . (2) when the applicant claims an interest relating to the property or transaction which is the subject of the action and the applicant is so situated that the disposition of the action may as a practical matter impair or impede the applicant's ability to protect that interest, unless the applicant's interest is adequately represented by existing parties.

Page 592

One of the disadvantages of sideline-sitting is that the bystander has no right to appeal from a judgment no matter how harmful it may be.

In this case the Court quite rightly concludes that the white firefighters who brought the second series of Title VII cases could not be deprived of their legal rights in the first series of cases because they had neither intervened nor been joined as parties. See Firefighters v. Cleveland. The consent decrees obviously could not deprive them of any contractual rights, such as seniority, cf. W.R. Grace & Co. v. Rubber Workers, 461 U.S. 757 (1983), or accrued vacation pay, cf. Massachusetts v. Morash, 109 S. Ct. 1668 (1989), or of any other legal rights, such as the right to have their employer comply with federal statutes like Title VII, cf. Firefighters v. Cleveland, *supra*.[4] There is no reason, however, why the consent decrees might not produce changes in conditions at the white firefighters' place of employment that, as a practical matter, may have a serious effect on their opportunities for employment or promotion even though they are not bound by the decrees in any legal sense. The fact that one of the effects of a decree is to curtail the job opportunities of nonparties does not mean that the nonparties have been deprived of legal rights or that they have standing to appeal from that decree without becoming parties.

Persons who have no right to appeal from a final judgment—either because the time to appeal has elapsed or because they never became parties to the case—may nevertheless collaterally attack a judgment on certain narrow grounds. If the court had no jurisdiction over the subject matter, or if the judgment is the product of corruption, duress, fraud, collusion, or mistake, under limited circumstances it may be set aside in an appropriate collateral proceeding. See Restatement (Second) of Judgments §§ 69-72 (1982). This rule not only applies to parties to the original action, but also allows inter-

---

4. As Chief Justice Rehnquist has observed:

Suppose, for example, that the Government sues a private corporation for alleged violations of the antitrust laws and then enters a consent decree. Surely, the existence of that decree does not preclude a future suit by another corporation alleging that the defendant company's conduct, even if authorized by the decree, constitutes an antitrust violation. The nonparty has an independent right to bring his own private antitrust action for treble damages or for injunctive relief. See 2 P. Areeda & D. Turner, Antitrust Law ¶330, p. 143 (1978). Similarly, if an action alleging unconstitutional prison conditions results in a consent decree, a prisoner subsequently harmed by prison conditions is not precluded from bringing suit on the mere plea that the conditions are in accordance with the consent decree. Such compliance might be relevant to a defense of good-faith immunity, but it would not suffice to block the suit altogether. Ashley v. City of Jackson, 464 U.S. 900, 902 (1983) (opinion dissenting from denial of certiorari).

In suggesting that compliance with a consent decree might be relevant to a defense of good-faith immunity, this passage recognizes that neither due process nor the Rules of Civil Procedure foreclose judicial recognition of a judgment that may have a practical effect on the interests of a nonparty.

ested third parties collaterally to attack judgments.[5] In both civil and criminal cases, however, the grounds that may be invoked to support a collateral attack are much more limited than those that may be asserted as error on direct appeal.[6] Thus, a person who can foresee that a lawsuit is likely to have a practical impact on his interests may pay a heavy price if he elects to sit on the sidelines instead of intervening and taking the risk that his legal rights will be impaired.

In this case there is no dispute about the fact that the respondents are not parties to the consent decrees. It follows as a matter of course that they are not bound by those decrees. Those judgments could not, and did not, deprive them of any legal rights. The judgments did, however, have a practical impact on respondents' opportunities for advancement in their profession. For that reason, respondents had standing to challenge the validity of the decrees, but the grounds that they may advance in support of a collateral challenge are much more limited than would be allowed if they were parties prosecuting a direct appeal.[8]

The District Court's rulings in this case have been described incorrectly. [T]his Court's opinion seems to assume that the District Court had interpreted its consent decrees in the earlier litigation as holding "that the white firefighters were precluded from challenging employment decisions taken pursuant to the decrees." It is important, therefore, to make clear exactly what the District Court did hold and why its judgment should be affirmed.

I

The litigation in which the consent decrees were entered was a genuine adversary proceeding. In 1974 and 1975, two groups of private parties and the United States brought three separate Title VII actions against the City of

---

5. See F. James & G. Hazard, Civil Procedure §12.15, p.681 (3d ed. 1985) (hereinafter James & Hazard). . . .
6. We have long held that proceedings brought before a court collaterally "are by no means subject to all the exceptions which might be taken on a direct appeal." Thompson v. Tolmie, 2 Pet. 157, 16 (1829). See also Teague v. Lane, 109 S. Ct. 1060 (1989) (petition for writ of habeas corpus).
8. . . . Professors James and Hazard describe the rule as follows:

Ordinarily, a nonparty has no legal interest in a judgment in an action between others. Such a judgment does not determine the nonparty's rights and obligations under the rules of res judicata and he may so assert if the judgment is relied upon against him. But in some situations one's interests, particularly in one's own personal legal status or claims to property, may be placed in practical jeopardy by a judgment between others. In such circumstances one may seek the aid of a court of equity, *but the grounds upon which one may rely are severely limited.* The general rule is that one must show either that the judgment was void for lack of jurisdiction of the subject matter or that it was the product of fraud directed at the petitioner. James & Hazard §12.15, p.681 (emphasis supplied) (footnotes omitted).

Birmingham (City), the Personnel Board of Jefferson County (Board), and various officials, alleging discrimination in hiring and promotion in several areas of employment, including the fire department. After a full trial in 1976, the District Court found that the defendants had violated Title VII and that a test used to screen job applicants was biased. After a second trial in 1979 that focused on promotion practices—but before the District Court had rendered a decision—the parties negotiated two consent decrees, one with the City defendants and the other with the Board. The United States is a party to both decrees. The District Court provisionally approved the proposed decrees and directed that the parties provide notice "to all interested persons informing them of the general provisions of the consent decrees . . . and of their right to file objections." Approximately two months later, the District Court conducted a fairness hearing, at which a group of black employees objected to the decrees as inadequate and a group of white firefighters—represented in part by the Birmingham Firefighters Association (BFA)—opposed any race-conscious relief. The District Court overruled both sets of objections and entered the decrees in August of 1981.

In its decision approving the consent decrees, the District Court first noted "that there is no contention or suggestion that the settlements are fraudulent or collusive." The court then explained why it was satisfied that the affirmative action goals and quotas set forth in the decrees were "well within the limits upheld as permissible" in Steelworkers v. Weber, and other cases. It pointed out that the decrees "do not preclude the hiring or promotion of whites and males even for a temporary period of time," and that the City's commitment to promote blacks and whites to the position of fire lieutenant at the same rate was temporary and was subject both to the availability of qualified candidates and "to the caveat that the decree is not to be interpreted as requiring the hiring or promotion of a person who is not qualified or of a person who is demonstrably less qualified according to a job-related selection procedure." It further found that the record provided "more than ample reason" to conclude that the City would eventually be held liable for discrimination against blacks at high-level positions in the fire and police departments. Based on its understanding of the wrong committed, the court concluded that the remedy embodied in the consent decrees was "reasonably commensurate with the nature and extent of the indicated discrimination." Cf. Milliken v. Bradley, 418 U.S. 717, 744 (1974). The District Court then rejected other specific objections, pointing out that the decrees would not impinge on any contractual rights of the unions or their members. Finally, after noting that it had fully considered the white firefighters' objections to the settlement, it denied their motion to intervene as untimely.

Several months after the entry of the consent decrees, the Board certified to the City that five black firefighters, as well as eight whites, were qualified to fill six vacancies in the position of lieutenant. A group of white firefighters

6. Procedures for Enforcing Title VII   Page 592

then filed suit against the City and Board challenging their policy of "certifying candidates and making promotions on the basis of race under the assumed protection of consent settlements." The complaint alleged, in the alternative, that the consent decrees were illegal and void, or that the defendants were not properly implementing them. The plaintiffs filed motions for a temporary restraining order and a preliminary injunction. After an evidentiary hearing, the District Court found that the plaintiff's collateral attack on the consent decrees was "without merit" and that four of the black officers were qualified for promotion in accordance with the terms of the decrees. Accordingly, it denied the motions, and, for the first time in its history, the City had a black lieutenant in its fire department.

The plaintiffs' appeal from that order was consolidated with the appeal that had been previously taken from the order denying the motion to intervene filed in the earlier litigation. The Court of Appeals affirmed both orders. While that appeal was pending, in September 1983, the *Wilks* respondents filed a separate action against petitioners. The *Wilks* complaint alleged that petitioners were violating Title VII, but it did not contain any challenge to the validity of the consent decrees. After various preliminary proceedings, the District Court consolidated these cases, along with four other reverse discrimination actions brought against petitioners, under the caption In re: Birmingham Reverse Discrimination Litigation. In addition, over the course of the litigation, the court allowed further parties to intervene.

On February 18, 1985, the District Court ruled on the City's motion for partial summary judgment and issued an opinion that, among other things, explained its understanding of the relevance of the consent decrees to the issues raised in the reverse discrimination litigation. [T]he District Court expressly "recognized that the consent decrees might not bar all claims of 'reverse discrimination' since [the plaintiffs] had not been parties to the prior suits." The court then took a position with respect to the relevance of the consent decrees that differed from that advocated by any of the parties. . . . [It ruled] that promotions required by—and made because of—the decrees were justified. However, it denied the City's summary judgment motion because it raised factual issues requiring a trial.

In December 1985, the court conducted a 5-day trial limited to issues concerning promotions in the City's fire and engineering departments. [At the conclusion of the trial, the District Court dismissed portions of the plaintiffs' complaints, orally ruling from the bench:]

> In that February order, it was my view as expressed then, that if the City of Birmingham made promotions of blacks to positions as fire lieutenant, fire captain and civil engineer, because the City believed it was required to do so by the consent decree, and if in fact the City was required to do so by the consent decree, then they would not be guilty of racial discrimination, either under

Title 7, Section 1981, 1983 or the 14th Amendment. That remains my conclusion given the state of the law as I understand it.

He then found as a matter of fact that petitioners had not promoted any black officers who were not qualified or who were demonstrably less qualified than the whites who were not promoted. He thus rejected respondents' contention that the City could not claim that it simply acted as required by terms of the consent decree.[17] . . .

The written conclusions of law that he adopted are less clear than his oral opinion. [H]e did state that "plaintiffs cannot collaterally attack the Decree's validity." Yet, when read in context—and particularly in light of the court's finding that the decree was lawful under Eleventh Circuit and Supreme Court precedent—it is readily apparent that, at the extreme, this was intended as an alternative holding. More likely, it was an overstatement of the rule that collateral review is narrower in scope than appellate review. In any event, and regardless of one's reading of this lone sentence, it is absolutely clear that the court did not hold that respondents were bound by the decree.[18] . . .

II

Regardless of whether the white firefighters were parties to the decrees granting relief to their black co-workers, it would be quite wrong to assume that they could never collaterally attack such a decree. If a litigant has standing, he or she can always collaterally attack a judgment for certain narrowly defined defects. On the other hand, a district court is not required to retry a case—or to sit in review of another court's judgment—every time an interested nonparty asserts that some error that might have been raised on direct appeal was committed. Such a broad allowance of collateral review would destroy the integrity of litigated judgments, would lead to an abundance of vexatious litigation, and would subvert the interest in comity between courts. Here, respondents have offered no circumstance that might justify reopening the District Court's settled judgment.

The implementation of a consent decree affecting the interests of a miltitude of nonparties, and the reliance on that decree as a defense to a charge of discrimination in hiring and promotion decisions, raise a legitimate

---

17. Paragraph 2 of the city consent decree provides, in pertinent part:

Nothing herein shall be interpreted as requiring the City to . . . promote a person who is not qualified . . . or promote a less qualified person, in preference to a person who is demonstrably better qualified based upon the results of a job related selection procedure.

18. . . . Because I conclude that the District Court did not hold that respondents were bound by the consent decrees, I do not reach [the issue of whether a litigant can be bound by a prior decision because, although technically a nonparty, he had purposely bypassed an adequate opportunity to intervene.]

concern of collusion. No such allegation, however, has been raised. Moreover, there is compelling evidence that the decree was not collusive. . . .

Nor can it be maintained that the consent judgment is subject to reopening and further litigation because the relief it afforded was so out of line with settled legal doctrine that it "was transparently invalid or had only a frivolous pretense to validity." Walker v. Birmingham, 388 U.S. 307, 315, (1967) (suggesting that a contemnor might be allowed to challenge contempt citation on ground that underlying court order was "transparently invalid"). To the contrary, the type of race-conscious relief ordered in the consent decree is entirely consistent with this Court's approach to affirmative action. Given a sufficient predicate of racial discrimination, neither the Equal Protection Clause of the Fourteenth Amendment nor Title VII of the Civil Rights Act of 1964 erects a bar to affirmative action plans that benefit non-victims and have some adverse effect on non-wrongdoers. As Justice O'CONNOR observed in Wygant v. Jackson Bd. of Education, "[t]his remedial purpose need not be accompanied by contemporaneous findings of actual discrimination to be accepted as legitimate as long as the public actor has a firm basis for believing that remedial action is required." Such a belief was clearly justified in this case. After conducting the 1976 trial and finding against the City and after listening to the five days of testimony in the 1979 trial, the judge was well qualified to conclude that there was a sound basis for believing that the City would likely have been found to have violated Title VII if the action had proceeded to a litigated judgment.

Hence, there is no basis for collaterally attacking the judgment as collusive, fraudulent, or transparently invalid. Moreover, respondents do not claim — nor has there been any showing of — mistake, duress, or lack of jurisdiction. Instead, respondents are left to argue that somewhat different relief would have been more appropriate than the relief that was actually granted. Although this sort of issue may provide the basis for a direct appeal, it cannot, and should not, serve to open the door to relitigation of a settled judgment.

III

The facts that respondents are not bound by the decree and that they have no basis for a collateral attack, moreover, do not compel the conclusion that the District Court should have treated the decree as nonexistent for purposes of respondents' discrimination suit. That the decree may not directly interfere with any of respondents' legal rights does not mean that it may not affect the factual setting in a way that negates respondents' claim. The fact that a criminal suspect is not a party to the issuance of a search warrant does not imply that the presence of a facially valid warrant may not be taken as evidence that the police acted in good faith. See Malley v. Briggs, 475 U.S.

335, 334-345 (1986). Similarly, the fact that an employer is acting under court compulsion may be evidence that the employer is acting in good faith and without discriminatory intent. Cf. Ashley v. City of Jackson, 464 U.S. 900, 903 (1983) (Rehnquist, J., dissenting from denial of certiorari) (suggesting that compliance with a consent decree "might be relevant to a defense of good-faith immunity"); Restatement (Second) of Judgments §76, Comment a, p.217 (1982) ("If the judgment is held to be not binding on the person against whom it is invoked, it is then ignored in the determination of matters in issue in the subsequent litigation, unless it is relevant for some other purpose such as proving the good faith of a party who relied on it"). Indeed, the threat of a contempt citation provides as good a reason to act as most, if not all, other business justifications.[27]

After reviewing the evidence, the District Court found that the City had in fact acted under compulsion of the consent decree. Based on this finding, the court concluded that the City carried its burden of coming forward with a legitimate business reason for its promotion policy, and, accordingly, held that the promotion decisions were "not taken with the requisite discriminatory intent" necessary to make out a claim of disparate treatment under Title VII or the Equal Protection Clause. For this reason, and not because it thought that respondents were legally bound by the consent decree, the court entered an order in favor of the City and defendant-intervenors.

Of course, in some contexts a plaintiff might be able to demonstrate that reference to a consent decree is pretextual. For example, a plaintiff might be able to show that the consent decree was collusive and that the defendants simply obtained the court's rubber stamp on a private agreement that was in no way related to the eradication of pervasive racial discrimination. The plaintiff, alternatively, might be able to show that the defendants were not bound to obey the consent decree because the court that entered it was without jurisdiction. Similarly, although more tenuous, a plaintiff might argue that the parties to the consent judgment were not bound because the order was "transparently invalid" and thus unenforceable. If the defendants were as a result not bound to implement the affirmative-action program, then

---

27. Because consent decrees "have attributes both of contracts and judicial decrees," they are treated differently for different purposes. For example, because the content of a consent decree is generally a product of negotiations between the parties, decrees are construed for enforcement purposes as contracts. For purposes of determining whether an employer can be held liable for intentional discrimination merely for complying with the terms of a consent decree, however, it is appropriate to treat the consent decree as a judicial order. Unlike the typical contract, a consent decree, such as the one at issue here, is developed in the context of adversary litigation. Moreover, the court reviews the consent decree to determine whether it is lawful, reasonable, and equitable. In placing the judicial imprimatur on the decree, the court provides the parties with some assurance that the decree is legal and that they may rely on it. Most significantly, violation of a consent decree is punishable as criminal contempt. See 18 U.S.C. §§401, 402; Fed. Rule Crim. Proc. 42.

the plaintiff might be able to show that the racial preference was not a product of the court order.

In a case such as this, however, in which there has been no showing that the decree was collusive, fraudulent, transparently invalid, or entered without jurisdiction, it would be "unconscionable" to conclude that obedience to an order remedying a Title VII violation could subject a defendant to additional liability. Cf. Farmers v. WDAY, Inc., 360 U.S. 525, 531 (1959). Rather, all of the reasons that support the Court's view that a police officer should not generally be held liable when he carries out the commands in a facially valid warrant apply with added force to city officials, or indeed to private employers, who obey the commands contained in a decree entered by a federal court.[29] In fact, Equal Employment Opportunity Commission regulations concur in this assessment. They assert, "[t]he Commission interprets Title VII to mean that actions taken pursuant to the direction of a Court Order cannot give rise to liability under Title VII." 29 C.F.R. §1608.8 (1989).[30] Assuming that the District Court's findings of fact were not clearly erroneous—which of course is a matter that is not before us—it seems perfectly clear that its judgment should have been affirmed. Any other conclusion would subject large employers who seek to comply with the law by remedying past discrimination to a never-ending stream of litigation and potential liability. It is unfathomable that either Title VII or the Equal Protection Clause demands such a counter-productive result.

IV

The predecessor to this litigation was brought to change a pattern of hiring and promotion practices that had discriminated against black citizens in Birmingham for decades. The white respondents in this case are not responsible for that history of discrimination, but they are nevertheless beneficiaries of the discriminatory practices that the litigation was designed to correct. Any remedy that seeks to create employment conditions that would have obtained if there had been no violations of law will necessarily have an adverse impact on whites, who must now share their job and promotion with blacks. Just as white employees in the past were innocent beneficiaries of illegal discrimina-

---

29. Both warrants and consent decrees bear the indicium of reliability that a judicial officer has reviewed the proposed act and determined that it is lawful. See United States v. Alexandria, 614 F.2d 1358, 1361 (Ca5 1980) ("trial court must satisfy itself that the consent decree is not unlawful, unreasonable, or inequitable before it can be approved"). Unlike the police officer in receipt of facially valid warrant, however, an employer with notice of an affirmative injunction has no choice but to act. This added element of compulsion renders imposition of liability for acting pursuant to a valid consent decree all the more inequitable.

30. Section 1608.8 does not differentiate between orders "entered by consent or after contested litigation." 29 C.F.R. §1608.8 (1989). Indeed, the reasoning in the Court's opinion today would seem equally applicable to litigated orders and consent decrees. . . .

tory practices, so is it inevitable that some of the same white employees will be innocent victims who must share some of the burdens resulting from the redress of the past wrongs.

There is nothing unusual about the fact that litigation between adverse parties may, as a practical matter, seriously impair the interests of third persons who elect to sit on the sidelines. Indeed, in complex litigation this Court has squarely held that a sideline-sitter may be bound as firmly as an actual party if he had adequate notice and a fair opportunity to intervene and if the judicial interest in finality is sufficiently strong. See *Penn-Central Merger* and *N & W Inclusion* Cases.

There is no need, however, to go that far in order to agree with the District Court's eminently sensible view that compliance with the terms of a valid decree remedying violations of Title VII cannot itself violate that statute or the Equal Protection Clause.[32] The City of Birmingham, in entering into and complying with this decree, has made a substantial step toward the eradication of the long history of pervasive racial discrimination that has plagued its fire department. The District Court, after conducting a trial and carefully considering respondents' arguments, concluded that this effort is lawful and should go forward. Because respondents have thus already had their day in court and have failed to carry their burden, I would vacate the judgment of the Court of Appeals and remand for further proceedings consistent with this opinion.

NOTES

1. The "procedural" dispute resolved by *Martin* had important substantive consequences. While the rule of mandatory intervention, which the Supreme Court rejected in *Martin*, may appear innocuous, it was a serious barrier to "reverse discrimination" suits for two reasons. First, while some courts seemed to favor intervention, others were more hostile, frequently finding that the petition to intervene was untimely. E.g., Culbreath v. Dukakis, 630 F.2d 15 (1st Cir. 1980); Hefner v. New Orleans Pub. Serv., Inc., 605 F.2d 893 (5th Cir. 1979), *cert. denied*, 448 U.S. 955 (1980). As a result, a rule requiring

---

32. In professing difficulty in understanding why respondents are not "bound" by a decree that provides a defense to employment practices that would otherwise violate Title VII, the Court uses the word "bound" in a sense that is different from that used earlier in its opinion. A judgment against an employer requiring it to institute a seniority system may provide the employer with a defense to employment practices that would otherwise violate Title VII. In the sense in which the word "bound" is used in the cases cited by the Court, only the parties to the litigation would be "bound" by the judgment. But employees who first worked for the company 180 days after the litigation ended would be "bound" by the judgment in the sense that the Court uses when it responds to my argument. The cases on which the Court relies are entirely consistent with my position. Its facile use of the word "bound" should not be allowed to conceal the obvious flaws in its analysis.

mandatory intervention sometimes meant that no avenue of relief was open at all. Second, although some decisions were willing to permit suits that did not directly conflict with a decree's provisions, others held that any suit that required an interpretation of the decree constituted a collateral attack because the parties might be bound by inconsistent decisions.

2. While *Martin* involved a consent decree, the Court speaks throughout about the law of judgments. As the dissent points out, there is no basis for limiting the decision to consent decrees: any judgment, including one entered after full litigation, is also at risk in the sense that actions taken pursuant to it do not immunize the employer (or union) from liability under Title VII.

3. If plaintiff or defendant are concerned about possible third party rights, the *Martin* Court suggests that they can resolve all claims in one litigation merely by joining the absent parties under Rule 19. That rule is, to a large extent, the flip side of Rule 24. Both speak in similar terms about the requirements for adding a party to litigation — the outsider being having "an interest relating to the subject of the action" and being "so situated that the disposition of the action . . . may (i) as a practical matter impair or impede the person's ability to protect that interest." "Interests" for this purpose are much broader than legal rights: Although an employee at will has no "right" to continued employment, she nevertheless may have an expectation in fact that will justify intervention to protect it against the adverse consequences of a judgment. This strongly suggests that, applying the parallel language of Rule 19, either the plaintiff or the defendant may join those who have such an expectation.

4. Further, Rule 19 also permits adding a party when, regardless of any threat to that outsider's interests, not joining it would leave an insider "subject to a substantial risk of incurring double, multiple, or other inconsistent obligations by reason of the claimed interest." Thus, an outsider cannot avoid joinder merely by claiming that, after *Martin*, no possible decision by the court will affect his rights.

5. Rule 19 may be utilized to add a party to litigation even when there is no cause of action against that party. This is especially useful in employment discrimination because "reverse discriminatees" usually have not violated the statute (although in some cases unions may share liability with employers).

6. The majority in *Martin* recognized certain practical problems with joinder:

> Potential adverse claimants may be numerous and difficult to identify; if they are not joined, the possibility of inconsistent judgments exists. Judicial resources will be needlessly consumed in relitigation of the same question.

But not only did the Court believe that accepting these arguments "would require a rewriting rather than an interpretation of the relevant Rules," it saw the problem as more substantive than procedural: the accommodation of rights would generate difficulties regardless of whether Rule 19 or Rule 24 was the procedural mechanism used to bring all interested parties together in one action.

7. Is this true? The *Martin* case itself arose because various self-identified individuals sought to intervene or sue. If you were attorney for either plaintiff or defendant at the outset of the suit and wanted to use Rule 19, whom would you seek to join? All present employees? What about future employees, at least individuals who are employed during the course of the litigation? Could the practical difficulties of this be avoided by virtue of a "defendant class action," and, if so, how does one identify the proper class representative? Where there is a union, perhaps it might be joined and thereby unify all interests in a single suit. But for this resolution to be fully effective requires ultimately finding that all co-workers are in privity with the union such that a judgment binding it also binds them.

8. Is the dissent persuasive when it argues, essentially, that nonparties could not be "bound" by a consent decree in a legal sense, but nevertheless may find their interests affected by the decree in ways they are unable to challenge? Isn't Chief Justice Rehnquist right when he says that, if the decree becomes a defense to the employer—presumably, whether an absolute defense or merely one to monetary liability—"it is very difficult to see why respondents are not being 'bound' " by it.

9. Or is this so strange? Perhaps the dissent is simply saying that, absent either an extraordinary basis for collateral attack or timely intervention, the judgment becomes a fact of life with which the nonparty must live. Is this so unusual? In many contexts the law does not view individuals as "bound" to acts to which they are not parties, although they may be radically affected by them. To borrow an analogy from another area of Title VII, a disadvantaged employee is not viewed as legally "bound" by a seniority system agreed to by his union and the employer. Nevertheless, the system is a fact of life for her and in practice may substantially affect her interests. Indeed, on the very day that *Wilk* was decided, the Supreme Court held in Lorance v. AT & T Technologies, Inc., reproduced supra at p. 140, that a seniority system that intentionally discriminated against women could not be challenged unless a charge was timely filed measured from the period of its adoption. Are the untimely plaintiffs in *Lorance* "bound" by the decision to adopt the system, or merely subject to it?

10. If the dissent had prevailed on its notion of "bound," Justice Stevens would have upheld the district court: a motive to adhere to a court order negates the intent to discriminate requisite to a Title VII disparate treatment violation, and, absent some indication of "pretext," required dismissal of the suit of the white plaintiffs. Is this persuasive? Doesn't the employer still intend to treat persons differently because of their race?

6. Procedures for Enforcing Title VII
Page 592

11. In some cases, the technicalities of preclusion law may minimize the impact of *Martin*. For preclusive purposes a "party" to a proceeding includes not only named parties but also their "privies," and that is an amorphous concept. Some understanding of both the reach and limits of this principle can be gained from a Sixth Circuit decision that preceded *Martin*. In Detroit Police Officers Assn. v. Young, 824 F.2d 512 (6th Cir. 1987), the Court of Appeals approved of preclusive use of a prior determination that Detroit had intentionally discriminated against blacks in police hiring. Although the prior suit had involved white sergeants, the court found it proper to preclude relitigation by white patrolmen of that issue given the "strong community of interest" between the two classes and the substantial overlap in class membership. However, the court found that the prior litigation had not decided the question of the appropriate remedy—quota or otherwise—for the discrimination found; accordingly plaintiffs in the second suit were free to litigate that issue. See also NAACP v. Detroit Police Officers Assn., 821 F.2d 328 (6th Cir. 1987).

12. What about the timing of reverse discrimination suits. As noted, the Supreme Court decided *Martin* and Lorance v. AT & T Technologies, Inc., reproduced supra at p. 140, on the same day. *Lorance* was a challenge to a seniority system alleged to intentionally discriminate against women. A majority of the Court held that the suit was time barred: no charge was timely filed, as measured from the point of the system's adoption, although the charge was timely as measured by its impact on the plaintiffs. As applied to *Martin*, when must reverse discriminatees file a charge? Within 180/300 days of the entry of the consent decree or judgment? Or does the time not begin to run until the decree is implemented by the employer? Note that this problem does not arise in intervention: the white intervenors are not claiming that anyone has violated Title VII, and so are not limited by charge-filing requirements. But intervention is essentially a shield, while the lawsuit authorized by *Martin* is also a sword.

13. Although *Martin* reduced the necessity for such intervention for nonparties threatened by a judgment, the Court also encouraged intervention by such nonparties in Independent Federation of Flight Attendants v. Zipes, 109 S. Ct. 2732 (1989), which refused to impose attorneys' fees liability on intervenors who had unsuccessfully resisted a settlement with the employer. Despite the substantial fees that the plaintiffs had incurred in sustaining the proposed settlement against the intervenors' objections, a majority of the Court held that no award could be made under §706(k), which has been held to "presumptively" mandate an award to a prevailing plaintiff. If attorneys' fees were to be awarded, it could only be if the intervenor's position in the litigation was "frivolous, unreasonable, or without foundation." See discussion at p. 172.

14. Articles discussing the problem of nonparty interests in judgments

include Mengler, Consent Decree Paradigms: Models Without Meaning, 29 B.C.L. Rev. 291 (1988); Laycock, Consent Decrees Without Consent: The Rights of Nonconsenting Third Parties, 1987 U. Chi. Legal Forum 103 (1987); Comment, Collateral Attacks on Employment Discrimination Consent Decrees, 53 U. Chi. L. Rev. 147 (1986).

Beyond the technicalities of preclusion, it must be stressed that not every court order in favor of a black or a woman will adversely affect a white male. Consider the Supreme Court's decision in W.R. Grace & Co. v. Local 759, Rubber Workers, 461 U.S. 757 (1983). There, the employer entered into a conciliation agreement with the EEOC. That agreement was inconsistent with the governing collective bargaining agreement, and the union, although invited to participate in the settlement negotiations, refused to do so. Ultimately, the company laid off certain workers in order to comply with the conciliation agreement, which required maintenance of the existing proportion of women in the relevant bargaining unit. Those workers, on the basis of the collective bargaining agreement alone, would have retained their jobs. The union filed grievances under the governing arbitration clause, and the company went to court to bar the prosecution of such grievances. Although the company was successful in the district court, the Fifth Circuit refused to uphold an injunction. As a result, the arbitration was completed and an award was made requiring backpay for the workers whose rights under the collective bargaining agreement had been violated.

The Supreme Court recognized that the award was valid under normal principles governing court review of labor arbitrations but also recognized that the courts should not enforce an agreement that violates public policy. Accordingly, the Court had to decide whether the agreement, as interpreted by the arbitrator, violated such policy. The Court found no contrary public policy either in an interim order of the district court that the employer not violate the conciliation agreement, or in the conciliation agreement itself.

As for the court order, the Court recognized the company's dilemma in being subjected to conflicting obligations regarding layoffs. But the dilemma "was of the Company's own making. The Company committed itself to two conflicting contractual obligations." Id. at 767. The existence of one contract could not exonerate the company of liability for breach of the other. Further, while the court order might have required the actual layoffs to occur pursuant to the conciliation agreement, "nothing in the collective bargaining agreement as interpreted by [the arbitrator] required the company to violate that order." Id. at 768. The award did not require layoffs nor require that any layoffs be in accordance with the collective bargaining agreement. The arbitral award merely granted backpay for layoffs that were in violation of the labor agreement. The award, then, could not be struck down as "creat[ing] intolerable incentives to disobey a court order." Id. at 769.

Turning to the argument that the EEOC conciliation agreement itself evidenced a public policy that barred the enforcement of the arbitral award, the Court used much the same analysis. The Court noted that there was no showing that the collective bargaining agreement itself violated Title VII, it therefore explicitly refrained from addressing the issue of whether public policy would be violated by enforcing an arbitration award for breach of provisions ultimately found to violate Title VII. What was at issue, then, was whether a conciliation agreement could supercede another contract in the absence of any showing that that contract violated the law.

While recognizing the strong Title VII policy in favor of voluntary compliance, the *Grace* Court stressed that the union had never consented to any modification of its collective bargaining agreement, and "[a]bsent a judicial determination, the Commission, not to mention the company, cannot alter the collective bargaining agreement without the Union's consent." Id. at 771. Such a result would undermine federal labor policy designed to encourage collective bargaining.

Grace strongly suggests that in many cases a court decree—litigated or by consent—can co-exist with other rights. It will be neither binding on a nonparty in any technical sense nor adversely affect their rights in a practical sense. While it is true that the employer may be subject to double liability, that will simply be the consequence of its assuming (by consent or court order) two separate obligations.

Nevertheless any such double liability can be avoided by either including all affected parties in the settlement—which is the preferred Title VII resolution—or by using Rule 19 to join those who may be adversely affected in a practical sense. Further, Rule 19 is obviously an appropriate mechanism when the result of a decision may actually require two conflicting actions—awarding a particular position to a black and a white at the same time. For example, a judgment (whether by consent or litigation) that black plaintiffs were the victims of discrimination and ordering relief—including relief at the expense of white co-workers—would then be binding on everyone. Since each party would have had the opportunity to litigate the issues, there would be no unfairness to anyone.

Chapter 7

Title VII Remedies

B. Types of Relief

Page 603. Add the following at the end of Note 3:

The District of Columbia Circuit seems to think that "bumping" is appropriate whenever no substantially equivalent position is available for the discriminatee. Lander v. Lujan, 888 F.2d 153 (D.C. Cir. 1989).

Page 605. Add the following at the end of Note 6:

The First Circuit has adopted a somewhat more liberal attitude toward the availability of tenure awards. Brown v. Trustees of Boston Univ., 891 F.2d 337 (1st Cir. 1989).

Page 612. In Note 2, replace the first paragraph and the first sentence of the second paragraph with the following:

In Price Waterhouse v. Hopkins, reproduced in this supplement at p. 9, the Supreme Court concluded that even if gender was a motivating factor in an employment decision, the employer can escape "liability" under Title VII by proving by a preponderance of the evidence that the same decision would have been reached if the plaintiff's gender had not been taken into account.

Does *Price Waterhouse* preclude a backpay award in cases like Cohen v. West Haven Board of Police Commissioners, 638 F.2d 496 (2d Cir. 1980), and Rodriquez v. Taylor, reproduced at p. 875?

Page 613. Add the following at the end of Note 6:

In Loeffler v. Frank, 486 U.S. 549 (1988), the Supreme Court held that prejudgment interest can be awarded on a Title VII backpay award against the United States Postal Service. Congress, by launching the USPS into the commercial world and expressly providing that it may "sue and be sued," had waived the agency's sovereign immunity.

F. ATTORNEYS' FEES

Page 663. Add the following at the end of Note 1:

In its most recent decision, the Supreme Court held that a plaintiff can be a "prevailing party" even if he did not prevail on a "central issue" in his claim. Texas State Teachers Assn. v. Garland Independent School Dist., 109 S. Ct. 1486 (1989). The Court explained, "The touchstone of the prevailing party inquiry must be the material alteration of the legal relationship of the parties in a manner Congress sought to promote in the fee statute." 109 S. Ct. at 1493. The Court emphasized, however, that the plaintiff's victory must have been "significant" and that a "purely technical or *de minimis*" victory would not confer "prevailing party" status. The Court concluded that the plaintiff's failure to prevail on all of his claims goes to the amount of a reasonable fee award, not to its availability.

Page 665. Add the following at the end of Note 6:

In Missouri v. Jenkins, 109 S. Ct. 2463 (1989), the Supreme Court held that a fee award may be enhanced to compensate for delay in payment to the attorney.

7. Title VII Remedies   Page 665

Page 665. Add the following to the end of Note 8:

See also Missouri v. Jenkins, 109 S. Ct. 2463 (1989), which held that the Eleventh Amendment does not prohibit a §1988 fee award against a state from being enhanced to compensate for delay in payment.

Page 665. Add the following after Note 8:

9. Does a fee award by the court invalidate a contingent-fee contract? In Venegas v. Mitchell, 110 S. Ct. 1679 (1990), the Supreme Court held that a §1988 fee award to a prevailing plaintiff does not invalidate a contingent-fee contract that required the plaintiff to pay his attorney more than the amount of the fee award. The Court found nothing in the text of §1988 or its legislative history which suggested that the statute was intended to supersede private fee arrangements. Moreover, "depriving plaintiffs of the option of promising to pay more than the statutory fee if that is necessary to secure counsel of their choice would not further §1988's general purpose of enabling such plaintiffs in civil rights cases to secure competent counsel." Id. at 1684.

PART III

OTHER ANTIDISCRIMINATION STATUTES

Chapter 8

The Equal Pay Act

D. BREAKING A PRIMA FACIE CASE

Page 727. Add at end of first full paragraph:

Several recent cases involved job classifications in civil service positions. EEOC v. Delaware Dept. of Health and Social Services, 865 F.2d 1408 (3d Cir. 1989), was a challenge to a civil service classification in which a male Physician's Assistant (PA) was paid more than the female Public Health Nurses (PHN) working in the establishment. The Third Circuit reversed a judgment n.o.v. for defendants. Although the employer put on evidence as to the general structure of the civil service classification system, it "made no effort to explain how the point totals for PHNs and PAs were assigned or otherwise justify the discrepancy in pay grades." Id. at 1415. Since the employer had the burden of persuasion on the defense, a rational jury could have remained unpersuaded that the discrepancy in salary between two jobs doing equal work was merely the result of a neutral system. Further, the jury could have found that the reclassification of a male PA upward was evidence of discrimination in the administration of the system. Cf. Riordan v. Kempiners, 831 F.2d 690 (7th

Page 727.

Cir. 1987), which involved an employer's claim that a discrepancy disfavoring a woman supervisor as compared to two male subordinates was explained by the neutral application of civil service rules. Although remanding the EPA case on other grounds, the *Riordan* court seemed convinced that a directed verdict in favor of defendant with respect to these differences was justified. Both workers' state salaries were the result of their conversion from being federal employees at still higher salaries; an additional raise given one of them when he succeeded plaintiff as supervisor was mandatory under the civil service system when he received a promotion.

In Fallon v. State of Illinois, 882 F.2d 1206 (7th Cir. 1989), while affirming that District Court's finding that male Veterans Service Officers did work equal to female Veterans Service Office Associates, the Seventh Circuit remanded for a determination of whether the difference was justified as a factor other than sex. The state argued its limitation of VSO's to "wartime veterans" explained the difference in pay in the two classifications despite the equality of work. Apparently relying on the fact that not all such veterans were male, the Court of Appeals held the lower court was in error in rejecting this defense as a matter of law. What should the court do on remand? The case was also predicated on Title VII, but doesn't §712, 42 USCA §2000e-11, provide a complete defense to that cause of action?

Page 728. Add at end of carryover paragraph:

Glenn v. General Motors, 841 F.2d 1567 (11th Cir. 1988), *cert. denied*, 109 S. Ct. 378 (1988), rejected an employer's defense to paying three women less than certain male comparators. The defendant argued that the males had transferred from higher-paid positions within the company while the females were newly-hired or had transferred from lower-paid positions. It further argued that it had a policy of not requiring transferees to take a salary cut. The Eleventh Circuit affirmed a finding of liability: the employer was simply using the discredited "market force" theory. Although the court's reasoning is not explicit, it seemed to believe the employer was, in effect, drawing upon higher-paid males to fill the jobs in question when the market would not supply a sufficient number of women at the prevailing rates. The *Glenn* court criticized the Seventh Circuit's decision in Covington v. Southern Illinois University, 816 F.2d 317 (7th Cir.), *cert. denied*, 108 S. Ct. 146 (1987), as implicitly approving of market forces to support a "salary retention" policy at issue there. It is, however, not so clear that the cases are contrary to one another since the *Covington* court stressed that there was no evidence that the policy at issue was either discriminatingly applied or had a discriminatory effect. See generally Comment, When Prior Pay Isn't Equal Pay: A Proposed Standard for the Identification of "Factors Other Than Sex" Under the Equal Pay Act, 89 Colum. L. Rev. 1085 (1989).

8. The Equal Pay Act   Page 768

Page 730. Add at end of last full paragraph:

See also EEOC v. J.C. Penney, 843 F.2d 249 (6th Cir. 1988) (2-1); Colby v. J.C. Penney, 811 F.2d 1119 (7th Cir. 1987).

F. BEYOND THE EQUAL PAY ACT: USING TITLE VII ATTACK GENDER-BASED WAGE DISCRIMINATION

2. *Structuring Title VII Attacks in Gender-Based Wage Discrimination*

   a. **Where Work Is Equal**

Page 753. Add after "Contra" in Note 1, line 4:

State of Illinois v. Fallon, 882 F.2d 1206 (7th Cir. 1989);

Page 754. Add at end of Note 7:

Does Price v. Lockheed Space Operations, 856 F.2d 1503 (11th Cir. 1988), help you answer this question? In *Price* the defendant argued that, in order to be responsive to NASA in submitting its bids, it agreed with NASA not to reduce the salaries of employees it hired to work on the project in question from prior contractors. At the same time, as a way to keep costs down in order to submit the lowest bid, Lockheed decided not to pay such hires any more than their prior salary. The result was, presumably, a checkerboard of salaries. The appeals court upheld the defense in the sense that it believed that the case should go to the jury; the court, however, reversed the district court's grant of summary judgment to the defendants and explicitly held that use of prior salary was not a per se defense to an EPA claim. See also EEOC v. J.C. Penney, 843 F.2d 249 (6th Cir. 1988).

   b. **Where the Work Is Unequal**

Page 768. Add a new Note 16:

16. Beard v. Whitley Cty. REMC, 840 F.2d 405 (7th Cir. 1988), considered a challenge to an employer's giving different raises to two distinct

collective bargaining units, with the predominantly female unit receiving no increase while the predominantly male unit received 6%. Using a disparate treatment analysis, the court found no violation: direct evidence of bias towards the "girls'" unit was too ephemeral, and the employer's stated reliance on an area wage survey that showed that the female unit was overpaid was upheld as nondiscriminatory. The court stressed that, under disparate treatment, such a defense could be rejected only if it were used to "hide the truth" of sex discrimination. "It is insufficient merely to show that REMC erroneously relied on one wage survey as opposed to another or that it exercised poor business acumen." Id. at 412. Is this reasoning persuasive?

H. Equal Pay Act Remedies

Page 792. Replace Laffey v. Northwest Airlines with the following:

McLaughlin v. Richland Shoe Co.
486 U.S. 128 (1988)

Justice STEVENS delivered the opinion of the Court.

The question presented concerns the meaning of the word "willful" as used in the statute of limitations applicable to civil actions to enforce the Fair Labor Standards Act (FLSA). The statute provides that such actions must be commenced within two years "except that a cause of action arising out of a willful violation may be commenced within three years after the cause of action accrued." 29 U.S.C. §255(a).

I

Respondent, a manufacturer of shoes and boots, employed seven mechanics to maintain and repair its equipment. In 1984, the Secretary of Labor (Secretary) filed a complaint alleging that "in many work weeks" respondent had failed to pay those employees the overtime compensation required by the FLSA. As an affirmative defense, respondent pleaded the 2-year statute of limitations. The District Court found, however, that the 3-year exception applied because respondent's violations were willful. . . .

In resolving the question of willfulness, the District Court followed Fifth Circuit decisions that had developed the so-called *Jiffy June* standard. The District Court explained:

> The Fifth Circuit has held that an action is willful when "there is substantial evidence in the record to support a finding that the employer knew or suspected

8. The Equal Pay Act Page 792

that his actions might violate the FLSA. Stated most simply, we think the test should be: Did the employer know the FLSA was in the picture?"
Coleman v. Jiffy June Farms, Inc., 458 F.2d 1139, 1142 (5th Cir.) [*cert. denied*, 409 U.S. 948 (1972)]. . . .

On appeal respondent persuaded the Court of Appeals for the Third Circuit "that the *Jiffy June* standard is wrong because it is contrary to the plain meaning of the FLSA." Adopting the same test that we employed in Trans World Airlines, Inc. v. Thurston [reproduced on p. 882], the Court of Appeals held that respondent had not committed a willful violation unless "it knew or *showed reckless disregard for the matter of whether* its conduct was prohibited by the FLSA." . . .

The Secretary filed a petition for certiorari asking us to resolve the post-*Thurston* conflict among the Circuits concerning the meaning of the word "willful" in this statute. The petition noted that the statute applies not only to actions to enforce the overtime and recordkeeping provisions of the FLSA, but also to the Equal Pay Act . . . and the Age Discrimination in Employment Act (ADEA). Somewhat surprisingly, the petition did not endorse the *Jiffy June* standard that the Secretary had relied on in the District Court and the Court of Appeals, but instead invited us to adopt an intermediate standard. We granted certiorari, and now affirm.

II

Because no limitations period was provided in the original 1938 enactment of the FLSA, civil actions brought thereunder were governed by state statutes of limitations. In the Portal-to-Portal Act of 1947, 29 U.S.C. §§ 216, 251-262, however, as part of its response to this Court's expansive reading of the FLSA, Congress enacted the 2-year statute to place a limit on employers' exposure to unanticipated contingent liabilities. As originally enacted, the 2-year limitations period drew no distinction between willful and nonwillful violations.

In 1965, the Secretary proposed a number of amendments to expand the coverage of the FLSA, including a proposal to replace the 2-year statute of limitations with a 3-year statute. The proposal was not adopted, but in 1966, for reasons that are not explained in the legislative history, Congress enacted the 3-year exception for willful violations.

The fact that Congress did not simply extend the limitations period to three years, but instead adopted a two-tiered statute of limitations, makes it obvious that Congress intended to draw a significant distinction between ordinary violations and willful violations. It is equally obvious to us that the *Jiffy June* standard of willfulness—a standard that merely requires that an employer knew that the FLSA "was in the picture"—virtually obliterates any distinc-

187

tion between willful and nonwillful violations. As we said in Trans World Airlines, Inc. v. Thurston, "it would be virtually impossible for an employer to show that he was unaware of the Act and its potential applicability." Under the *Jiffy June* standard, the normal 2-year statute of limitations would seem to apply only to ignorant employers, surely not a state of affairs intended by Congress.

In common usage the word "willful" is considered synonymous with such words as "voluntary," "deliberate," and "intentional." See Roget's International Thesaurus § 622.7, p. 479; § 653.9, p. 501 (4th ed. 1977). The word "willful" is widely used in the law, and, although it has not by any means been given a perfectly consistent interpretation, it is generally understood to refer to conduct that is not merely negligent. The standard of willfulness that was adopted in *Thurston*—that the employer either knew or showed reckless disregard for the matter of whether its conduct was prohibited by the statute—is surely a fair reading of the plain language of the Act.

The strongest argument supporting the *Jiffy June* standard is that it was widely used for a number of years. The standard was not, however, consistently followed in all Circuits. In view of the fact that even the Secretary now shares our opinion that it is not supported by the plain language of the statute, we readily reject it.

We also reject the intermediate alternative espoused by the Secretary for the first time in this Court. Relying on the opinion of the Court of Appeals for the District of Columbia in Laffey v. Northwest Airlines, Inc., 567 F.2d 429, 461-462 (1976), *cert. denied*, 434 U.S. 1086 (1978), she argues that we should announce a two-step standard that would deem an FLSA violation willful "if the employer, recognizing it might be covered by the FLSA, acted without a reasonable basis for believing that it was complying with the statute." Brief for Petitioner 41. This proposal differs from *Jiffy June* because it would apparently make the issue in most cases turn on whether the employer sought legal advice concerning its pay practices. It would, however, permit a finding of willfulness to be based on nothing more than negligence, or, perhaps, on a completely good-faith but incorrect assumption that a pay plan complied with the FLSA in all respects. We believe the Secretary's new proposal, like the discredited *Jiffy June* standard, fails to give effect to the plain language of the statute of limitations.[13]

---

13. We recognize that there is some language in Trans World Airlines v. Thurston, 469 U.S. 111 (1985), not necessary to our holding, that would seem to permit a finding of unreasonableness to suffice as proof of knowing or reckless disregard, and thus that would render petitioner's standard an appropriate statement of the law. Our decision today should clarify this point: If an employer acts reasonably in determining its legal obligation, its action cannot be deemed willful under either petitioner's test or under the standard we set forth. If an employer acts unreasonably, but not recklessly, in determining its legal obligation, then, although its action would be considered willful under petitioner's test, it should not be so considered under *Thurston* or the identical standard we approve today.

8. The Equal Pay Act Page 797

Ordinary violations of the FLSA are subject to the general 2-year statute of limitations. To obtain the benefit of the 3-year exception, the Secretary must prove that the employer's conduct was willful as that term is defined in both *Thurston* and this opinion.

The judgment of the Court of Appeals is Affirmed.

Justice MARSHALL, with whom Justice BRENNAN and Justice BLACKMUN join, dissenting. . . .

Page 795. Replace Note 1 with the following:

1. Was the Supreme Court correct in adopting the *Thurston* definition of "willful"? *Thurston* concerned §7(b) of the ADEA, 29 U.S.C. §626(b), which authorizes liquidated damages for a "willful violation." Moreover, *Thurston* expressly recognized that the ADEA liquidated damages award has a punitive purpose. Should the three-year limitation period in PPA §6(a) be regarded as punitive?

Page 796. Replace Note 2 with the following:

2. Does adoption of the *Thurston* definition of "willful" mean that it is "easier to get double damages [in an EPA action] than to extend the statute of limitations"? EEOC v. Madison School District, 818 F.2d 577, 586 (7th Cir. 1987). Do you think Congress intended this result?

Page 797. Add the following at the end of Note 4:

In EEOC v. Penton Industrial Publishing Co., 851 F.2d 835 (6th Cir. 1988), the court said the cause of action accrues at the initial discriminatory act but is tolled when there is a "continuing violation." The court recognized two types of "continuing violations": (1) where the employer is presently continuing to pay unequal wages to the plaintiff and (2) where the employer has a long-standing policy of paying unequal wages. Is this approach correct?

Chapter 9

The Age Discrimination in Employment Act of 1967

A. INTRODUCTION

Page 800. Add at end of footnote **:

With the amendments to the ADEA exempting police and firefighters, there have been renewed constitutional attacks. These have generally not fared well. E.g., Gondelman v. Commonwealth of Pennsylvania, 50 EPD ¶ 39,039 (Pa. S. Ct. 1988), *cert. denied*, 110 S. Ct. 146 (1989); Maresca v. Cuomo, 64 N.Y.2d 242, 485 N.Y.S.2d 724, 475 N.E.2d 95 (Ct. App. NY 1984), *app. dismissed* 474 U.S. 802 (1985). See also Apkin v. Treasurer and Receiver General, 401 Mass. 427, 517 N.E.2d 141 (1988) (Congress did not intend to pre-empt state law regarding mandatory retirement of judges). In Zombro v. Baltimore Police Department, 868 F.2d 1364 (4th Cir. 1989) (2-1), *cert. denied*, 110 S. Ct. 147 (1989), the Fourth Circuit added another barrier, holding that a police officer's challenge to a transfer allegedly due to his age could not be brought under §1983 because the ADEA was the exclusive remedy for age discrimination against public employees. The court did not directly address whether it would reach a contrary decision under the ADEA, as amended in 1986, which prospectively exempts law enforcement officers from coverage.

B. COVERAGE OF THE ADEA

Page 802. Add at end of carryover paragraph:

One of the more intriguing constructions of statutory coverage arose after amendments to that law eliminated mandatory retirement at any age. The question was the effects of that law on state statutes and constitutional provisions calling for mandatory retirement of state judges, typically at 70. Although in many states judges are elected, thus falling within the "elected officials" exception, in a number of states judges are appointed. The first appellate decision to address this question held that such judges are outside the ADEA because they are "appointees on the policymaking level." EEOC v. Commonwealth of Massachusetts, 858 F.2d 52 (1st Cir. 1988). See also Stillians v. State of Iowa, 843 F.2d 276 (8th Cir. 1988) (ADEA) (Director of the Iowa Arts Council, a gubernatorial appointee, was a policymaker). Another decision, dealing with judges chosen by the state legislature (and therefore "appointed" within the meaning of the ADEA) applied the doctrine of legislative immunity. Schlitz v. Commonwealth of Virginia, 854 F.2d 43 (4th Cir. 1988). In that case, since the state no longer had a mandatory retirement law, determining whether the legislature's refusal to reappoint the plaintiff was discriminatory would have required an inquiry into the state of mind of legislators about a "core legislative function." The court therefore found the suit barred.

C. THE CONCEPT OF AGE DISCRIMINATION

1. Individual Disparate Treatment Age Discrimination

Page 816. Add a new Note 9a:

9a. Many cases will turn on the question of plaintiff's absolute or relative qualifications. While some ADEA decisions have faulted the plaintiff

9. The Age Discrimination in Employment Act   Page 818

for not establishing his qualifications to a sufficient degree to establish a prima facie case, more cases require only a showing of minimal qualifications by the plaintiff, postponing any real focus on her deficiencies to the employer's rebuttal. E.g., Brown v. M&M/Mars, 883 F.2d 505 (7th Cir. 1989); Bienkowski v. American Airlines, Inc., 851 F.2d 1503 (5th Cir. 1988); Branson v. Price River Coal Co., 853 F.2d 768 (10th Cir. 1988); Healy v. New York Life Ins. Co., 860 F.2d 1209 (3d Cir. 1988). The Supreme Court confirmed this approach with respect to racial discrimination, and also stressed that it may be possible for a plaintiff to demonstrate that the defendant's reason is pretextual without demonstrating that she is better qualified. Patterson v. McLean Credit Union, 109 S. Ct. 316 (1989).

Page 817. Add at end of Note 13:

See also Schuler v. Polaroid Co., 848 F.2d 276 (1st Cir. 1988); Hebert v. Mohawk Rubber Co., 872 F.2d 1104 (1st Cir. 1989); Bodnar v. Synpol, 843 F.2d 190 (5th Cir.), *cert. denied*, 109 S. Ct. 260 (1988). See generally, McMorrow, Retirement and Worker Choice: Incentives to Retire and the Age Discrimination in Employment Act, 29 B.C.L. Rev. 347 (1988); Note, Early Retirement Incentives: "Golden Handshake" for Some, Age Discrimination for Others, 54 Brooklyn L. Rev. 927 (1988); Comment, Voluntary Acceptance of Early Retirement Offers: Golden Handshake or Gilded Shove, 20 Ariz. St. L.J. 797 (1988).

Page 818. Add in Note 15 after "Golumb" citation:

Such a showing is not necessarily conclusive of pretext, however, since the real question is not whether the reason is objectively true but instead whether the employer believed it was true and acted on it rather than on the basis of the employee's age. E.g., Bienkowski v. American Airlines, Inc., 851 F.2d 1503 (5th Cir. 1988); Menard v. First Security Services Corp., 848 F.2d 281 (5th Cir. 1988); Grohs v. National Gypsum Co., Gold Bond Building Prod. Div., 859 F.2d 1283 (7th Cir. 1988), *cert. denied*, 109 S. Ct. 1934 (1989). However, there is obviously a strong inference if a reason is in fact false that the employer knew it was false and therefore that it was a pretext. This may be the basis for some courts stating that a finding that the proffered reason is false is sufficient to impose liability.

Page 818. Add at end of Note 15:

Such a showing may not be dispositive, however, since the employer might have been unaware of the violations by others. Mechnig v. Sears, Roebuck & Co., 864 F.2d 1359 (7th Cir. 1988).

Page 819. Add before "Note on Causation . . .":

See generally Note, Summary Judgment and the ADEA Claimant: Problems and Patterns of Proof, 21 Conn. L. Rev. 99 (1988).

Page 820. Delete last paragraph; replace with:

The Supreme Court adopted precisely this view in the Title VII context in Price Waterhouse v. Hopkins, 109 S. Ct. 1775 (1989). Although that case did not hold on the ADEA, there is little doubt that it will apply to that statute. Indeed, the dissent in *Price Waterhouse* was to some extent predicated on its perception that application of this rule in ADEA cases involving jury trials would be too confusing.

3. Systemic Disparate Impact

Page 844. Add at end of carryover paragraph:

In Lowe v. Commack Union Free School Dist., 886 F.2d 1364 (2d Cir. 1989), *cert. denied*, 110 S. Ct. 1470 (1990), the court rejected the use of disparate impact analysis within the protected group; for intragroup discrimination, only disparate treatment is available. Looking to race and sex cases, the Second Circuit noted that the Supreme Court had always spoken in terms of impact on the protected group. It argued, reductio ad absurdum, that otherwise an 85 year old plaintiff could use disparate impact against all younger persons, including those who were in their 70's. On this point, one judge dissented, arguing that this holding would tend to exclude older persons within the protected group even though they were the object of the greatest congressional concern. Nor did the dissent find the "octagenarian vs. septuagenerian hypothetical" persuasive: the difference in ages might sometimes be too slight to be significant, but if it were not, the plaintiff aged 85 was entitled to the full protection of the act.

Page 844. Add new text immediately before Section D:

4. The Interaction of the Theories

METZ v. TRANSIT MIX, INC.,
828 F.2d 1202 (7th Cir. 1987)

Before BAUER, Chief Judge, and CUDAHY and EASTERBROOK, Circuit Judges.

CUDAHY, Circuit Judge. . . .

I

Transit Mix is in the business of selling concrete to construction contractors. Metz worked for Transit Mix as manager of its plant in Knox, Indiana, a satellite of Transit Mix's principal office and larger plant in Plymouth, Indiana. During the three years prior to Metz's discharge, Transit Mix experienced financial problems which the district court attributed to the decline in the local construction business. In November 1983, Will Lawrence, the president of Transit Mix, notified Metz that due to Transit Mix's poor sales, the Knox plant would be closed for the winter starting in December and Metz would be laid off. At that time, Lawrence had not decided whether he would close the Knox facility permanently or only for the winter.

In February 1984, Lawrence sent the assistant manager of the Plymouth plant, Donald Burzloff, to Knox to inspect the plant and make any necessary repairs. Burzloff obtained permission to take orders from the plant's regular customers while he was there. Burzloff later requested that he be allowed to manage the Knox facility. Lawrence approved this request and in April 1984 discharged Metz.

At the time of his layoff in December 1983, Metz had an annual salary of $26,000, or about $15.75 an hour. He was among the highest paid of Transit Mix employees and, having worked for Transit Mix for twenty-seven years, was the second most senior employee there.[1] Metz's relatively high salary was a direct result of his many years of employment by Transit Mix; Lawrence testified at trial that Metz was given a raise each year, including years when Transit Mix was losing money. Burzloff was forty-three and had worked for Transit Mix for seventeen years when he replaced the fifty-four-year-old Metz as manager. Burzloff's salary as manager was about $8.05 an hour.

---

1. The most senior employee was Lawrence's mother.

II

The ADEA prohibits employers from discriminating against employees on the basis of age. Its objective in part is to promote employment of older workers on the basis of their abilities rather than their age. 29. U.S.C. §621. The statute does not, however, prevent an employer from terminating an older worker based on reasonable factors other than age. 29 U.S.C. §623(f)(1). When, as in the present case, a plaintiff is proceeding on a disparate treatment analysis, the plaintiff may recover only if the defendant in discharging the plaintiff was motivated by a discriminatory animus; that is, the plaintiff may recover only if his or her age was a determining factor in the employer's decision.

Proving intentional discrimination is often difficult, so a plaintiff may do so by presenting either direct or indirect evidence of discrimination. In order to permit recovery for an ADEA claim through indirect means, this circuit has adopted a variation of the burden-shifting analysis set forth by the Supreme Court in the Title VII context for establishing a prima facie case of employment discrimination. See McDonnell Douglas Corp. v. Green. As applied to an ADEA claim, this analysis requires that a plaintiff show that he or she: 1) belongs to the protected class (age forty or older); 2) was qualified for his or her position; 3) was terminated; and 4) was replaced by a younger person. After the plaintiff has established a prima facie case, the defendant employer then has the burden of presenting evidence that the plaintiff's discharge was a result of "some legitimate, nondiscriminatory reason." If the defendant meets this burden of production, the burden shifts to the plaintiff to prove that the reasons proffered by the employer for the discharge were merely a pretext for discrimination. Throughout the trial, the burden remains with the plaintiff to prove there was discrimination, rather than with the employer to prove the absence of discrimination.

The district court found that Metz had established a prima facie case of age discrimination. The court further found that a determining factor in Transit Mix's decision to replace Metz with Burzloff was a desire to save the higher cost of Metz's salary and that this factor "bore a relationship to Mr. Metz's age."[5]

---

[5]. The district court found that the decision to terminate Metz was also motivated by the "greater flexibility afforded by Mr. Burzloff," who, in contrast to Metz, was able to return to the Plymouth plant provided the operations at the Knox satellite plant did not improve. The court characterized this consideration (as well as the salary/cost concern) as a "determining factor" in the firing decision. The dissent argues that this finding is sufficient to support the court's verdict independent of the issue presented by the defendant's stated salary concerns. We disagree. The district court did not find that absent the desire to save the higher cost of Metz's salary, Transit Mix nevertheless would have replaced Metz because of the flexibility motivation. The more reasonable interpretation is that the court found that both factors combined to provide a nondiscriminatory reason for the dismissal. That is, in the absence of salary concern, Metz would not have been replaced by Burzloff. For example, the court states that the salary issue "permeated the eventual decision" to replace Metz. Indeed, this is the only interpretation which adequately explains the extended discussion of the salary issue by the district court.

The court held, however, that this was not age discrimination in violation of the ADEA because it was based on an assessment of the cost of employing an individual employee, namely, Metz, rather than an impermissible assessment of the costs of employing Transit Mix's older employees as a group. The sole issue on appeal is whether the salary savings that can be realized by replacing a single employee in the ADEA age-protected range with a younger, lower-salaried employee constitutes a permissible, nondiscriminatory justification for the replacement.

III

Congress enacted the ADEA in response to the problems that the older worker faces in the job market, including the obstacles that the long-term employee encounters when he or she is suddenly without work. See generally Report of Secretary of Labor to Congress, The Older American Worker: Age Discrimination in Employment 11-17 (1965), reprinted in EEOC, Legislative History of the Age Discrimination in Employment Act, 16, 28-34 (1981). These difficulties have been attributed in large part to the worker's development of firm-specific skills not easily transferable to a different job setting. National Commission for Employment Policy, 9th Annual Report, Rep. No. 17, Older Workers: Prospects, Problems and Policies 4 (1985). Therefore, while the older employee's higher salary reflects the value of improved skills and the increased productivity that results, it is also indicative of one of the very problems the ADEA was intended to address: the likelihood that the employee will be less employable in other settings.[6]

The ADEA has consistently been interpreted by the administrative agencies charged with its enforcement and the courts to prohibit an employer from replacing higher paid employees with lower paid employees in order to save money. The Equal Employment Opportunity Commission guidelines expressly provide that "A differentiation based on the average cost of employing older employees as a group is unlawful except with respect to employee benefit plans which qualify for the section 4(f)(2) exception to the Act." 29 C.F.R. §1625.7(f) (1986). This position is consistent with that adopted by the Department of Labor when it administered the ADEA. . . . Courts have also emphatically rejected business practices in which "the plain intent and effect . . . was to eliminate older workers who had built up, through years of satisfactory service, higher salaries than their younger counterparts." Leftwich v. Harris-Stowe State College, 702 F.2d 686, 691 (8th Cir. 1983); see

---

6. As Willie Loman, of Arthur Miller's Death of a Salesman, exclaimed to his boss upon being suddenly fired after thirty-four years of employment, "You can't eat the orange and throw the peel away—a man is not a piece of fruit!" A. Miller, Death of a Salesman 82 (1949).

also EEOC v. Chrysler Corp., 733 F.2d 1183 (6th Cir. 1984); Dace v. ACF Indus., Inc., 722 F.2d 374 (8th Cir. 1983), aff'd on rehearing, 728 F.2d 976 (1984); Geller v. Markham. See generally 1 H. Eglit, Age Discrimination §16.32 (1985).

Neither the district court nor Transit Mix on appeal takes issue with this interpretation of the ADEA in the context of policies that eliminate older employees as a group based on their higher salaries. Rather, they argue for a distinction based on whether the employer's employment action, motivated by a desire to save costs, affects a group of employees or an individual employee. The district court held that while the former would be impermissible age discrimination, the latter is a legitimate, nondiscriminatory reason for replacing an employee. . . . Neither the policies behind the ADEA nor the relevant case law supports making this distinction and we find it to be an inappropriate distinction as applied to Metz's claim.

The ADEA is aimed at protecting the individual employee. Section 623(a)(1) prohibits practices that "discriminate against *any individual* . . . because of such individual's age." (Emphasis added). The statute's language indicates that it shares the same focus as Title VII legislation: "fairness to individuals rather than fairness to classes." City of Los Angeles Dept. of Water & Power v. Manhart; see also Connecticut v. Teal. The same ADEA policy concern that forms the basis for rejecting cost-based employer practices that have an adverse impact upon older workers as a group is present in the case of Metz's discharge: Given the correlation between Metz's higher salary and his years of satisfactory service, allowing Transit Mix to replace Metz based on the higher cost of employing him would defeat the intent of the statute.

This position is consistent with past decisions that have found in favor of employees' ADEA claims as well as those that have found for the employer. In *Leftwich*, an employer defending an ADEA claim argued that although its employment selection plan had a detrimental disparate impact on older employees, the plan was justified because it was adopted as a cost-saving measure. The Eighth Circuit found that this cost justification did not establish a business necessity defense

> Here, the defendants' selection plan was based on tenure status rather than explicitly on age. Nonetheless, because of the close relationship between tenure status and age, the plain intent and effect of the defendants' practice was to eliminate older workers who had built up, through years of satisfactory service, higher salaries than their younger counterparts. If the existence of such higher salaries can be used to justify discharging older employees, then the purpose of the ADEA will be defeated.

Although *Leftwich* involved a disparate impact claim, the reasoning behind its holding can apply equally to a discriminatory treatment claim brought by an individual employee where, because of the high correlation

9. The Age Discrimination in Employment Act   Page 844

between age and salary, it would undermine the goals of the ADEA to recognize cost-cutting as a nondiscriminatory justification for an employment decision. The Eighth Circuit itself applied the reasoning in *Leftwich* to an ADEA claim of discriminatory treatment brought by a single employee. Dace v. ACF Indus., Inc., 722 F.2d 374 (8th Cir. 1983), *aff'd on rehearing*, 728 F.2d 976 (1984). In upholding a jury verdict in favor of the plaintiff, the court quoted the portion of *Leftwich* that we have reprinted above and characterized *Leftwich* as holding "that discrimination on the basis of factors, like seniority, that invariably would have a disparate impact on older employees is improper under the ADEA." In a third case, the Eighth Circuit found that although an employer has the right to abolish a position held by an older worker and combine that position's repsonsibilities with the duties of a younger person, it distinguished such a situation from one in which "*the position remained the same*" and the employer knew the replacement would save money. Holley v. Sanyo Mfg., Inc., 771 F.2d 1161, 1168 (8th Cir.1985) (emphasis added). The court stated that there would be a much stronger claim for recovery in the latter case. . . .

In Geller v. Markham the Second Circuit held that a school board policy that limited teacher hiring to persons with less then five years' experience violated the ADEA. The court further found that the plaintiff, an older teacher replaced under the school board's policy, could recover on theories of both disparate impact, based on the plaintiff's membership in a group unfairly affected by the policy, and disparate treatment, based on her individual replacement by a younger teacher. The court . . . rejected the defendants' defense that the policy "was supportable as a necessary cost-cutting gesture in the face of tight budgetary constraints."

The Sixth Circuit has held that "the prospect of imminent bankruptcy" may qualify as a "reasonable factor other than age" and thus justify, for example, a forced retirement policy. EEOC v. Chrysler Corp., 733 F.2d 1183, 1186 (6th Cir.1984). The court described two tests that the employer must meet to establish a reasonable-factor-other-than-age defense based on the economic needs of a failing company. "First, the necessity for drastic cost reduction obviously must be real. . . . Second, the forced early retirements must be the least-detrimental-alternative means available to reduce costs." Even if we were to adopt a similar economic necessity exception in the present case, Transit Mix would not satisfy this two-part test. We are not convinced that Transit Mix's financial solvency was sufficiently in jeopardy to meet *Chrysler*'s first requirement. More important, Transit Mix clearly has not satisfied the second requirement. Transit Mix did not pursue obvious less-detrimental alternatives to replacing Metz, such as offering Metz continued employment at a lower salary or in a different position. The district court expressly found that Transit Mix "did not ask Mr. Metz to take a pay cut or to take a different job within the company."

IV

The dissent presents a number of interesting insights into the nature of age discrimination and the role of productivity as a legitimate factor in employment decisions. But, while sweeping in its approach, the dissent fails to come to grips with the specific facts of this case.

Metz's relatively high salary was the result of annual raises that were given to him by Transit Mix regardless of how the company was doing financially. Metz's salary therefore reflected his twenty-seven years of service to Transit Mix. When Lawrence, the president of Transit Mix, decided that the company's poor performance no longer justified the salary that the company had given Metz, Lawrence replaced Metz because of that salary without first asking Metz to take a pay cut. Given these facts, Lawrence's desire to save costs was not a permissible, nondiscriminatory reason for replacing Metz with the younger, less-costly Burzloff; by thus replacing Metz, Transit Mix violated Metz's rights under the ADEA.

We, of course, recognize that our use of pay as a "proxy" for age, although inescapable in this particular case, is of limited application and may be employed only on a case-by-case basis where the facts support its use. We do not agree with the dissent that cross-sectional studies of pay in relation to age have much value here. There are any number of reasons why the average fifty-five-year-old might be earning less than the average forty-year-old. For example, as the dissent suggests, younger employees as a group may be better educated and therefore better qualified when entering the workforce than are older employees. Employees may also invest more time and resources in improving their skills through training and education during their early years of employment. Employees may choose less demanding, and therefore lower paying, work as they grow older. In addition, many high-paying jobs require strength, speed, dexterity, endurance and other physical attributes and may even be compensated on a piece-work basis. At fifty-five many employees may be physically disqualified from or limited in high-speed, physically demanding tasks in such places as automobile plants or packinghouses. They may by that age have been down-graded to janitors. And there are not many fifty-five-year-olds playing major league baseball. By age fifty-five many people may have been laid-off or discharged from formerly high-paying factory or transportation jobs and may find work as security guards. Finally, age discrimination on the part of employers may account for some of the decline in the average salary of older workers. In any event, no matter what the facts, only federal judges under the Constitution have guaranteed earnings regardless of productivity until they die.

In the case of Metz, however, the facts are much narrower. He and Burzloff were both plant managers—apparently of equivalent competence. Their work is of the sort where declining physical effectiveness through aging

9. The Age Discrimination in Employment Act   Page 844

is not apparently of consequence and may be more than offset by growth in experience. The facts suggest, as is usual with this type of work, that seniority is a factor in compensation and age and seniority are, of course, strongly correlated. Metz is paid more—as are most middle managers—because he has been there longer. There may be other reasons for the pay disparity but certainly seniority is an important one.

The dissent postulates output or productivity per wage dollar as a legitimate factor in discharge decisions. The dissent is then able to equate high pay with low productivity per wage dollar and thereby legitimate high pay as a reason for lay-off. The dissent maintains that since Metz, who is senior, is paid more because of his seniority (age), he may be fired for that reason alone. Because of his higher pay, awarded for seniority, he is automatically less productive per wage dollar and therefore becomes subject to termination. By this way of thinking, seniority (and hence age) is translated into a perfectly acceptable excuse for firing everyone who receives seniority pay raises.

Thus, if a company has twenty foremen, all of exactly equal ability, and the oldest ten make more money than the others because their average seniority is much higher, according to the dissent the employer would have a complete defense to an age discrimination charge when it fires the ten graybeards. In middle management jobs we would expect pay to reflect seniority and hence to be something of a proxy for age. This is how the civil service works and private industry usually is not much different.[9] To accept the approach of the dissent is to make totally vulnerable the employees who are paid a little more because they have been with the company a little longer. All this has nothing to do with whether older employees across the economy make more or less on average than younger ones (which would presumably be revealed by cross-sectional analysis).

Nor do we accept the view of the dissent that discharge and reduction in pay must be regarded as equivalents under the ADEA for the purposes of this case. After all, discharge is "the industrial equivalent of capital punishment." And, as the dissent makes clear, economic imperatives must be continually balanced against the requirements of the age discrimination law. At least two things are clear: most older employees (who have difficulty getting new jobs) would prefer a wage reduction to being fired, and many employers, knowing of the morale problems created by wage cuts, would prefer to terminate older employees rather than have them remain at work with their morale in serious disarray because their pay was reduced. For this reason, we think general pay reductions are less a threat to senior employees than terminations would be (in part because employers are less likely to cut pay unless economic circum-

---

9. Our dissenting colleague is perhaps not acquainted with the old Army saying that, "There are two methods of promotion: seniority and favoritism."

stances absolutely require it). Certainly, however, in the case before us, we lay down no general rules about what circumstances might justify pay cuts for older employees. We only suggest that the language of the statute does not require that in this case we regard discharge or reduction in pay as the same thing (although they may have economic similarities and, under proper circumstances, they can both result in a successful ADEA claim). It is common knowledge that older employees tend to protect their jobs at all costs—even at the cost of a reduction in pay.[10]

The essential problem with the dissent's approach is that pay for middle management jobs is, at least in the short run and within the broad limits of competition, under the control of the employer. The logic of the dissent's position is that an employer may reward years of service for middle management employees with raises in the paycheck. If this is the practice, as it frequently is, when the middle managers reach age fifty or sixty, they may all be terminated since all will be making more money than younger managers with equivalent jobs. If we assume that all managers at a given level are of equivalent proficiency, as we must for purposes of analysis in the instant case, under the dissent's analysis the managers who are paid the most are by definition the least productive per wage dollar. Through its control over productivity per wage dollar, the management would effectively decide who could be terminated as its employees reach a relatively advanced age.

The dissent's approach to "productivity" as a rationale for discharge is inconsistent with the policies chosen by Congress in enacting the ADEA. As this circuit has previously recognized, the ADEA imposes some costs on employers and deprives employers of some decisionmaking autonomy in order to treat our nation's older employees fairly. . . .

The dissent mentions the higher cost of some fringe benefits for older employees, which is noted in the legislative history of the ADEA. The cost of some fringe benefits does increase with age and it might be said that the cost of these benefits reduces the productivity per fringe dollar of older employees. For example, after fifty, employees may incur higher costs for the provision of health insurance and health care and, under most benefit plans, more senior employees are entitled to longer vacations. But it has not been argued that these higher costs, and by hypothesis lower productivity per dollar, should be reason for exposing older employees to discharge in the face of the age discrimination law. There is even less reason for firing because of higher salaries than because of higher fringes. Salaries are, within a substantial range, in the control of the employer, while fringes—medical costs, for

---

10. We assume (and we do not understand the dissent to disagree) that what aging middle managers would receive from their longtime employers is not necessarily what they could expect to command on the street.

example — may not be. Hence, as a basis for discharge we believe that cost factors must be evaluated critically.

We are, of course, aware that employers must control costs if they are to remain competitive and that this imperative of survival will inevitably create tensions with the legal prohibitions against age discrimination. We think it would be unwise, however, to translate this imperative into a rule that an older employee can be fired and replaced by an equally proficient younger employee merely because the older employee happens to be earning more money at the moment. There are a number of less burdensome measures that can be introduced if necessary before "industrial capital punishment" is brought into play. We therefore reverse the judgment of the district court. . . .

EASTERBROOK, Circuit Judge, dissenting.

Transit Mix laid off Metz and closed the Knox cement plant, which he was managing, because that plant's sales were insufficient to justify its operation. Five months later it reopened the plant under the management of Burzloff, who made a little more than half of Metz's $26,000 salary. The district court found that "Metz's salary was too high to justify in light of the poor performance of the Knox plant." The court also found that because of "differences of opinion and style between Mr. Metz and those who populate the Plymouth plant [Transit Mix's other, larger, plant], it was legitimate and nondiscriminatory" not to employ Metz at Plymouth or to ask Metz to put the Knox plant back in operation. Burzloff, who had worked for 18 years at the Plymouth plant, could be recalled to Plymouth if Knox should prove unprofitable again; Metz could not be detailed to Plymouth. The district court concluded "that each of these reasons — the greater flexibility afforded by Mr. Burzloff and the salary savings — was a determining factor in the decision to terminate Mr. Metz." My colleagues do not hold that any of these findings is clearly erroneous.

I

The district court expressed the view that Transit Mix was entitled to take Metz's salary into account. The majority disagrees. But we review judgments, not opinions, and it is hard to see how Metz's salary mattered. The district court found that both salary and flexibility were "determining" factors. It is clear from the context that the court meant sufficient rather than necessary conditions. That is, Transit Mix was not going to reopen the Knox plant unless its manager could work at Plymouth too. My colleagues do not disturb this finding. Because causation is an essential part of the plaintiff's burden in a disparate treatment case, Metz loses no matter what we make of the district court's approval of the salary business. So although I see why my colleagues disagree with the district court's opinion, I do not understand why they disagree with its judgment.

The district court also found that Transit Mix was not going to pay $26,000 to a manager at Knox, because the plant did not do enough business to support such a salary. The sales of the Knox plant were less than $300,000 in each of 1982 and 1983, falling from earlier levels. "Metz's salary was too high to justify in light of the poor performance of the Knox plant." We have held, in common with every other court to consider the issue, that a firm may lay off or fire employees of any age when economic conditions make that prudent. E.g., Tice v. Lampert Yards, Inc., 761 F.2d 1210 (7th Cir. 1985); Dorsch v. L.B. Forster Co., 782 F.2d 1421 (7th Cir. 1986). "Economic conditions" implies a comparison of the employees' wages with their product; a plant that is unprofitable when the average wage is $20 per hour may be a bonanza for the firm when the average wage is $10. If Transit Mix had said: "We are losing money at Knox, in part because of your high salary, so we are closing that plant", Metz could not have complained. If Transit Mix had known what the court holds today — that it is forbidden to replace Metz with another employee at lower salary — it would have kept the Knox plant shuttered. Metz still would be out of work. He would have been fired had he been 35 years old and everything else the same. This is age discrimination?

Metz's victory today is Pyrrhic — not for him, but for older employees in general. The court tells employers to keep their plants closed. Throw overpaid employees out of work because their salaries are high (as *Tice* permits) but don't you dare hire anyone else at a lower salary to do the work. If that rule were widely followed, the Metzes of the world would be no better off, and the Burzloffs (also in the protected age group) would be worse off. They would be denied advancement, and other employees whom the Burzloffs would manage at Knox would never be hired. If Congress wants such a stultifying result, if Congress wants to hurt older workers, so be it. But judges should not go out of their way to injure protected groups. The ADEA as it exists does not prohibit consideration of the relation between an employee's salary and his productivity.

II

My colleagues' treatment of "wage discrimination" under the ADEA has the support of several other courts. Fair arguments may be made on both sides. But I am persuaded that my brethren, and these other courts, have settled on an approach that is too broad, and I shall try to explain why. Wage discrimination is age discrimination only when wage depends directly on age, so that the use of one is a pretext for the other; high covariance is not sufficient, and employers always should be entitled to consider the relation between a particular employee's wage and his productivity. . . .

9. The Age Discrimination in Employment Act   Page 844

Section 4(f)(1), 29 U.S.C. §623(f)(1), adds that it is lawful "to take any action . . . where the differentiation is based on reasonable factors other than age". A natural reading is that an employer may take into account wages, which are "factors other than age". Many people under 40 (the lower bound of the protected group) earn $26,000 or more; if such a salary exposes them to discharge on economic grounds, then it should expose older employees to discharge. You do not get immunity from an otherwise lawful employment decision by growing old. As my colleagues say, the "ADEA is aimed at protecting the individual employee", but what it protects each employee against is age discrimination. The Act prohibits adverse personnel actions based on myths, stereotypes, and group averages, as well as lackadaisical decisions in which employers use age as a proxy for something that matters (such as gumption) without troubling to decide employee-by-employee who can still do the work and who can't. The ADEA does not protect anyone against decisions based on actual performance.

The contrary view starts from the belief that wage and age are correlated. But age and ability also are correlated. For many years employees add to their skills and as a result do better work; eventually the tables turn, as mental and motor skills slip away. This proceeds at different paces for different people; the ADEA ensures that employers examine each employee's actual performance rather than the average performance of a group defined by age. No one doubts, however, that an employer may discharge an employee, of any age, who no longer performs the job with acceptable skill. But one could say about performance on the job *exactly* what my colleagues say about wages: a test based on performance hurts the old relative to the young. Does it follow that this adverse impact makes inquiry into performance impermissible?

The customary response is that no one is protected by the ADEA unless qualified for the job. An older employee whose skills have diminished is not qualified. Yet there are degrees of skill; an employee is not "qualified" one day and "unqualified" the next. In business the question is not "is Jones qualified?" but "can Jones do the job well enough to cover his wage?" A welder good enough to work on simple sheet metal at $10 per hour may be unqualified for a welding job, paying $30 per hour, in a nuclear plant or on a bridge where lives depend on the quality of the joint and other, better welders compete for the position. There is no "qualified welder" in the abstract, and there is no "qualified manager of a cement plant" either. To say that someone is "qualified" to manage the Knox plant is to say that he can handle the manufacture and sale of concrete well enough that he adds to the value of the enterprise at least the cost of his salary. If he cannot do this, he is unqualified for the particular job at the particular time. It is therefore not possible to divorce the ability to do a job from the wage demanded. If the ADEA allows employers to make decisions based on performance—surely it does, even though performance is systematically related to age—then it also allows employers to make decisions based on the interaction of performance and wage. If the wage is too high for the performance, the employer may act.

My colleagues concede as much when they say that Transit Mix could have cut Metz's salary. Cases such as *Tice* and *Dorsch* hold that employers also may fire workers whose productivity does not justify their wage. If these things are true, however, then the rule the majority creates—that employers cannot act on the basis of salary—cannot be right. More, the language of the ADEA will not sustain a difference between firing an employee based on salary (which my colleagues think forbidden) and reducing an employee's salary based on salary (which my colleagues think OK). The premise of the court's opinion is that wage is the equivalent of age, and to treat an employee adversely because of his high wage is illegal because it has a disproportionately large effect on older employees. Reducing the salary of higher-paid employees also affects older employees adversely, and therefore should be equally illegal. Section 4(a)(1) lists compensation as one forbidden ground. It would be a shocking violation of the ADEA to reduce by 50% the wages of all employees 50 and up; yet my colleagues suggest that Transit Mix should have done just that to Metz. Discharge and a reduction in salary are treated the same under §4(a)(1). If one is off limits, so is the other; neither the language nor the structure of the Act creates the sort of distinction my colleagues suggest. One of the principal reasons for enacting the ADEA was a belief that people dismissed at advanced ages cannot obtain jobs at equivalent pay elsewhere; most employees care about the discharge because of its financial consequences, not because of a sentimental attachment to their employers; discharge is really no different from a reduction in income to the salary paid by the next employer; yet the court ironically says that it is fine to reduce the pay of older employees, so long as it is reduced "at home."

My colleagues view salary reduction as a less restrictive alternative and therefore preferable. Perhaps it is, but we have held that the ADEA does not require employers to use less restrictive alternatives such as offering employees other jobs rather than firing them. E.g., *Tice*. The disparate impact model of race discrimination law on which my brethren draw instead demands that tests or devices with disparate effects be validated or justified by a business necessity. See Griggs v. Duke Power Co.; Dothard v. Rawlinson. The majority waters down the disparate impact approach even as it borrows.

If we apply disparate impact analysis rigorously to decisions based on wages, we will require some fundamental changes in the operation of American business. A firm may not close a plant or curtail its operations on the basis of high wage costs. At a minimum, the court must determine whether a general wage reduction would have restored the plant's profitability. A firm may not give lower-paid employees a wage increase without doing the same for higher-paid employees. Many times an increase will help the lower-paid employees catch up with others; if wage discrimination is age discrimination, this differential increase is presumptively unlawful. (I pass the question whether the ADEA would require an equal percentage increase or an equal dollar increase — whether, indeed, an across-the-board percentage increase might be called discrimination against the younger employees in the protected group who receive lower absolute dollar increases.) In times of corporate austerity, firms may freeze or reduce the salaries of their managers and other well-paid employees; no more, because that is age discrimination.

III

I would accept all of this if the ADEA required it. The language of the Act does not, however, and neither does the analogy to disparate impact cases under Title VII of the Civil Rights Act of 1964. It is time to unscramble the strands of doctrine involved in this and similar cases.

Anti-discrimination law uses two forms of inquiry: disparate treatment and disparate impact. (This ugly use of "impact" instead of "effect" is ingrained, and I follow the convention.) . . .

Metz filed and litigated this case under the disparate treatment model. He was accordingly required to show intent and causation — which, as I have pointed out, he failed to do. My colleagues bail him out by merging the two models. They allow him to get into court with a prima facie case rather than with the daunting statistical showing of a class-wide disparate impact. Then they require the employer to refute this ersatz disparate impact case; it is not enough, they say, for the employer to advance a legitimate reason. And at the end, they conclude, the trier of fact must (not just may) infer intent from the unrefuted disparate impact case, so that Metz prevails. This mixture gives Metz the benefit of the easy parts of both models. Only by using the aspects of the disparate treatment and disparate impact routes most favorable to plaintiffs, and discarding the aspects of each approach favorable to employers, does the court find a violation in today's case.

The two methods of proof should be kept separate. They are built on different premises: disparate treatment on the premise that employees are identical, so that differential treatment must be attributed to use of the prohibited characteristic, and disparate impact on the premise that because of a history of discrimination employees are different, so that employers must be prevented from using arbitrary tests and devices that play on that regrettable difference without advancing any legitimate interest. Putting the two theories together yields nothing but confusion. See Douglas Laycock, Statistical Proof and Theories of Discrimination, 49 L. & Contemp. Prob. 66 (Aut. 1986). This case shows why.

As a disparate treatment case, Metz's claim falls short. Transit Mix articulated two justifications other than Metz's age: the need to have a manager at Knox who also could work at Plymouth, and the relation between Metz's salary and the revenues of the Knox plant. The district court credited the first as an accurate and sufficient reason. The second, too, was a sufficient reason; although perhaps related to Metz's age in a statistical sense, such relatedness does not show discriminatory intent in a disparate treatment case. As a disparate impact case Metz's claim is equally weak. A disparate impact claim depends on groupwide adverse effects, which Metz never offered to show. It also depends on the outcome of a validation study and an inquiry into business necessity, which no court has conducted.

The consequences of scrambling the two models are most apparent in the court's treatment of intent. The plaintiff in a disparate treatment case must show discriminatory intent. There is no finding that Transit Mix treated Metz adversely because of his age; there is only a finding that Transit Mix considered something that is correlated with age. Yet the majority allows disparate impact to substitute for intent, although all the disparate impact cases reflect the belief that disparate impact and intent are different. They allow liability in the absence of discriminatory intent. See *Griggs*. Intent means doing something because of, not in spite of, a particular consequence. Personnel Administrator v. Feeney. That means using wage to get at age. Metz did not claim that Transit Mix used his wage as a smokescreen; the record shows, and the district court found, that Transit Mix used Metz's wage with indifference to his age, rather than because of it. *Feeney* and Washington v. Davis, reject the equation between disparate impact and intent on which my colleagues' conclusion depends. Both cases reverse decisions that had equated the two, or used disparate effect as the sole basis of inferring intent.

The two approaches are related in the sense that if in a disparate impact case a court declares that a particular employer may not insist that bricklayers have high school degrees, that employer could not respond to a later disparate treatment claim by saying "I did not hire Smith because he lacked a high school degree." But it is not the law that if Duke Power Co. cannot demand a high school degree of its janitors, Boeing cannot demand a high school degree of its engineers. Each new job, each new employer, requires a separate inquiry. My colleagues have fused disparate treatment and disparate impact rules in such a way that one employer's loss in a disparate impact case means that no employer can use a particular ground of decision in a disparate treatment case. . . . The melding of the two strands of discrimination law effectively relieved Metz of his burden—indeed has allowed him to prevail even though the employer advanced, and the trier of fact credited, a sufficient reason utterly unrelated to his age. This unfortunate outcome is the wages of conceptual confusion.

IV

Perhaps, however, we could abandon the disparate treatment model in cases of this sort. I now inquire how Metz should fare if we were to explore that possibility. . . . Let us assume for the moment, however, that because of the parallel language in Title VII and §4(a) of the ADEA [the disparate impact] approach governs and ask whether it applies to decisions based on the relation between an employee's wage and his productivity. I return toward the end of this opinion to the question whether there should be a disparate impact model in ADEA cases. . . .

Disparate impact analysis under *Griggs* has three steps: (1) identifying a test, device, or practice; (2) establishing that the test, device, or practice adversely affects a group protected by the statute; (3) assessing the validity or business necessity of a test that has disparate impact. The application of this approach to wage discrimination encounters problems at each step.

Where is the class-wide test, practice, or device? Decisions based on the relation between the value of the employee's work and the pay he receives for it are scarcely arbitrary; to the contrary, they are essential in every business. This is individualized decisionmaking, the opposite of the rote and pointless tests the Supreme Court had in mind in *Griggs*. It is not a test, device, or practice at all.

Where is the disparate impact of considering wages? It is true, as my colleagues observe, that the average employee's income tends to increase with age. Some employees regress (for example, lawyers earn less as judges than in the practice) but the usual direction is up. See Gary S. Becker, Human Capital: A Theoretical and Empirical Analysis, with Special Reference to Education 219 (2d ed. 1975) (time series analysis of people who completed their education in a single year); Jacob Mincer, Schooling, Experience, and Earnings 64-82, 101 (1974) (many time series analyses for different levels of education). This may occur because people do better work as time goes by, because they are better matched to their jobs, see Boyan Jovanovic, Job Matching and the Theory of Turnover, 87 J. Pol. Econ. 972 (1979), or because of other factors. Robert Topel, Job Mobility, Search, and Earnings Growth: A Reinterpretation of Human Capital Earnings Functions, 8 Research in Labor Economics 199 (1986).

The change in each person's income with time is not the sense relevant to disparate impact analysis, however. We want to know whether wages for the body of employees rise with age: that is, do 50-year-old employees earn more than 40-year-olds at any given moment? Would an employer, bent on slashing costs, find older employees' wages the most attractive target? This is a question about the profile of an employer's wage bill by the age of its employees. The wage-age profile in a cross-sectional analysis (that is, the data obtained from a snapshot of everyone's wages at an instant of time) shows wages rising through age 40 and thereafter declining. E.g., Lloyd G. Reynolds, Stanley H. Masters & Colletta H. Moser, Labor Economics and Labor Relations 234 (9th ed. 1986) (national cross section of annual wages of all employees in 1982). In 1982, employees age 60 had roughly the same average income as employees age 30. This is so in part because younger employees are better educated and therefore start at higher wages than employees did a generation ago. Data from 1981, reproduced in the National Commission for Employment Policy's Ninth Annual Report: Older Workers: Prospects, Problems and Policies 16 (1985), have a similar pattern, though they show that employees aged 40-44 have the highest earnings. See Figure 1. The Bureau of Labor Statistics' estimate for March 1987 has the same pattern. BLS News (Apr. 28, 1987).

No matter why the cross-section looks as it does, however, the foundation for a disparate impact analysis is shaky; the most one can say is that the average wage at (say) 50 is higher than the average wage at 25, even though

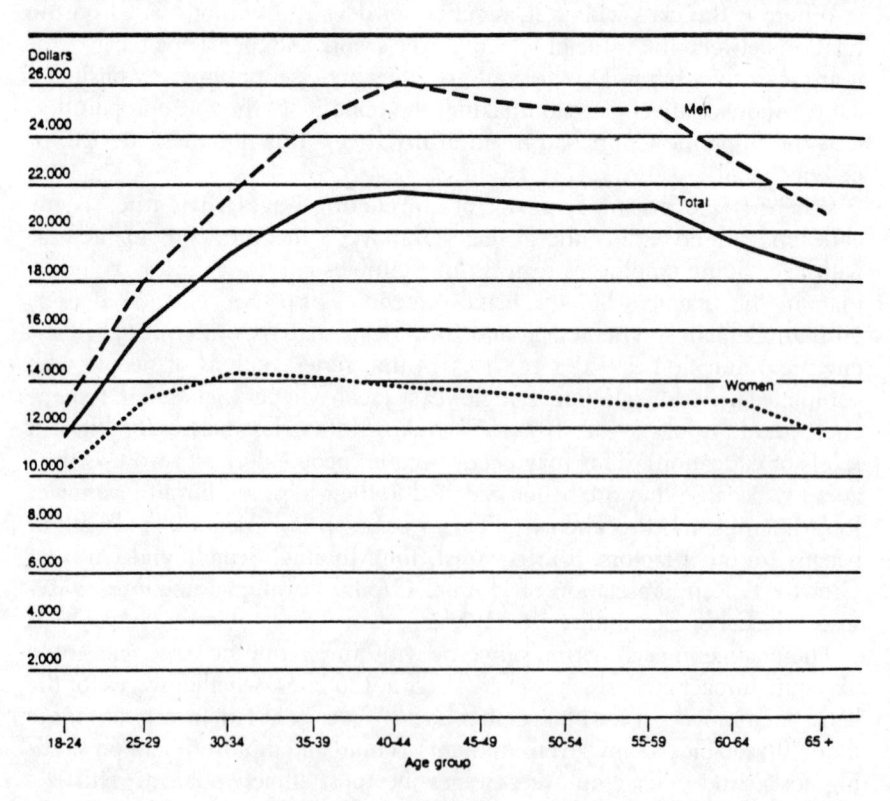

Figure 1.
Earnings of Year Round Full-Time Workers, by Age and Sex, 1981 Source: U.S. **Bureau of the Census**

9. The Age Discrimination in Employment Act

the cross-section shows leveling off or decline after age 40. The data for hourly wages show much the same pattern. Census data from 1984 covering workers paid by the hour give median wages as follows:

Ages	Hourly Wage
16-19	$3.64
20-24	$4.94
25-29	$6.52
30-34	$7.23
35-39	$7.37
40-44	$7.17
45-49	$7.23
50-54	$7.20
55-59	$6.85
60-64	$6.45
65-69	$4.95
70+	$4.38

Department of Labor, Bureau of Labor Statistics, Monthly Labor Review 22 (Feb. 1986) (median covers all races and both sexes). No evidence in the record of this case shows that the wage-age profile at Transit Mix has an upward slope. If Metz wanted to use a disparate impact analysis, he should have built the statistical foundation. It is not appropriate to take judicial notice of a wage-age profile that creates a disparate impact problem — especially when the court is "noticing" something that is not true. See Fed. R. Evid. 201(b)(1) (judicial notice appropriate only when the fact is "not subject to reasonable dispute").

Finally, what happened to the search for validation or business necessity? *Griggs* does not condemn all tests or devices with disparate impact; it forbids only those that are not valid (job-related) or supported by strong business reasons. It is hard to imagine how the use of wages could not be valid; wages correspond precisely to the costs of doing business, and hence to profitability. We might have a validity problem if an employer tried to slash wages without regard to the employee's performance. For example, a wage reduction for all employees over 60 could reflect the stereotypical belief that no one over 60 can do the job well. . . . But a use of wage in relation to job performance — which is how Transit Mix used Metz's wage — is "valid" almost by definition. This is why the district court was right to see a difference between across-the-board decisions and employee-by-employee decisions. My colleagues, however, have written validation out of the disparate impact test. Their opinion does not suggest that it matters whether Transit Mix had a sound business reason for taking Metz's wages into account. Indeed, the holding of this case is that an employer may not replace an employee with one willing to accept lower pay, even though it has a sound business reason. Nothing in *Griggs* or any other case in the Supreme Court's disparate impact sequence supports this.

If neither the text of the ADEA nor the disparate impact cases under Title VII support Metz, what about the ADEA's legislative history? Little of the history is pertinent. None of the committee reports discusses the extent to which employers may take salary into account in making decisions. To the extent the legislative history addresses the subject, it suggests that employers may consider the costs of hiring older employees — and §4(f)(2), 29 U.S.C. §623(f)(2), writes into the statute the permission to use age as a ground of decision when costs so dictate. Section 4(f)(2) provides that employers may use age in, for example, designing insurance plans: term life insurance costs much more for 65-year-old employees than for 25-year-old employees, and §4(f)(2) permits employers to consider that in designing packages of benefits. . . .

The assumption behind §4(f)(2) is that without an explicit privilege to use age in the design of welfare and pension plans, the higher costs of fringe benefits for older persons would be a legitimate reason not to employ them. Secretary of Labor Wirtz, the Johnson Administration's chief spokesman on the ADEA, made that point explicitly in both the Senate and the House hearings. . . .

The floor debate was inconclusive. Several members of Congress expressed concern that employers were taking the higher cost of older labor into account, but in the context of remarks that the employers did not appreciate that older workers still did good work. What were these members getting at?: that it is forbidden to look at an employee's salary, or that it is forbidden to judge an employee by his age rather than by his ability to perform the work? The latter theme predominates.

The structure of the Act accords with its history. Section 4(a) parallels Title VII in some respects but is different in others. One striking difference is §4(f)(1), which says that "reasonable factors other than age" may be the basis of decision — implying strongly that the employer may use a ground of decision that is not age, even if it varies with age. What else could be the purpose of this language? Surely it does not mean simply that "only age discrimination is age discrimination." "The prohibition and the exception appear identical. The sentence is incomprehensible unless the prohibition forbids disparate treatment and the exception authorizes disparate impact." Douglas Laycock, Continuing Violations, Disparate Impact in Compensation, and Other Title VII Issues, 49 L. & Contemp. Prob. 53, 55 (Aut. 1986).

There are other differences between Title VII and the ADEA. For example, §4(f)(2) allows age to be used explicitly. Then there is §4(f)(3), stating that an employer may discharge anyone for "cause" — another clause missing from Title VII. "Cause," like "qualified," is a continuous rather than dichotomous variable; not being productive enough to cover your wage is "cause." . . .

All of this does not deny the force of the position, expressed in *Chrysler* and similar cases, including Leftwich v. Harris-Stowe State College, that the ADEA forbids use of wage as a euphemism for age. [W]hen wage is "directly dependent on" age, the use of one is no better than the use of the other. Some colleges (and law firms) use lock-step compensation systems. The wage is a function of age and age only. For such an employer the statements "we are firing all professors with salaries above $35,000" and "we are firing all professors older than 65" are identical. Courts should treat them as identical. That is not remotely what Transit Mix did, however: it shut a poorly performing plant and fired its manager.

A growing literature on education, training, employment, and other aspects of human capital suggests that there may be times when employers will pay wages that do not represent the employees' marginal products. For example, while receiving firm-specific training the employee may receive a wage exceeding his product; this is how the firm finances the training (for which the employee will not pay, because it has no use outside the firm). Later the firm will recoup its investment by paying less than the marginal product. See Becker, Human Capital 26-37, 216-23. Other firms that give their employees access to trade secrets or put them in positions of trust may try to cement the employees' loyalty (or honesty) with "golden handcuffs"—wages in excess of the employees' marginal product, a form of special compensation the employee forfeits if he leaves the firm. E.g., Gary S. Becker & George J. Stigler, Law Enforcement, Malfeasance, and Compensation of Enforcers, 3 J. Legal Studies 1 (1974). Still other firms may pay employees slightly less than their marginal product early in their careers, knowing that as each employee's productivity declines at the end of his career, the firm will be paying more than marginal product (thus paying the employee his due over the life cycle). This gives employees strong reasons to stick with their firms and be more productive throughout their careers, which in turn yields society the benefit of everyone's abilities. Edward P. Lazear, Agency, Earnings Profiles, Productivity and Hours Restrictions, 71 Am. Econ. Rev. 606 (1981); Robert Hutchens, Delayed Payment Contracts and a Firm's Propensity to Hire Older Workers, 4 J. Labor Econ. 439 (1986). But cf. Peter Kuhn, Wages, Effort, and Incentive Compatibility in Life-Cycle Employment Contracts, 4 J. Labor Econ. 28 (1986).

Whenever the age-wage profile of a class of employees includes a period of compensation at more than marginal product, the firm may be inclined to behave opportunistically—to fire the employee as soon as his current productivity no longer covers his current wage. A firm's desire to attract new employees will curtail this opportunism, to the extent new hires learn of the firm's reputation (or depend on a union to police the firm's behavior). When the firm encounters economic trouble or for some other reason plans to shrink, it need not worry about scaring away bright new employees; it is out of that market. The distressed or shrinking firm may try to dispose of higher paid, older employees, cheating them out of the high compensation at the end of their careers. A disparate impact approach under the ADEA might help to curtail this opportunism. Whether it would do so well enough in light of the substantial error costs the inquiry would entail, I need not consider, for this approach would not assist Metz even if it were the law. Metz does not contend that Transit Mix was changing the structure of its compensation so as to exploit its older employees. And my colleagues apparently would allow Transit Mix to do so, if it wanted — it could reduce Metz's salary, they say.

The court's invitation to employers to cut wages the next time they are in a situation like the one Transit Mix encountered not only fails to protect older employees against the principal danger they face but also creates an anomaly. If it would have been legitimate to reduce Metz's wage, why can he collect damages in this case? Presumably Transit Mix would be entitled to reduce Metz's wage to what he could command in the market from another employer. Metz in fact took another job two months after Transit Mix put Burzloff in charge of the Knox plant. His new job, with the Starke County Highway Commission, pays about $12,500 per year. Metz wants the difference between $26,000 (his salary at Transit Mix) and $12,500; but if Metz was worth only $12,500 in the market and Transit Mix could have cut his salary to that level, he should collect nothing. . . .

NOTES

1. Viewing Metz's relatively high salary as a function of his 27 years of employment with the company, the majority held that the employer's attempt to save salary costs was not a nondiscriminatory reason. In short, the court used higher pay as a proxy for age when the level of compensation was inextricably entwined with long years of service. Although it cautioned that using relatively high salary as a proxy for age is justifiable only on a case-by-case basis, the majority failed to indicate what was distinctive about that use in the case before it. Will the situation in *Metz* be the rule or the exception?

2. Suppose an employer freely admits that it selected higher paid workers for layoff; not only may this not defeat a claim of age discrimination, it may actually establish a violation. When will this be true? See also White v. Westinghouse Electric Co., 862 F.2d 56 (3d Cir. 1988) (termination of employee just short of critical pension dates raised factual issue of age discrimination in view of high correlation between advanced age and higher compensation).

3. But the *Metz* court did not leave the employer helpless when faced with straitened economic circumstances and high labor costs. The opinion suggested that a wage reduction, rather than discharge, might be the appropriate

solution, although it cautioned that a wage reduction may itself sometimes violate the ADEA. When is such a reduction permissible? When is it a violation?

4. Judge Easterbrook's dissent is broadly permissive of employment decisions based on "productivity," with productivity viewed as a cost-benefit concept. If two workers are equally productive in terms of output but one is paid more than the other, the higher-paid worker is less productive per dollar of employer input. The employer, therefore, may freely terminate higher-paid workers without regard to the ADEA so long as the decisions are really based on a cost-benefit calculus. For the dissent, is any employer decision on these grounds essentially immune from attack, regardless of the extent to which higher salaries correlate with age or seniority, and without any concern for less restrictive alternatives to discharge? If the dissent's position exposes older workers to discharge on a wholesale basis because equal absolute productivity with younger workers would not suffice to save higher-paid older workers, would the Congress which enacted the ADEA find this interpretation acceptable? What about the possibility that "productivity" judgments could frequently disguise decisions which were truly based on age?

5. Is Easterbrook's position predicated on the data showing that salaries decrease with age? By the way, was this data taken from the record of the case, or was Judge Easterbrook taking judicial notice of this "fact"? It is at best counter-intuitive since most of us in our daily lives see an imperfect but strong correspondence between increased age and higher salaries within any organization or profession.

6. Judge Easterbrook argues that wage discrimination is not necessarily age discrimination — it is only "when wage depends directly on age, so that the use of one is a pretext for the other." This must be correct under the disparate treatment model: intent is critical. But he goes on to argue that "high covariance is not sufficient." Isn't "high covariance" evidence of intentional discrimination in the sense that, *absent another explanation,* the proper inference from a statistically significant showing of a relationship between increased age and adverse employment decisions *is* intent to discriminate? Isn't the critical point that Easterbrook would uphold the district court's finding of only a productivity decision, despite the high covariance? In short, there was an innocent explanation for the high covariance. But suppose the district court found that the high covariance established age discrimination, would Easterbrook also vote to affirm that finding?

7. Note that Judge Easterbrook believes there would be a violation of the ADEA when firms "use lock-step compensation systems. The wage is a function of age and age only." Doesn't this merge the "intent to discriminate" question with that of "high covariance"? If the correlation is perfect, the use of wage *is* age discrimination. Why should this be true if the employer truly intended to save money (a legitimate justification which happened to affect only older workers), as opposed to ridding itself of older workers (an illegitimate one)?

8. Is *Metz* really a disparate impact case? The dissent criticizes the majority for confusing the disparate treatment and disparate impact models. Is this criticism justified? Maybe this is what courts are doing when they use something as a "proxy" for age—seniority or seniority-related higher salary. Under this view, the majority applied a kind of informal disparate impact analysis and quickly came to the conclusion that, regardless of the business necessity for cutting costs, there was a less restrictive alternative to discharge—reduction of salary—which met the employer's needs as well as did the termination of the older worker.

9. Viewed as a disparate impact case, the dissent first suggests that disparate impact may not be applicable to wage decisions, but ultimately seems to rest its result on the absence of impact of such a rule on older workers. This is the point of the cross-sectional data. Is Judge Easterbrook saying that a policy of firing workers with higher salaries could never harm older workers because, as a group, they have lower salaries? But isn't this wrong-headed? The data show that older workers are comparatively less well off than younger workers. Wouldn't it be a strange kind of discrimination law analysis which would permit employees to *heighten* that relative disadvantage by discharging older workers who (atypically) happened to higher pay when there is a close correspondence (covariance) between their higher pay and their age?

10. At another point, Judge Easterbrook seems to suggest that such cross-sectional data is not necessarily fatal since plaintiff could have made out a prima facie disparate impact case by showing that "the wage-age profile at Transit Mix has an upward slope." Is the cross-sectional data intended simply to show that such a slope should not be presumed or taken judicial notice of? But surely there was evidence in the record that Transit Mix had an upward-sloping age-wage curve: (1) the employer testified that raises were given yearly; (2) Easterbrook agreed with his colleagues "that the average employee's income tends to increase with age;" and (3) there was such a relationship between the two individuals in question.

11. At its broadest, the *Metz* majority has converted an employer's "wage-productivity" defense to an admission of liability; at its narrowest, Judge Easterbrook's dissent would permit an employer to fire all workers earning more than a certain amount, despite any age impact. Will either polar position be adopted? If not, what intermediate rule should emerge?

Page 844. Add new Notes:

12. In Arnold v. United States Postal Service, 863 F.2d 994 (D.C. Cir. 1988) (2-1), *cert. denied*, 110 S. Ct. 140 (1989), the court considered a challenge to a postal service rule, the Career Path Policy or CCP, designed to staff less-desirable geographic areas. After providing for volunteers and for promotion inducements for volunteering, the rule specified that, with certain

9. The Age Discrimination in Employment Act

exceptions, the most senior of the "level 23 inspectors" would be reassigned to the needed positions. The plaintiffs challenged this "reverse seniority" rule as having a disparate impact on older workers, both because it applied to relatively senior level 23 inspectors and because the most senior persons in that group were to be mandatorily reassigned. Without deciding that disparate impact is available under the ADEA, the *Arnold* court found no age-related impact on those 40 and older.

It was common ground to the parties that the senior-first rule, viewed by itself, had a disparate impact on those over 40. But the defendant argued, and the appeals court agreed, that the proper focus was on the entire transfer rule, including the provisions for volunteers and for encouraging volunteers by incentives. Comparing the proportion of over-40 inspectors against the number of level 23 inspectors overall (34.4 percent), the court noted that a slightly smaller percentage of such older workers were transferred (33.8 percent) when voluntary and involuntary transfers were considered. The Supreme Court's holding in Connecticut v. Teal, 457 U.S. 440 (1982), a Title VII case, that disparate impact could be applied to each component of a selection process, was ruled inapposite to the case at hand: the senior-first rule, unlike the test at issue in *Teal*, "was not a free-standing element of an employment program. Under the CCP, every level 23 employee was expected to spend five years in a [less desirable location]. Thus, each level 23 employee can fulfill this requirement through *either* an early voluntary or later involuntary transfer. Those individuals who are subject to involuntary transfers and protected by the ADEA, were not excluded from the voluntary transfer stage." 863 F.2d at 999. Because everyone was subject to the entire rule, it was improper to break down the CPP into its component parts in order to conduct a disparate impact analysis. Judge Garth dissented. He found Connecticut v. Teal controlling: fairness to a group cannot justify unfairness to individuals.

13. The Supreme Court's recent shift of the burden of persuasion on business necessity from the defendant to the plaintiff, and its recent redefinition of the defense in Title VII, Wards Cove v. Atonio, reproduced at p. 46, will presumably also apply to Age Act cases. Would *Geller* be decided differently under *Wards Cove*?

D. STATUTORY EXCEPTIONS

2. Seniority Systems

Page 845, add before "Nevertheless" in second paragraph, line 6:

For that reason, violations of seniority systems to the disadvantage of older workers are strong evidence of age discrimination. See Ayala v. Mayfair

Molder Products Corp., 831 F.2d 1314 (7th Cir. 1987). But see Arnold v. United States Postal Service, 863 F.2d 994 (D.C. Cir. 1988), *cert. denied*, 110 S. Ct. 140 (1989) (viewed in context, a policy requiring senior workers to transfer to undesirable assignments showed no discrimination because of age); Mauter v. Hardy Corp., 825 F.2d 1554 (11th Cir. 1987).

3. Bona Fide Benefit Plans

Page 846. Delete from *"Benefit Plan" up to "4. Good Cause . . ."* **on p. 849 and replace with the following:**

PUBLIC EMPLOYEES RETIREMENT SYSTEM OF OHIO V. BETTS
109 S. Ct. 2854 (1989)

Justice KENNEDY delivered the opinion of the Court.

The Age Discrimination in Employment Act of 1967 (ADEA) forbids arbitrary discrimination by public and private employers against employees on account of age. Under §4(f)(2) of the Act, 29 U.S.C. §623(f)(2), however, age-based employment decisions taken pursuant to the terms of "any bona fide employee benefit plan such as a retirement, pension, or insurance plan, which is not a subterfuge to evade the purposes of" the Act, are exempt from the prohibitions of the ADEA. In the case before us, we must consider the meaning and scope of the §4(f)(2) exemption.

I

A

In 1933, the State of Ohio established the Public Employees Retirement System of Ohio (PERS) to provide retirement benefits for state and local government employees. Public employers and employees covered by PERS make contributions to a fund maintained by PERS to pay benefits to covered employees. Under the PERS statutory scheme, two forms of monthly retirement benefits are available to public employees upon termination of their public employment. Age-and-service retirement benefits are paid to those employees who at the time of their retirement (1) have at least 5 years of service credit and are at least 60 years of age; (2) have 30 years of service credit; or (3) have 25 years of service credit and are at least 55 years of age. Ohio Rev. Code Ann. §§ 145.33, 145.34 (1984 and Supp. 1988). Disability retirement benefits are available to employees who suffer a permanent disabil-

9. The Age Discrimination in Employment Act

ity, have at least five years of total service credit, and are under the age of 60 at retirement. §145.35. The requirement that disability retirees be under age 60 at the time of their retirement was included in the original PERS statute, and has remained unchanged since 1959.

Employees who take disability retirement are treated as if they are on leave of absence for the first five years of their retirement. Should their medical conditions improve during that time, they are entitled to be rehired. §145.39. Employees receiving age-and-service retirement, on the other hand, are not placed on leave of absence, but they are permitted to apply for full-time employment with any public employer covered by PERS after 18 months of retirement. Ohio Rev. Code Ann. §145.381(C) (1984). Once an individual retires on either age-and-service or disability retirement benefits, he or she continues to receive that type of benefit throughout retirement, regardless of age.

B

Appellee June M. Betts was hired by the Hamilton County Board of Mental Retardation and Developmental Disabilities as a speech pathologist in 1978. The Board is a public agency, and its employees are covered by PERS. In 1984, because of medical problems, appellee became unable to perform her job adequately and was reassigned to a less demanding position. Appellee's medical condition continued to deteriorate, however, and by May 1985, when appellee was 61 years of age, her employer concluded that she was no longer able to perform adequately in any employment capacity. Appellee was given the choice of retiring or undergoing medical testing to determine whether she should be placed on unpaid medical leave. She chose to retire, an option which gave her eligibility for age-and-service retirement benefits from PERS. Because she was over 60 at the time of retirement, however, appellee was denied disability retirement benefits, despite her medical condition.

Before 1976, the fact that appellee's age disqualified her for disability benefits would have had little practical significance, because the formula for calculating disability benefits was almost the same as the formula used to determine age-and-service benefits. In 1976, however, the PERS statutory scheme was amended to provide that disability retirement payments would in no event constitute less than 30 percent of the disability retiree's final average salary. Ohio Rev. Code Ann. §145.36 (1984). No such floor applies in the case of employees receiving age-and-service retirement payments. The difference was of much significance in appellee's case: her age-and-service retirement benefits amount to $158.50 per month, but she would have received nearly twice that, some $355 per month, had she been permitted to take disability retirement instead. . . .

II

. . . On its face, the PERS statutory scheme renders covered employees ineligible for disability retirement once they have attained age 60. PERS' refusal to grant appellee's application for disability benefits therefore qualifies as an action "to observe the terms of" the plan. All parties apparently concede, moreover, that PERS' plan is "bona fide," in that it " 'exists and pays benefits.' " United Air Lines, Inc. v. McMann. Finally, whatever the precise meaning of the phrase "any . . . employee benefit plan such as a retirement, pension, or insurance plan," it is apparent that a disability retirement plan falls squarely within that category. Cf. 29 C.F.R. §1625.10(f)(1)(ii) (1988).

Accordingly, PERS is entitled to the protection of the §4(f)(2) exemption unless its plan is "a subterfuge to evade the purposes of" the Act. We first construed the meaning of "subterfuge" under §4(f)(2) in United Air Lines, Inc. v. McMann. In *McMann*, the employer's retirement plan required employees to retire at the age of 60. . . . With respect to mandatory retirement, we found that the statutory language and legislative history provided no support for the proposition that Congress intended to forbid age-based mandatory retirement.

Turning to the claim that the mandatory retirement provision was a "subterfuge to evade the purposes of" the Act, we rejected the conclusion of the court below that forced retirement on the basis of age must be deemed a subterfuge absent some business or economic purpose for the age-based distinction. Instead, we held that the term "subterfuge" must be given its ordinary meaning as "a scheme, plan, stratagem, or artifice of evasion." Viewed in this light, the retirement plan at issue could not possibly be characterized as a subterfuge to evade the purposes of the Act, since it had been established in 1941, long before the Act was enacted. As we observed, "[t]o spell out an intent in 1941 to evade a statutory requirement not enacted until 1967 attributes, at the very least, a remarkable prescience to the employer. We reject any such per se rule requiring an employer to show an economic or business purpose in order to satisfy the subterfuge language of the Act."

As an initial matter, appellee asserts that *McMann* is no longer good law. She points out that in 1978, less than a year after *McMann* was decided, Congress amended §4(f)(2) to overrule *McMann's* validation of mandatory retirement based on age. The result of that amendment was the addition of what now is the final clause of §4(f)(2).

The legislative history of the 1978 amendment contains various references to the definition of subterfuge, and according to appellee these reveal clear congressional intent to disapprove the reasoning of *McMann*. The Conference Committee Report on the 1978 amendment, for example, expressly discusses and rejects *McMann*, stating that "[p]lan provisions in effect prior to the date of enactment are not exempt under section 4(f)(2) by virtue of the fact that they antedate the act or these amendments." H.R. Conf. Rep. No. 95-950, p.8 (1978), U.S. Code Cong. & Admin. News 1978, pp. 504, 511. . . .

The 1978 amendment to the ADEA did not add a definition of the term "subterfuge" or modify the language of §4(f)(2) in any way, other than by inserting the final clause forbidding mandatory retirement based on age. We have observed on more than one occasion that the interpretation given by one Congress (or a committee or member thereof) to an earlier statute is of little assistance in discerning the meaning of that statute. Congress changed the specific result of *McMann* by adding a final clause to §4(f)(2), but it did not change the controlling, general language of the statute. As Congress did not amend the relevant statutory language, we see no reason to depart from our holding in *McMann* that the term "subterfuge" is to be given its ordinary meaning, and that as a result an employee benefit plan adopted prior to enactment of the ADEA cannot be a subterfuge.

According to PERS, our reaffirmation of *McMann* should resolve this case. The PERS system was established by statute in 1933, and the rule that employees over age 60 may not qualify for disability retirement benefits has remained unchanged since 1959. The ADEA was not made applicable to the States until 1974. Since the age-60 requirement pre-dates application of the ADEA to PERS, PERS argues that, under *McMann*, its plan cannot be a subterfuge to evade the purposes of the ADEA.

While *McMann* remains of considerable relevance to our decision here, we reject the argument that it is dispositive. It is true that the age-60 rule was adopted before 1974, and is thus insulated under *McMann* from challenge as a subterfuge. The plan provision attacked by appellee, however, is the rule that disability retirees automatically receive a minimum of 30 percent of their final average salary upon retirement, while disabled employees who retire after age 60 do not. The 30 percent floor was not added to the plan until 1976, and to the extent this new rule increased the age-based disparity caused by the pre-Act age limitation, *McMann* does not insulate it from challenge. . . .

III

Appellee and her *amici* say that §4(f)(2) protects age-based distinctions in employee benefit plans only when justified by the increased cost of benefits for older workers. They cite an interpretive regulation promulgated by the Department of Labor, the agency initially charged with enforcing the Act, in 1979. 29 C.F.R. §1625.10 (1988). The regulation recites that the purpose of the exemption "is to permit age-based reductions in employee benefit plans where such reductions are justified by significant cost considerations," and that "benefit levels for older workers may be reduced to the extent necessary to achieve approximate equivalency in cost for older and younger workers." §1625.10(a)(1). With respect to disability benefits in particular, the regulation provides that "[r]eductions on the basis of age in the level or duration of benefits available for disability are justifiable only on the basis of age-related

221

cost considerations. . . ." Under these provisions, employers may reduce the value of the benefits provided to older workers as necessary to equalize costs for workers of all ages, but they cannot exclude older workers from the coverage of their benefit plans altogether.

The requirement that employers show a cost-based justification for age-related reductions in benefits appears nowhere in the statute itself. The EEOC as *amicus* contends that this rule can be drawn either from the statutory requirement that age-based distinctions in benefit plans not be a subterfuge to evade the purposes of the Act, or from the portion of §4(f)(2) limiting its scope to actions taken pursuant to "any bona fide employee benefit plan such as a retirement, pension, or insurance plan." We consider these alternatives in turn.

A

The regulations define "subterfuge" as follows: "In general, a plan or plan provision which prescribes lower benefits for older employees on account of age is not a 'subterfuge' within the meaning of section 4(f)(2), provided that the lower level of benefits is justified by age-related cost considerations." 29 C.F.R. §1625.10(d) (1988). Various lower courts have accepted this definition. As the analysis in *McMann* makes apparent, however, this approach to the definition of subterfuge cannot be squared with the plain language of the statute. Although *McMann*'s holding, that pre-Act plans can never be a subterfuge, is not dispositive here, its reasoning is nonetheless controlling, for we stated in that case that "subterfuge" means "a scheme, plan, stratagem, or artifice of evasion," which, in the context of §4(f)(2), connotes a specific "intent . . . to evade a statutory requirement." The term thus includes a subjective element that the regulation's objective cost-justification requirement fails to acknowledge.

Ignoring this inconsistency with the plain language of the statute, appellee and the EEOC suggest that the regulation represents a contemporaneous and consistent interpretation of the ADEA by the agencies responsible for the Act's enforcement, and is therefore entitled to special deference. But, of course, no deference is due to agency interpretations at odds with the plain language of the statute itself. Even contemporaneous and longstanding agency interpretations must fall to the extent they conflict with statutory language.

[The majority also concluded that the cost-justification requirement was not in fact adopted contemporaneously with enactment of the ADEA by interpreting the original version of the regulations as simply establishing a cost-justification rule as "a safe-harbor." Not until 1979, was "this regulatory safe-harbor . . . transformed into the exclusive means of escaping classification as a subterfuge."]

Appellee and her *amici* rely in large part on the legislative history of the

9. The Age Discrimination in Employment Act

ADEA and the 1978 amendments. In view of our interpretation of the plain statutory language of the subterfuge requirement, however, this reliance on legislative history is misplaced. . . .

B

The second possible source of authority for the cost-justification rule is the statute's requirement that the §4(f)(2) exemption be available only in the case of "any bona fide employee benefit plan such as a retirement, pension, or insurance plan." The EEOC argues, and some courts have held, that the phrase "such as a retirement, pension, or insurance plan" is intended to limit the protection of §4(f)(2) to those plans which have a cost justification for all age-based differentials in benefits. See EEOC v. Westinghouse Electric Corp., 725 F.2d 211, 224 (CA 3 1983), *cert. denied*, 469 U.S. 820, (1984). The argument is as follows: the types of plans listed in the statute share the common characteristic that the cost of the benefits they provide generally rises with the age of their beneficiaries. This common characteristic suggests that Congress intended the §4(f)(2) exemption to cover only those plans in which costs rise with age. The obvious explanation for the limitation on the scope of §4(f)(2), the argument continues, is that the purpose of the exemption is to permit employers to reduce overall benefits paid to older workers only to the extent necessary to equalize costs for older and younger workers.

There are a number of difficulties with this explanation for the cost-justification requirement. Perhaps most obvious, it requires us to read a great deal into the language of this clause of §4(f)(2), language that appears on its face to be nothing more than a listing of the general types of plans that fall within the category of "employee benefit plan." The statute's use of the phrase "any employee benefit plan" seems to imply a broad scope for the statutory exemption, and the "such as" clause suggests enumeration by way of example, not an exclusive listing. Nor is it by any means apparent that the types of plans mentioned were intentionally selected because the cost to the employer of the benefits provided by these plans tends to increase with age. Indeed, many plans that fall within these categories do not share that particular attribute at all, defined-contribution pension plans perhaps being the most obvious example.[5] We find it quite difficult to believe that Congress

---

5. A defined contribution plan is one in which "the employer's contribution is fixed and the employee receives whatever level of benefits the amount contributed on his behalf will provide." See 29 U.S.C. §1002(34). Under this type of plan, the cost of making contributions for any given employee is completely unrelated to that employee's age. The dissent therefore is quite wrong to suggest that these plans "commonly — indeed, almost invariably — entail costs that rise with the age of the beneficiary. . . ."

would have chosen such a circuitous route to the result urged by respondent and the EEOC. . . .

For these reasons, we conclude that the phrase "any bona fide employee benefit plan such as a retirement, pension, or insurance plan" cannot reasonably be limited to benefit plans in which all age-based reductions in benefits are justified by age-related cost considerations. Accordingly, the interpretive regulation construing §4(f)(2) to include a cost-justification requirement is contrary to the plain language of the statute, and is invalid.

IV

Having established that the EEOC's definition of subterfuge is invalid, we turn to the somewhat more difficult task of determining the precise meaning of the term as applied to post-Act plans. We begin, as always, with the language of the statute itself.

The protection of §4(f)(2) is unavailable to any employee benefit plan "which is a subterfuge to evade the purposes of" the Act. As set forth in §2(b) of the ADEA, the purposes of the Act are "to promote employment of older persons based on their ability rather than age; to prohibit arbitrary age discrimination in employment; to help employers and workers find ways of meeting problems arising from the impact of age on employment." 29 U.S.C. §621(b). On the facts of this case, the only purpose that the PERS plan could be a "subterfuge to evade" is the goal of eliminating "arbitrary age discrimination in employment."

As the presence of the various exemptions and affirmative defenses contained in §4(f) illustrates, Congress recognized that not all age discrimination in employment is "arbitrary." In order to determine the type of age discrimination that Congress sought to eliminate as arbitrary, we must look for guidance to the substantive prohibitions of the Act itself, for these provide the best evidence of the nature of the evils Congress sought to eradicate. Indeed, our decision in *McMann* compels this approach, for it rejected the contention that the purposes of the Act can be distinguished from the Act itself. . . . Accordingly, a post-Act plan cannot be a subterfuge to evade the ADEA's purpose of banning arbitrary age discrimination unless it discriminates in a manner forbidden by the substantive provisions of the Act.

Section 4(a), the ADEA's primary enforcement mechanism against age discrimination by employers, forbids employers [inter alia, to "discriminate against any individual with respect to his compensation, terms, conditions, or privileges of employment, because of such individual's age."]

The phrase "compensation, terms, conditions, or privileges of employment" in §4(a)(1) can be read to encompass employment benefit plans of the type covered by §4(f)(2). Such an interpretation, however, would in effect render the §4(f)(2) exemption nugatory with respect to post-Act plans. Any benefit plan that by its terms mandated discrimination against older workers would also be facially irreconcilable with the prohibitions in §4(a)(1) and, therefore, with the purposes of the Act itself. It is difficult to see how a plan provision that expressly mandates disparate treatment of older workers in a manner inconsistent with the purposes of the Act could be said not to be a subterfuge to evade those purposes, at least where the plan provision was adopted after enactment of the ADEA.

On the other hand, if §4(f)(2) is viewed as exempting the provisions of a bona fide benefit plan from the purview of the ADEA so long as the plan is not a method of discriminating in other, nonfringe-benefit aspects of the employment relationship, both statutory provisions can be given effect. This interpretation of the ADEA would reflect a congressional judgment that age-based restrictions in the employee benefit plans covered by §4(f)(2) do not constitute the "arbitrary age discrimination in employment" that Congress sought to prohibit in enacting the ADEA. Instead, under this construction of the statute, Congress left the employee benefit battle for another day, and legislated only as to hiring and firing, wages and salaries, and other nonfringe-benefit terms and conditions of employment.

To be sure, this construction of the words of the statute is not the only plausible one. But the alternative interpretation would eviscerate §4(f)(2). . . .

Not surprisingly, the legislative history does not support such a self-defeating interpretation, but to the contrary shows that Congress envisioned a far broader role for the §4(f)(2) exemption. When S. 830, the bill that was to become the ADEA, was originally proposed by the Administration in January 1967, it contained no general exemption for benefit plans that differentiated in benefits based on age. Senator Javits, one of the principal moving forces behind enactment of age discrimination legislation, generally favored the Administration's bill, but believed that a broader exemption for employee benefit plans was needed. Accordingly, he proposed an amendment substantially along the lines of present-day §4(f)(2). 113 Cong. Rec. 7077 (1967).

One factor motivating Senator Javits' amendment was the concern that, absent some exemption for benefit plans, the Act might "actually encourage employers, faced with the necessity of paying greatly increased premiums, to look for excuses not to hire older workers when they might have done so under a law granting them a degree of flexibility with respect to such matters." Reducing the cost of hiring older workers was not the only purpose of the proposed amendment, however. Its goals were far more comprehensive. As Senator Javits put it, "the age discrimination law is not the proper place to fight" the battle of ensuring "adequate pension benefits for older workers," and §4(f)(2) was therefore intended to be "a fairly broad exemption . . . for bona fide retirement and seniority systems." Later, referring to the effect of his proposed amendment on the provisions of employee benefit plans, Senator Javits stated that "[i]f the older worker chooses to waive all of those provisions, then the older worker can obtain the benefits of this act. . . ." And finally, in his individual views accompanying the Senate Report on S. 830, Senator Javits observed: "I believe the bill has also been improved by the adoption of language, based on an amendment which I had offered, *exempting the observance of bona fide seniority systems and retirement, pension, or other employment benefit plans from its prohibitions.*" S. Rep. No. 723, 90th Cong., 1st Sess., 14 (1967) (emphasis added).

Other Members of Congress expressed similar views. . . .

While the Committee Reports on the ADEA do not address the matter in any detail, they do state that §4(f)(2) "serves to emphasize the primary purpose of the bill—hiring of older workers—by permitting employment without necessarily including such workers in employee benefit plans." S. Rep. No. 723, supra, at 4; H.R. Rep. No. 805, 90th Cong., 1st Sess., 4 (1967). That explanation does not support a narrow reading of the §4(f)(2) exemption. The Committee Reports, moreover, refute a reading of §4(f)(2) that would limit its protection to pre-Act plans, for they make it clear that the exemption "applies to new and existing employee benefit plans, and to both the establishment and maintenance of such plans." S. Rep. No. 723, supra, at 4; H.R. Rep. No. 805, supra, at 4. In short, the legislative history confirms that the broader reading of §4(f)(2) is the correct one, and that Congress intended to exempt employee benefit plans from the coverage of the Act except to the extent plans were used as a subterfuge for age discrimination in other aspects of the employment relation.

While this result permits employers wide latitude in structuring employee benefit plans, it does not render the "not a subterfuge" proviso a dead letter. Any attempt to avoid the prohibitions of the Act by cloaking forbidden discrimination in the guise of age-based differentials in benefits will fall outside the §4(f)(2) exemption. Examples of possible violations of this kind can be given. Under §4(d) of the ADEA, for example, it is unlawful for an employer to discriminate against an employee who has "opposed any action made unlawful by" the Act or has participated in the filing of any age-discrimination complaints or litigation. Nothing in §4(f)(2) would insulate from liability an employer who adopted a plan provision formulated to retaliate against such an employee. See 29 C.F.R. §1625.10(d)(5) (1988). Similarly, while §4(f)(2) generally protects age-based reductions in fringe benefits, an employer's decision to reduce salaries for all employees while substantially increasing benefits for younger workers might give rise to an inference that the employer was in fact utilizing its benefits plan as a subterfuge for age-based discrimination in wages, an activity forbidden by §4(a)(1). These examples are not exhaustive, but suffice to illustrate the not-insignificant protections provided to older employees by the subterfuge proviso in the §4(f)(2) exemption.

V

As construed above, §4(f)(2) is not so much a defense to a charge of age discrimination as it is a description of the type of employer conduct that is prohibited in the employee benefit plan context. By requiring a showing of actual intent to discriminate in those aspects of the employment relationship protected by the provisions of the ADEA, §4(f)(2) redefines the elements of a plaintiff's prima facie case instead of establishing a defense to what otherwise would be a violation of the Act. Thus, when an employee seeks to challenge a benefit plan provision as a subterfuge to evade the purposes of the Act, the employee bears the burden of proving that the discriminatory plan provision actually was intended to serve the purpose of discriminating in some nonfringe-benefit aspect of the employment relation.

This result is supported by our longstanding interpretation of the analogous provision of Title VII, the statute from which "the prohibitions of the ADEA were derived in haec verba.". . . Despite the fact that §703(h) [establishing, inter alia, a seniority system exception] like §4(f)(2), appears on first reading to describe an affirmative defense, we have "regarded [§703(h)] not as a defense . . . but as a provision that itself 'delineates which employment practices are illegal and thereby prohibited and which are not.' " Lorance v. AT & T Technologies, Inc., 109 S. Ct. 2261 (1989). Although the use of the phrase "subterfuge to evade the purposes of [the Act]" in §4(f)(2) renders the scope of its protection for employee benefit plans broader than the scope of the protection for seniority systems provided by §703(h), the similar structure and purpose of the two provisions supports the conclusion that ADEA plaintiffs must bear the burden of showing subterfuge.

Applying this structure to the facts here, it follows that PERS' disability retirement plan is the type of plan subject to the §4(f)(2) exemption, and PERS' refusal to grant appellee's request for disability benefits was required by the terms of the plan. Because appellee has failed to meet her burden of proving that the reduction in benefits at age 60 was the result of an intent to discriminate in some nonfringe-benefit aspect of the employment relation, summary judgment for appellee was inappropriate. On remand, the District Court should give appellee an opportunity to demonstrate the existence of a genuine issue of material fact on this issue. . . .

Justice MARSHALL, with whom Justice BRENNAN joins, dissenting.

The majority today immunizes virtually all employee benefit programs from liability under the Age Discrimination in Employment Act of 1967 (ADEA or Act). Henceforth, liability will not attach under the ADEA even if an employer is unable to put forth any justification for denying older workers the benefits younger ones receive, and indeed, even if his only reason for discriminating against older workers in benefits is his abject hostility to, or his unfounded stereotypes of them. In reaching this surprising result, the majority casts aside the estimable wisdom of all five Courts of Appeals to consider the ADEA's applicability to benefit programs, of the two federal agencies which have administered the Act, and of the Solicitor General as *amicus curiae*, all of whom have concluded that it contravenes the text and history of the Act to immunize discrimination against older workers in benefit plans which is not justified by any business purpose. Agreeing with these authorities, and finding the majority's "plain language" interpretation impossibly tortured and antithetical to the ADEA's goal of eradicating baseless discrimination against older workers, I dissent.

It is common ground that appellant Public Employees Retirement System of Ohio (PERS) discriminated against appellee June Betts on account of her age. Had Betts become disabled before, rather than after, turning 60, PERS would be paying her $355.02 a month in disability benefits for the rest of her life, more than double the $158.50 a month she is now entitled to collect. It is also common ground that PERS' facially discriminatory provision was enacted after the ADEA's passage in 1967, and therefore is subject to the Act's broad antidiscrimination command, and the PERS is liable to Betts for the difference between the monthly sums noted above unless PERS' benefit plan falls within the §4(f)(2) exemption. Finally, it is common ground that, based on PERS' refusal to offer any explanation for the age-specific benefits it provides, its disparate treatment of older employees lacked any business justification whatsoever; indeed, the cost to PERS of its disability plan varied not at all with an employee's age.[2] For want of a better explanation, one is left to conclude that PERS denied benefits to those employees who became disabled after turning 60 solely because it wished to cut its overall disability outlays—and that PERS viewed older workers as a convenient target for its budgetary belt-tightening.

This case thus presents the issue of whether a benefit plan which arbitrarily imposes disparate burdens on older workers can claim succor under §4(f)(2) from age discrimination liability. The majority arrives at the novel conclusion that the ADEA exempts from liability all discriminatory benefit programs, regardless of their justification, unless the discrimination implicates aspects of the employment relationship unrelated to the provision of benefits, and then only if the discrimination violates "the substantive provisions of the Act." The majority acknowledges that this reading shelters from the ADEA's

---

2. It is no answer to surmise that providing disability benefits to an older worker costs more than providing equivalent benefits to a younger worker, as is typically the case with life insurance benefits. PERS, after all, provided full monthly benefits to employees over 60, so long as they had become disabled prior to attaining that age. The sole distinction PERS drew was based on an employee's age at disability, a factor that does not correlate with the cost to an employer of providing benefits. Indeed, insofar as an employer is concerned about the cumulative cost of providing benefits during the remaining life of a disabled employee, this concern militates in favor of older workers, whose predicted life-spans are shorter than those of younger workers.

9. The Age Discrimination in Employment Act

purview all but a few hypothetical types of benefit-plan age discrimination, leaving older workers unprotected from baseless discrimination insofar as it affects the often considerable portion of overall compensation comprised by employee benefits. The majority thus scuttles the heretofore consensus, and in my view correct, interpretation that the §4(f)(2) exemption is limited to those programs whose disparate treatment is justified by a plausible business purpose. . . .

Beginning with the text, the only thing plain about §4(f)(2)'s spare language is that it offers no explicit command as to what heuristic test those applying it should use. In dispatching the consensus reading, the majority makes much of the fact that "[t]he requirement that employers show a cost-based justification for age-related reductions in benefits appears nowhere in the statute itself." This truism, is, however, equally applicable to the complex construction the majority adopts, under which all but certain limited species of benefit plan discrimination are exempted from the ADEA, and under which the burden of proving non-exemption is shouldered by the ADEA plaintiff. Indeed, the fact that §4(f)(2) enumerates various types of benefit programs eligible for exemption from the ADEA's nondiscrimination command but makes no mention of disability programs strongly undercuts the majority's assertion that the text compels exemption here. This is a case in which only so much blood can be squeezed from the textual stone, and in which one therefore must turn to other sources of statutory meaning.

The structure of §4(f)(2), on the other hand, provides considerable support for the business purpose interpretation. The majority views §4(f)(2) as involving two separate clauses, with the first enumerating, for no apparent reason, three types of benefit plans, and the second, the "subterfuge" clause, making §4(f)(2)'s exemption applicable except where a benefit plan is created with a "specific 'intent . . . to evade' " the ADEA. This reading has the perverse consequence of denying the §4(f)(2) exemption only to subtle acts of discrimination effected through a stratagem or other artifice of discrimination, while leaving it intact for those age-based distinctions like PERS which, though arbitrary, are so brazenly discriminatory in disentitling older workers to benefits that they cannot possibly warrant the "subterfuge" characterization. It is difficult to believe that Congress, in passing the ADEA, intended to immunize acts of unabashed discrimination against older workers.

A far more sensible structural interpretation regards the §4(f)(2) sentence as a synthetic whole. Under this reading, the initial enumeration of "a retirement, pension, or insurance plan" serves a concrete purpose: it gives content to the ensuing word "subterfuge." All the enumerated benefit plans commonly— indeed, almost invariably—entail costs that rise with the age of the beneficiary; thus, an employer whose benefit plan treats older workers less favorably than younger ones though spending the same amount on each employee, typically has a cost-based reason for doing so. By this reading, an employer with an economic justification cannot properly be viewed as having resorted to subterfuge to evade the ADEA's command against irrelevant age distinctions. Unlike the majority's artificial bifurcation of §4(f)(2), this holistic interpretation does not excuse express acts of unjustified age discrimination like PERS', while punishing only evasive or subtle discrimination. Significantly, all the courts of appeals to consider §4(f)(2) have concluded that the enumeration of benefit plans where age and cost generally correlate sheds considerable light on the scope of the exemption. And once the possibility of this interpretation is admitted, the majority's sole ground for rejecting the business purpose interpretation—that it clashes with the "plain language of the statute," necessarily falls away. . . .

[The legislative] history convincingly supports the holistic reading and the business purpose interpretation derived therefrom. As initially introduced by Senator Ralph Yarborough in 1967, §4(f)(2) did not recognize any circumstances that might authorize age discrimination in the provision of fringe benefits. Instead, it sheltered only the employer who "separate[s] involuntarily an employee under a retirement policy or system where such policy or system is not merely a subterfuge to evade the purposes of this Act." S. 830, 90th Cong., 1st Sess.

Several Senators, however, led by Senator Jacob Javits, urged that employers, in fashioning benefit programs, be allowed to consider cost differentials between benefits provided to older employees and those provided to younger ones. During Senate hearings on the bill which became the ADEA, Senator Javits criticized the initial version of §4(f)(2), stating that that version did "not provide any flexibility in the amount of pension benefits payable to older workers depending on their age when hired." Age Discrimination in Employment: Hearings on S. 830 and S. 788 before the Subcommittee on Labor of the Senate Committee on Labor and Public Welfare, 90th Cong., 1st Sess., 27 (1967). Employers "faced with the necessity of paying greatly increased premiums," Senator Javits feared, might "look for excuses not to hire older workers." Senator George Smathers, a co-sponsor of the initial bill, acknowledged in response that the bill would not permit employers to vary benefit levels to take into account the greater expense of providing some fringe benefits to older workers. He proposed amending it to permit such variations. The following day, Senator Javits proposed, as a means of incorporat[ing] his and Senator Smathers' concerns, an amendment which incorporated essentially the present language enumerating specific types of benefit plans. 113 Cong. Rec. 7077 (1967). The Javits proposal, which was ultimately adopted and which underwent only peripheral changes before the Act's enactment, was designed to ensure, in its sponsor's words, that "an employer will not be compelled to afford older workers exactly the same pension, retirement, or insurance benefits as younger workers and thus employers will not, *because of the often extremely high cost of providing certain types of benefits to older* workers, *actually be discouraged from hiring older workers.*" 113 Cong. Rec. 31254-31255 (1967) (emphasis added).

The history of §4(f)(2) militates in favor of the business purpose interpretation in several respects. First, it demonstrates that the sponsors of the exemption intended to protect benefit plans with economic justifications for treating older workers disparately, and did not intend categorically to immunize benefit plans from liability for unjustified discrimination.[8] Second, this history undercuts the majority's contention that the §4(f)(2) term "subterfuge to evade the purposes of the Act" supports the broad exemption of benefit plans from coverage. That phrase predated the Javits amendment, and was part of the bill when it did not authorize any age-based discrimination in the provision of benefits. The language broadening the exemption must come instead from the enumeration language added at Senator Javits' behest, language most properly read to import only the business purpose test. Third, at no point during the debate on §4(f)(2) did any legislator come even remotely close to endorsing the construction of §4(f)(2) chosen by the majority. . . .

Even if I did not strongly believe that the text and structure of the §4(f)(2) exemption, as informed by its legislative history, limits the exemption to benefit plans whose discrimination against older workers rests on some business justification, I would still conclude that adoption of the business purpose test is mandated . . . to defer to enforcement agencies' reasonable interpretations of ambiguous statutory provisions. See Western Air Lines, Inc. v. Criswell (deferring to Department of Labor and EEOC on interpretation of ADEA). . . .

NOTES

1. The central question concerning §623(f) was when benefit plans may—short of "excus[ing] the failure to hire any individual" or "requir[ing] or permit[ting] the involuntary retirement of any individual"—discriminate

---

8. The majority attempts to appropriate Senator Javits by stringing together fragments of his comments on the Senate floor. The majority cites his statement that " 'the age discrimination battle is not the proper place to fight' the battle of ensuring 'adequate pension benefits for older workers.' " But as the Solicitor General notes, this remark, read in proper context, does not suggest "that *any* type of discrimination in the provision of employee benefits should be permissible under the ADEA," but makes the more limited point that certain existing pension plans with lengthy vesting periods "should be changed by comprehensive pension legislation rather than by an age discrimination statute." (emphasis added). Senator Javits eventually proposed, and won the enactment of, such legislation. See 29 U.S.C. §1053. Similarly, Senator Javits' statement that amended §4(f)(2) provides " 'a fairly broad exemption . . . for bona fide retirement and seniority systems,' " fully accords with the business purpose test. That test exempts from §4(f)(2)'s coverage any act of age discrimination with some legitimate business basis—leaving unprotected only the presumably narrow band of benefit programs, like PERS, which practice unjustified age discrimination.

Page 846   9. The Age Discrimination in Employment Act

on the basis of age. The *Betts* answer is, always. The decision is radical since the relevant regulations, and all the lower court decisions, had read §623(f) narrowly. Generally speaking, the lower courts started from the premise that Congress intended to allow employers to discriminate in their benefit plans only to the extent that increased age generated increased costs or at least after showing some business purpose for the discrimination.

2. The majority's approach does eliminate the tension that otherwise existed between the ADEA's basic prohibitions and §623(f). The tension arose because the mere fact that a plan discriminated on the basis of age by providing less benefits for older workers did not prevent it from being bona fide, since Congress believed that certain discriminations in benefits were justified. On the other hand, the requirement of bona fideness (and the prohibition of subterfuges) did not provide very useful guidelines as to the extent of the discriminations permitted. By basically reading "benefit plans" out of the statute, the *Betts* decision may force Congress to be more explicit in its commands.

3. Why did the Court spend so much time discussing the extent to which pre-Act benefit plans are immune; after all, isn't the bottom line of the decision that so are post-Act plans?

4. Does the majority's decision hinge on the language of *McMann* that "subterfuge" is a state-of-mind concept, thus rejecting any objective cost-justification test? If so, was *McMann* correct on this point when it was decided? Even if it was, should the Court have been more deferential to the views of the Congress which amended the ADEA in 1978?

5. Assuming that "subterfuge" is a state-of-mind concept, may not "cost justification" play a role in determining whether the employer's intent was to discriminate against older workers? What was PERS' reason for the discrimination challenged by June Betts?

6. Did the majority deal adequately with the argument that the Act's description of the kinds of benefit plans included within the exemption — "such as a retirement, pension, or insurance plan" — implicitly adopted a cost-justification component? It is true that a common kind of benefit plan — the defined contribution plan — does not have increased costs associated with age. But if an employer contributed less for older workers, perhaps that would show subterfuge — indicating an intent to discriminate. In short, maybe the two arguments — cost justification and kind of plan — work together.

7. Perceiving a fundamental conflict between a literal reading of the statute's prohibition of age discrimination in compensation and §623(f), the Court brought the two provisions into harmony by basically immunizing benefit plan discrimination. While recognizing that "this construction of the words of the statute is not the only plausible one," the Court felt it necessary since "the alternative interpretation would eviscerate" §623(f). In order to avoid eviscerating that section, did the Court choose to eviscerate the statu-

9. The Age Discrimination in Employment Act

tory prohibition of age discrimination in compensation? Is this an appropriate construction of a remedial statute?

8. Who has the better of the legislative history argument, the majority or the dissent?

9. What about the dissent's claim that the majority's interpretation "has the perverse consequence of denying the §4(f)(2) exemption only to subtle acts of discrimination effected through a strategem or other artifice of discrimination, while leaving it intact for those age-based distinctions . . . which, though arbitrary, are *so* brazenly discriminatory in disentitling older workers to benefits that they cannot possibly warrant the 'subterfuge' characterization"?

10. Oddly enough, neither the majority nor the dissent focused on the 1986 amendment to the ADEA by which Congress prohibited employers from discriminating against older workers by wholly excluding them from further participation in retirement plans after they reached "normal retirement age" under ERISA (typically, 65). Effective January 1, 1988, it was unlawful "to establish or maintain an employee pension benefit plan which requires or permits" any age-based reduction in employee benefit accrual (for defined benefit plans) or any age-based reduction in allocations to the employer's account (for defined contribution plans). Omnibus Budget Reconciliation Act of 1986, P.L. 99-509, *amending* 29 U.S.C.A. §623, section 4, of the ADEA by adding a new paragraph (i). Does that amendment bear on the original meaning of §623(f)? If so, which way?

11. Putting *Betts* together with the amendment, is the rule now that age discriminations in fringe benefit plans are permissible unless they result in a defined reduction in a pension plan or are a pretext for non-benefit plan discrimination?

12. Unless Congress alters the *Betts* result, it will be critical to the application of the decision to decide what falls within the §623(f) exemption. Obviously, one must distinguish between "benefits" and other aspects of employment, such as compensation. Although the term "fringe benefit" is not one of art, clearly Congress was concerned with plans "such as a retirement, pension, or insurance plan" rather than employer systems dealing with base compensation or other privileges of employment. The *Betts* majority recognized this distinction by using as one illustration of a "subterfuge" the possibility that an employer would underpay both older and younger workers in basic compensation while compensating younger workers (but not older ones) with enhanced benefits. This would be "compensation" discrimination, and so actionable.

13. If an employer "froze" salaries for all workers while simultaneously increasing "benefits" for younger workers, how would one decide whether this was illegal compensation discrimination or legal benefit plan discrimination? Would the only test be whether the employer's plan had the purpose (or effect?) of driving older workers out of the company?

14. On remand in *Betts*, the Sixth Circuit surprisingly held that Ms. Betts had been the victim of illegal age discrimination. Betts v. Hamilton County Board of Mental Retardation, 897 F.2d 1380 (6th Cir. 1990). The majority reasoned that, when the plaintiff became disabled, she was offered two choices under the Ohio scheme: an unpaid medical leave or length of service retirement. Had she been under 60 years old, she would have been offered a third choice — disability benefits with the option of returning to work should she recover. The court viewed the unpaid leave alternative as essentially forcing Betts to elect retirement, a choice she would not have been compelled to make had she been younger than 60 because she would then have been able to receive some compensation during her disability. The dissenting judge thought the majority incorrectly viewed Ms. Betts as being forced to retire. Whom do you agree with? What is the remedy Betts obtains under the majority's view?

15. Does "plan" mean anything? Prior to *Betts*, a one-time ad hoc arrangement was held not the kind of on-going plan that Congress intended as a plan. EEOC v. Bordens, Inc., 724 F.2d 1390 (9th Cir. 1984). See also Fort Halifax Packing Co. v. Coyne, 482 U.S. 1 (1987) (one time benefit payment not an employee benefit plan under ERISA).

16. Presumably, denials of benefits must also be "pursuant to" a plan to be immunized. Prior to *Betts*, courts rejected attempted defenses when the benefits in question were denied wholly apart from the plan, Alford v. City of Lubbock, 664 F.2d 1263 (5th Cir. 1982) (denying sick leave to employees not covered by the retirement plan was not part of the plan); EEOC v. County of Santa Barbara, 666 F.2d 373 (9th Cir. 1982).

17. In *Betts*, there was no dispute that the plan was bona fide in that it existed and paid benefits. Is that the extent of the concept of bona fide?

18. Consider the impact of *Betts* on a case decided before it was handed down in Karlen v. City Colleges of Chicago, 837 F.2d 314 (7th Cir.), *cert. denied*, 486 U.S. 1044 (1988), the plan at issue permitted persons taking early retirement before age 64 to continue group insurance coverage until age 70, a benefit denied those retiring after 65. The *Karlen* court was not concerned about the mere fact of age-based disparities within the protected group per se, but was concerned that the plan treated older workers within the protected group worse than younger ones. Using a cost-based model, the *Karlen* opinion concluded that there was a jury question about whether the reduction of benefits was sufficiently linked to increased costs not to constitute a "subterfuge."

This analysis presumably does not survive *Betts*. But the *Karlen* court's interest went beyond cost factors. It noted the college's historic commitment to a mandatory retirement at 65 by resisting a state law which (prior to ADEA amendments lifting the upper age limit) would have invalidated its mandatory retirement policy. The court also noted the employer's "defense" of its plan as a means of inducing early retirement of those over 65:

9. The Age Discrimination in Employment Act

> This strikes us as a damaging admission rather than a powerful defense. To withhold benefits from older persons in order to induce them to retire seems precisely the form of discrimination at which the Age Discrimination in Employment Act is aimed. Rather than offering a carrot to all workers 55 or older as in the *Henn* case, the City Colleges are offering the whole carrot to workers 55 to 64 and taking back half for workers 65 to 69. The reason is that the Colleges want to induce workers to retire by 65. In effect they have two retirement plans; a munificent one for workers 55 to 64 and a chintzy one for workers 65 to 69. [Id. at 320.]

In the post-*Betts* era, if the employer's motive in reducing benefits is to induce older workers to leave, presumably the plan is not within §623(f). That may in fact permit disfavored employees to obtain the benefits provided the favored workers.

19. Does this analysis suggest that employers' most serious benefit plan problem will arise with respect to early retirement programs? While such plans provide a benefit to eligible workers, they may be structured to suggest a goal of removing older workers. Such plans may nevertheless be legal either if eligibility rules do not discriminate on the basis of age or if such plans are truly a carrot and not a stick.

7. *Temporary Exception for Police and Firefighters*

Page 854. Add at end of first full paragraph:

See EEOC v. Commonwealth of Massachusetts, 864 F.2d 933 (1st Cir. 1988) (Motor Vehicle "examiners" in Massachusetts were "law enforcement officers" in light of their authority to carry deadly weapons, their training, and the duties of at least large numbers of examiners).

F. ENFORCEMENT PROCEDURES FOR ADEA RIGHTS

1. *Private Suit*

Page 866. Add after "NOTE":

While *Oscar Mayer* had held that a timely state filing was not necessary for purposes of the ADEA, in EEOC v. Commercial Office Products Co., 486

U.S. 107 (1988), the Court held that that a timely state filing was also unnecessary under Title VII, thus definitively bringing that statute into line with the ADEA. More significantly for present purposes, *Commercial Office Products* also held that the 300-day period for filing with the EEOC in deferral states controls in Title VII suits regardless of whether there has been a filing with the state agency that is timely under state law. This, coupled with the Court's tendency to align its ADEA decisions with Title VII authority, strongly suggests that a timely state filing is unnecessary for application of the 300-day period under the ADEA. See also McKelvy v. Metal Container Corp., 854 F.2d 448 (11th Cir. 1988).

Page 867. In tenth line, delete from "See generally" to end of paragraph and replace with the following:

In Hoffman-La Roche, Inc. v. Sperling, 110 S. Ct. 482 (1989), a majority of the Court held that a district court may "authorize and facilitate notice of the pending action," thus resolving a conflict among the circuits. In 1985, the employer reduced its work force, discharging or demoting 1,200 workers. Plaintiff Sperling filed an age discrimination charge with the EEOC for himself and all employees similarly situated. He and other employees formed a group known as Roche Age Discriminatees Asking Redress (R.A.D.A.R.) which mailed a letter to some 600 employees inviting them to join the suit by completing an enclosed consent form. Over 400 consents were received. After suit was filed, the plaintiffs sought discovery of the names and addresses of all similarly situated employees, and successfully requested the court to send notice to all potential plaintiffs who had not yet filed consent. Defendant resisted both the discovery and the court notices, and objected to the R.A.D.A.R. letter.

The Supreme Court held that "district courts have discretion, in appropriate cases, to implement 29 U.S.C. §216(b) in ADEA actions by facilitating notice to potential plaintiffs." Id. at 486. Although not addressing the terms of the notice used in the case before it, the majority upheld discovery of names and addresses of class members because the ADEA, through incorporation of §216(b), expressly authorizes collective age discrimination actions. Therefore, the Court reasoned, Congress intended to accord age discrimination plaintiffs "the advantage of lower individual costs to vindicate rights by the pooling of resources," and make suits more efficient by combining them in one action. Since these advantages depend on employees "receiving accurate and timely notice concerning the pendency of the collective action," the district court necessarily is granted authority "to manage the process of joining multiple parties in a manner that is orderly, sensible, and not otherwise

9. The Age Discrimination in Employment Act   Page 870

contrary to statutory commands or the provisions of the Federal Rules of Civil Procedure." Id. Court management also can avoid potential misuse of the class device, as by misleading communications. The Court cautioned, however, that

> In exercising the discretionary authority to oversee the notice-giving process, courts must be scrupulous to respect judicial neutrality. To that end, trial courts must take care to avoid even the appearance of judicial endorsement of the merits of the action.

Id. at 488.

Justice Scalia wrote a dissent, joined by the Chief Justice, which found "no source of authority for such an extraordinary exercise of the federal judicial power." Id. His central theme was that the broad judicial authority to "manage" cases is limited to the judge's authority to adjudicate them, and therefore did not reach cases which had not yet been filed—the claims of individuals not yet parties to the action. See generally Note, Sending Notice to Potential Plaintiffs in Class Actions Under the Age Discrimination in Employment Act: The Trial Court's Role, 54 Fordham L. Rev. 631 (1986). See also Lusardi v. Lechner, 855 F.2d 1062 (3d Cir. 1988).

4. Federal Employee Suits Under the ADEA

Page 869. Add at end of page:

This, of course, raises the question of what conduct constitutes an irrevocable election of remedies. The courts have generally held that filing an administrative complaint triggers the administrative remedies branch, Bornholdt v. Brady, 869 F.2d 57 (2d Cir. 1989); Rivera v. United States Postal Service, 830 F.2d 1037 (9th Cir. 1987), *cert. denied*, 108 U.S. 1737 (1988); Castro v. United States, 775 F.2d 399 (1st Cir. 1985); contra, Langford v. U.S. Army Corps of Engineers, 839 F.2d 1192 (6th Cir. 1988), but that resort to informal precomplaint counselling is not sufficient to be an election of administrative remedies. Proud v. United States, 872 F.2d 1066 (D.C. Cir. 1989).

Page 870. Add after "See" signal in the first paragraph:

Bornholdt v. Brady, 869 F.2d 57 (2d Cir. 1989) (6th Cir. 1988);

Page 875   9. The Age Discrimination in Employment Act

G. REMEDIES

Page 875. Add the following at the end of Note 5:

However, despite the legislative history and contrary case authority, the EEOC has recently amended its procedural regulations to provide that §7(e)(2) is also applicable to private suits. 54 Fed. Reg. §33,501 (1989) (*to be codified at* 29 C.F.R. §1626.15(b)).

Page 881. Add the following at the end of Note 2:

Several later appellate decisions have concluded that the judge decides whether damages in lieu of reinstatement should be awarded, but the jury decides the amount of such an award. E.g., Hansard v. Pepsi-Cola Metropolitan Bottling Co., 865 F.2d 1461 (5th Cir.), *cert. denied*, 110 S. Ct. 129 (1989); Fite v. First Tenn. Prod. Credit Assn., 861 F.2d 884 (6th Cir. 1988).

Page 886. Add the following at the end of Note 4:

In Williamson v. Handy Button Machine Co., 817 F.2d 1290 (7th Cir. 1987), the court held that interest cannot be recovered on sums constituting lost future wages and pensions.

Chapter 10

Reconstruction-Era Civil Rights Legislation

B. SECTION 1981

2. The Meaning of Discrimination Under Section 1981

Page 915. Add the following at the end of the page:

PATTERSON v. MCLEAN CREDIT UNION
109 S. Ct. 2363 (1989)

Justice KENNEDY delivered the opinion of the Court. . . .

I

Petitioner Brenda Patterson, a black woman, was employed by respondent McLean Credit Union as a teller and a file coordinator, commencing in May 1972. In July 1982, she was laid off. After the termination, petitioner commenced this action in District Court. She alleged that respondent, in violation of 42 U.S.C. §1981, had harassed her, failed to promote her to an intermediate accounting clerk position, and then discharged her, all because of her race. . . .

We granted certiorari to decide whether petitioner's claim of racial harassment in her employment is actionable under §1981, and whether the jury instruction given by the District Court on petitioner's §1981 promotion claim was error. After oral argument on these issues, we requested the parties to brief and argue an additional question:

> Whether or not the interpretation of 42 U.S.C. §1981 adopted by this Court in Runyon v. McCrary, 427 U.S. 160 (1976), should be reconsidered.

We now decline to overrule our decision in Runyon v. McCrary. We hold further that racial harassment relating to the conditions of employment is not actionable under §1981 because that provision does not apply to conduct which occurs after the formation of a contract and which does not interfere with the right to enforce established contract obligations. Finally, we hold that the District Court erred in instructing the jury regarding petitioner's burden in proving her discriminatory promotion claim.

II

In *Runyon*, the Court considered whether §1981 prohibits private schools from excluding children who are qualified for admission, solely on the basis of race. We held that §1981 did prohibit such conduct, noting that it was already well established in prior decisions that §1981 "prohibits racial discrimination in the making and enforcement of private contracts." [C]iting Johnson v. Railway Express Agency, Inc., 421 U.S. 454, 459-460 (1975); Tillman v. Wheaton-Haven Recreation Assn., Inc., 410 U.S. 431, 439-440 (1973). The arguments about whether *Runyon* was decided correctly in light of the language and history of the statute were examined and discussed with great care in our decision. It was recognized at the time that a strong case could be made for the view that the statute does not reach private conduct, but that view did not prevail. Some Members of the Court believe that *Runyon* was decided incorrectly, and others consider it correct on its own footing, but the question before us is whether it ought now to be overturned. We conclude after reargument that *Runyon* should not be overruled, and we now reaffirm that §1981 prohibits racial discrimination in the making and enforcement of private contracts.

[The Court's discussion of stare decisis is omitted]

III

Our conclusion that we should adhere to our decision in *Runyon* that §1981 applies to private conduct is not enough to decide this case. We must decide also whether the conduct of which petitioner complains falls within one of the enumerated rights protected by §1981.

A

Section 1981 reads as follows:

> All persons within the jurisdiction of the United States shall have the same right in every State and Territory to make and enforce contracts, to sue, be parties, give evidence, and to the full and equal benefit of all laws and proceedings for the security of persons and property as is enjoyed by white citizens, and shall be subject to like punishment, pains, penalties, taxes, licenses, and exactions of every kind, and to no other. Rev. Stat. §1977.

The most obvious feature of the provision is the restriction of its scope to forbidding discrimination in the "mak[ing] and enforce[ment]" of contracts alone. Where an alleged act of discrimination does not involve the impairment of one of these specific rights, §1981 provides no relief. Section 1981 cannot be construed as a general proscription of racial discrimination in all aspects of contract relations, for it expressly prohibits discrimination only in the making and enforcement of contracts. . . .

By its plain terms, the relevant provision in §1981 protects two rights: "the same right . . . to make . . . contracts" and "the same right . . . to . . . enforce contracts." The first of these protections extends only to the formation of a contract, but not to problems that may arise later from the conditions of continuing employment. The statute prohibits, when based on race, the refusal to enter into a contract with someone, as well as the offer to make a contract only on discriminatory terms. But the right to make contracts does not extend, as a matter of either logic or semantics, to conduct by the employer after the contract relation has been established, including breach of the terms of the contract or imposition of discriminatory working conditions. Such postformation conduct does not involve the right to make a contract, but rather implicates the performance of established contract obligations and the conditions of continuing employment, matters more naturally governed by state contract law and Title VII.

The second of these guarantees, "the same right . . . to . . . enforce contracts . . . as is enjoyed by white citizens," embraces protection of a legal process, and of a right of access to legal process, that will address and resolve contract-law claims without regard to race. In this respect, it prohibits discrimination that infects the legal process in ways that prevent one from enforcing contract rights, by reason of his or her race, and this is so whether this discrimination is attributed to a statute or simply to existing practices. It also covers wholly private efforts to impede access to the courts or obstruct nonjudicial methods of adjudicating disputes about the force of binding obligations, as well as discrimination by private entities, such as labor unions, in enforcing the terms of a contract. Following this principle and consistent with our holding in *Runyon* that §1981 applies to private conduct, we have held that certain private entities such as labor unions, which bear explicit responsibilities to process grievances, press claims, and represent members in disputes over the terms of binding obligations that run from the employer to the employee, are subject to liability under §1981 for racial discrimination in the enforcement of labor contracts. See Goodman v. Lukens Steel Co. The right to enforce contracts does not, however, extend beyond conduct by an employer which impairs an employee's ability to enforce through legal process his or her established contract rights. As Justice WHITE put it with much force in *Runyon*, one cannot seriously "contend that the grant of the other rights enumerated in §1981 [that is, other than the right to "make" contracts,] *i.e.*, the rights 'to sue, be parties, give evidence,' and '*enforce* contracts' accomplishes anything other than the removal of *legal* disabilities to sue, be a party, testify or enforce a contract. Indeed, it is impossible to give such language any other meaning." (dissenting opinion) (emphasis in original).

B

Applying these principles to the case before us, we agree with the Court of Appeals that petitioner's racial harassment claim is not actionable under §1981. Petitioner has alleged that during her employment with respondent, she was subjected to various forms of racial harassment from her supervisor. As summarized by the Court of Appeals, petitioner testified that "[her supervisor] periodically stared at her for several minutes at a time; that he gave her too many tasks, causing her to complain that she was under too much pressure; that among the tasks given her were sweeping and dusting, jobs not given to white employees. On one occasion, she testified, [her supervisor] told [her] that blacks are known to work slower than whites. According to [petitioner, her supervisor] also criticized her in staff meetings while not similarly criticizing white employees."

Petitioner also alleges that she was passed over for promotion, not offered training for higher level jobs, and denied wage increases, all because of her race.[2] With the exception perhaps of her claim that respondent refused to

---

2. In addition, another of respondent's managers testified that when he recommended a different black person for a position as a data processor, petitioner's supervisor stated that he did not "need any more problems around here," and that he would "search for additional people who are not black."

10. Reconstruction-Era Civil Rights Legislation Page 915

promote her to a position as an accountant, none of the conduct which petitioner alleges as part of the racial harassment against her involves either a refusal to make a contract with her or the impairment of her ability to enforce her established contract rights. Rather, the conduct which petitioner labels as actionable racial harassment is postformation conduct by the employer relating to the terms and conditions of continuing employment.

This is apparent from petitioner's own proposed jury instruction on her §1981 racial harassment claim. . . . Without passing on the contents of this instruction, it is plain to us that what petitioner is attacking are the conditions of her employment. This type of conduct, reprehensible though it be if true, is not actionable under §1981, which covers only conduct at the initial formation of the contract and conduct which impairs the right to enforce contract obligations through legal process. Rather, such conduct is actionable under the more expansive reach of Title VII of the Civil Rights Act of 1964. . . . Racial harassment in the course of employment is actionable under Title VII's prohibition against discrimination in the "terms, conditions, or privileges of employment." . . . While this Court has not yet had the opportunity to pass directly upon this [question], the lower federal courts have uniformly upheld this view,[3] and we implicitly have approved it in a recent decision concerning sexual harassment, Meritor Savings Bank v. Vinson. As we said in that case, "harassment [which is] sufficiently severe or pervasive 'to alter the conditions of [the victim's] employment and create an abusive working environment,' " is actionable under Title VII because it "affects a 'term, condition, or privilege' of employment."

Interpreting §1981 to cover postformation conduct unrelated to an employee's right to enforce her contract, such as incidents relating to the conditions of employment, is not only inconsistent with that statute's limitation to the making and enforcement of contracts, but would also undermine the detailed and well-crafted procedures for conciliation and resolution of Title VII claims. In Title VII, Congress set up an elaborate administrative procedure, implemented through the EEOC, that is designed to assist in the investigation of claims of racial discrimination in the workplace and to work towards the resolution of these claims through conciliation rather than litigation. Only after these procedures have been exhausted, and the plaintiff has obtained a "right to sue" letter from the EEOC, may she bring a Title VII action in court. Section 1981, by contrast, provides no administrative review or opportunity for conciliation.

Where conduct is covered by both §1981 and Title VII, the detailed procedures of Title VII are rendered a dead letter, as the plaintiff is free to

---

3. See, e.g., Firefighters Institute for Racial Equality v. St. Louis, 549 F.2d 506, 514-515 (CA8), *cert. denied sub nom.* Banta v. United States, 434 U.S. 819 (1977); Rogers v. EEOC, 454 F.2d 234 (CA5 1971), *cert. denied,* 406 U.S. 957 (1972).

pursue a claim by bringing suit under §1981 without resort to those statutory prerequisites. We agree that, after *Runyon,* there is some necessary overlap between Title VII and §1981, and that where the statutes do in fact overlap we are not at liberty "to infer any positive preference for one over the other." Johnson v. Railway Express Agency, Inc. We should be reluctant, however, to read an earlier statute broadly where the result is to circumvent the detailed remedial scheme constructed in a later statute. See United States v. Fausto, 484 U.S. 439 (1988). The egregious racial harassment of employees is forbidden by a clearly applicable law (Title VII), moreover, should lessen the temptation for this Court to twist the interpretation of another statute (§1981) to cover the same conduct. . . .

By reading §1981 not as a general proscription of racial discrimination in all aspects of contract relations, but as limited to the enumerated rights within its express protection, specifically the right to make and enforce contracts, we may preserve the integrity of Title VII's procedures without sacrificing any significant coverage of the civil rights laws.[4] Of course, some overlap will remain between the two statutes: specifically, a refusal to enter into an employment contract on the basis of race. Such a claim would be actionable under Title VII as a "refus[al] to hire" based on race, 42 U.S.C. §2000e-2(a), and under §1981 as an impairment of "the same right . . . to make . . . contracts . . . as . . . white citizens," 42 U.S.C. §1981. But this is precisely where it would make sense for Congress to provide for the overlap. At this stage of the employee-employer relation Title VII's mediation and conciliation procedures would be of minimal effect, for there is not yet a relation to salvage.

c

The Solicitor General and Justice Brennan offer two alternative interpretations of §1981. The Solicitor General argues that the language of §1981, especially the words "the same right," requires us to look outside §1981 to the terms of particular contracts and to state law for the obligations and covenants to be protected by the federal statute. Under this view, §1981 has no actual substantive content, but instead mirrors only the specific protections that are afforded under the law of contracts of each State. Under this view, racial harassment in the conditions of employment is actionable when, and only

---

4. Unnecessary overlap between Title VII and §1981 would also serve to upset the delicate balance between employee and employer rights struck by Title VII in other respects. For instance, a plaintiff in a Title VII action is limited to a recovery of backpay, whereas under §1981 a plaintiff may be entitled to plenary compensatory damages, as well as punitive damages in an appropriate case. Both the employee and employer will be unlikely to agree to a conciliatory resolution of the dispute under Title VII if the employer can be found liable for much greater amounts under §1981.

when, it amounts to a breach of contract under state law. We disagree. For one thing, to the extent that it assumes that prohibitions contained in §1981 incorporate only those protections afforded by the States, this theory is directly inconsistent with *Runyon*, which we today decline to overrule. A more fundamental failing in the Solicitor's argument is that racial harassment amounting to breach of contract, like racial harassment alone, impairs neither the right to make nor the right to enforce a contract. It is plain that the former right is not implicated directly by an employer's breach in the performance of obligations under a contract already formed. Nor is it correct to say that racial harassment amounting to a breach of contract impairs an employee's right to enforce his contract. To the contrary, conduct amounting to a breach of contract under state law is precisely what the language of §1981 does not cover. That is because, in such a case, provided that plaintiff's access to state court or any other dispute resolution process has not been impaired by either the State or a private actor, see Goodman v. Lukens Steel Co., the plaintiff is free to enforce the terms of the contract in state court, and cannot possibly assert, by reason of the breach alone, that he has been deprived of the same right to enforce contracts as is enjoyed by white citizens.

In addition, interpreting §1981 to cover racial harassment amounting to a breach of contract would federalize all state-law claims for breach of contract where racial animus is alleged, since §1981 covers all types of contracts, not just employment contracts. Although we must do so when Congress plainly directs, as a rule we should be and are "reluctant to federalize" matters traditionally covered by state common law. Santa Fe Industries, Inc. v. Green, 430 U.S. 462, 479 (1977); see also Sedima S.P.R.L. v. Imrex Co., 473 U.S. 479, 507 (1985) (Marshall, J., dissenting). By confining §1981 to the impairment of the specific rights to make and enforce contracts, Congress cannot be said to have intended such a result with respect to breach of contract claims. It would be no small paradox, moreover, that under the interpretation of §1981 offered by the Solicitor General, the more a State extends its own contract law to protect employees in general and minorities in particular, the greater would be the potential displacement of state law by §1981. We do not think §1981 need be read to produce such a peculiar result.

Justice Brennan, for his part, would hold that racial harassment is actionable under §1981 when "the acts constituting harassment [are] sufficiently severe or pervasive as effectively to belie any claim that the contract was entered into in a racially neutral manner." We do not find this standard an accurate or useful articulation of which contract claims are actionable under §1981 and which are not. The fact that racial harassment is "severe or pervasive" does not by magic transform a challenge to the conditions of employment, not actionable under §1981, into a viable challenge to the employer's refusal to make a contract. We agree that racial harassment may be used as evidence that a divergence in the explicit terms of particular contracts is explained by racial animus. Thus, for example, if a potential employee is offered (and accepts) a contract to do a job for less money than others doing like work, evidence of racial harassment in the workplace may show that the employer, at the time of formation, was unwilling to enter into a nondiscriminatory contract. However, and this is the critical point, the question under §1981 remains whether the employer, at the time of the formation of the contract, in fact intentionally refused to enter into a contract with the employee on racially neutral terms. The plaintiff's ability to plead that the racial harassment is "severe or pervasive" should not allow him to bootstrap a challenge to the conditions of employment (actionable, if at all, under Title VII) into a claim under §1981 that the employer refused to offer the petitioner the "same right to . . . make" a contract. We think it clear that the conduct challenged by petitioner relates not to her employer's refusal to enter into a contract with her, but rather to the conditions of her employment.

IV

Petitioner's claim that respondent violated §1981 by failing to promote her, because of race, to a position as an intermediate accounting clerk is a different matter. [T]he question whether a promotion claim is actionable under §1981 depends upon whether the nature of the change in position was such that it involved the opportunity to enter into a new contract with the employer. If so, then the employer's refusal to enter the new contract is actionable under §1981. In making this determination, a lower court should give a fair and natural reading to the statutory phrase "the same right . . . to make . . . contracts," and should not strain in an undue manner the language of §1981. Only where the promotion rises to the level of an opportunity for a new and distinct relation between the employee and the employer is such a claim actionable under §1981. Cf. Hishon v. King & Spaulding (refusal of law firm to accept associate into partnership) (Title VII). Because respondent has not argued at any stage that petitioner's promotion claim is not cognizable under §1981, we need not address the issue further here.

This brings us to the question of the District Court's jury instructions on petitioner's promotion claim. We think the District Court erred when it instructed the jury that petitioner had to prove that she was better qualified than the white employee who allegedly received the promotion. In order to prevail under §1981, a plaintiff must prove purposeful discrimination. General Building Contractors Assn., Inc. v. Pennsylvania. We have developed, in analogous areas of civil rights law, a carefully designed framework of proof to determine, in the context of disparate treatment, the ultimate issue of whether the defendant intentionally discriminated against the plaintiff. See Texas Dept. of Community Affairs v. Burdine; McDonnell Douglas Corp. v.

Green. We agree with the Court of Appeals that this scheme of proof, structured as a "sensible, orderly way to evaluate the evidence in light of common experience as it bears on the critical question of discrimination," should apply to claims of racial discrimination under §1981.

Although the Court of Appeals recognized that the *McDonnell Douglas/Burdine* scheme of proof should apply in §1981 cases such as this one, it erred in describing petitioner's burden. Under our well-established framework, the plaintiff has the initial burden of proving, by the preponderance of the evidence, a prima facie case of discrimination. *Burdine.* The burden is not onerous. Here, petitioner need only prove by a preponderance of the evidence that she applied for and was qualified for an available position, that she was rejected, and that after she was rejected respondent either continued to seek applicants for the position, or, as is alleged here, filled the position with a white employee. See id; *McDonnell Douglas.*

Once the plaintiff establishes a prima facie case, an inference of discrimination arises. See *Burdine.* In order to rebut this inference, the employer must present evidence that the plaintiff was rejected, or the other applicant was chosen, for a legitimate nondiscriminatory reason. Here, respondent presented evidence that it gave the job to the white applicant because she was better qualified for the position, and therefore rebutted any presumption of discrimination that petitioner may have established. At this point, as our prior cases make clear, petitioner retains the final burden of persuading the jury of intentional discrimination.

Although petitioner retains the ultimate burden of persuasion, our cases make clear that she must also have the opportunity to demonstrate that respondent's proffered reasons for its decision were not its true reasons. In doing so, petitioner is not limited to presenting evidence of a certain type. This is where the District Court erred. The evidence which petitioner can present in an attempt to establish that respondent's stated reasons are pretextual may take a variety of forms. Indeed, she might seek to demonstrate that respondent's claim to have promoted a better-qualified applicant was pretextual by showing that she was in fact better qualified than the person chosen for the position. The District Court erred, however, in instructing the jury that in order to succeed petitioner was required to make such a showing. There are certainly other ways in which petitioner could seek to prove that respondent's reasons were pretextual. Thus, for example, petitioner could seek to persuade the jury that respondent had not offered the true reason for its promotion decision by presenting evidence of respondent's past treatment of petitioner, including the instances of the racial harassment which she alleges and respondent's failure to train her for an accounting position. While we do not intend to say this evidence necessarily would be sufficient to carry the day, it cannot be denied that it is one of the various ways in which petitioner might seek to prove intentional discrimination on the part of respondent. She may not be forced to pursue any particular means of demonstrating that respondent's stated reasons are pretextual. It was, therefore, error for the District Court to instruct the jury that petitioner could carry her burden of persuasion only by showing that she was in fact better qualified than the white applicant who got the job. . . .

Justice BRENNAN, with whom Justice MARSHALL and Justice BLACKMUN join, and with whom Justice STEVENS joins as to Parts II-B, II-C, and III, concurring in the judgment in part and dissenting in part.

What the Court declines to snatch away with one hand, it takes with the other. Though the Court today reaffirms §1981's applicability to private conduct, it simultaneously gives this landmark civil rights statute a needlessly cramped interpretation. The Court has to strain hard to justify this choice to confine §1981 within the narrowest possible scope, selecting the most pinched reading of the phrase "same right to make a contract," ignoring powerful historical evidence about the Reconstruction Congress' concerns, and bolstering its parsimonious rendering by reference to a statute enacted nearly a century after §1981, and plainly not intended to affect its reach. When it comes to deciding whether a civil rights statute should be construed to further our Nation's commitment to the eradication of racial discrimination, the Court adopts a formalistic method of interpretation antithetical to Congress' vision of a society in which contractual opportunities are equal. I dissent from the Court's holding that §1981 does not encompass Patterson's racial harassment claim.

I

[The opinion faults the Court for even questioning the proposition that §1981 reaches private contracts, and then contends that the best reasons for reaffirming the prior precedents were not stare decisis but "that *Runyon* was correctly decided, and that in any event Congress has ratified our construction of the statute." Justice Brennan noted congressional refusal to overrule *Runyon*, but viewed as more important (1) Congress' 1972 rejection of an amendement to Title VII "that would have rendered §1981 unavailable in most cases as a remedy for private employment discrimination," and (2) its 1976 enactment of a statute providing for attorney's fees in §1981 actions with full knowledge that the Court had interpreted §1981 to reach private discrimination.]

II

I turn now to the two issues on which certiorari was originally requested and granted in this case. The first of these is whether a plaintiff may state a cause of action under §1981 based upon allegations that her employer harassed her because of her race. In my view, she may. The Court reaches a contrary conclusion by conducting an ahistorical analysis that ignores the circumstances and legislative history of §1981. The Court reasons that Title VII or modern state contract law "more naturally gover[n]" harassment actions—nowhere acknowledging the anachronism attendant upon the implication that the Reconstruction Congress would have viewed state law, or a federal civil rights statute passed nearly a century later, as the primary bases for challenging private discrimination.

A

The legislative history of §1981—to which the Court does not advert—makes clear that we must not take an overly narrow view of what it means to have the "same right . . . to make and enforce contracts" as white citizens. The very same legislative history that supports our interpretation of §1981 in *Runyon* also demonstrates that the 39th Congress intended, in the employment context, to go beyond protecting the freedmen from refusals to contract for their labor and from discriminatory decisions to discharge them. Section 1 of the Civil Rights Act was also designed to protect the freedmen from the imposition of working conditions that evidence an intent on the part of the employer not to contract on nondiscriminatory terms.* Congress realized that, in the former Confederate States, employers were attempting to "adher[e], as to the *treatment of the laborers*, as much as possible to the traditions of the old system, *even where the relations between employers and laborers had been fixed by contract*." Report of C. Schurz, S. Exec. Doc. No. 2, 39th Cong., 1st Sess., p.19 (1865) (emphasis added). These working conditions included the use of the whip as an incentive to work harder—the common-

---

*[Dissent's Note 4.] Report of C. Schurz, S. Exec. Doc. No. 2, 39th Cong., 1st Sess. (1865). The Schurz report is replete with descriptions of private discrimination, relating both to the freedmen's ability to enter into contracts, and to their treatment once under contract. It notes, for example, that some planters had initially endeavored to maintain "the relation of master and slave, partly by concealing from [their slaves] the great changes that had taken place, and partly by terrorizing them into submission to their behests." It portrays as commonplace the use of "force and intimidation" to keep former slaves on the plantations: "In many instances negroes who walked away from the plantations, or were found upon the roads, were shot or otherwise severely punished, which was calculated to produce the impression among those remaining with their masters that an attempt to escape from slavery would result in certain destruction."
. . . It must therefore have been evident to members of the 39th Congress that, quite apart from the Black Codes, the freedmen would not enjoy the same right as whites to contract or to own or lease property so long as private discrimination remained rampant. This broad view of the obstacles to the freedmen's enjoyment of contract and property rights was similarly expressed in the Howard Report on the operation of the Freedmen's Bureau, H.R. Exec. Doc. No. 11, 39th Cong., 1st Sess. (1865). It likewise appears in the hearings conducted by the Joint Committee on Reconstruction contemporaneously with Congress' consideration of the civil rights bill. See Report of the Joint Committee on Reconstruction, 39th Cong., 1st Sess., pts. I-IV (1866). . . .

place result of an entrenched attitude that "[y]ou cannot make the negro work without physical compulsion"—and the practice of handing out severe and unequal punishment for perceived transgressions. ("The habit [of corporal punishment] is so inveterate with a great many persons as to render, on the least provocation, the impulse to whip a negro almost irresistible.") Since such "acts of persecution" against employed freedmen, were one of the 39th Congress' concerns in enacting the Civil Rights Act, it is clear that in granting the freedmen the "same right . . . to make and enforce contracts" as white citizens, Congress meant to encompass post-contractual conduct.

B

The Court holds that §1981, insofar as it gives an equal right to make a contract, "covers only conduct at the initial formation of the contract." This narrow interpretation is not, as the Court would have us believe, the inevitable result of the statutory grant of an equal right "to make contracts." On the contrary, the language of §1981 is quite naturally read as extending to cover postformation conduct that demonstrates that the contract was not really made on equal terms at all. It is indeed clear that the statutory language of §1981 imposes some limit upon the type of harassment claims that are cognizable under §1981, for the statute's prohibition is against discrimination in the making and enforcement of contracts; but the Court mistakes the nature of that limit.[12] In my view, harassment is properly actionable under the language of §1981 . . . if it demonstrates that the employer has in fact imposed discriminatory terms and hence has not allowed blacks to make a contract on an equal basis.

The question in a case in which an employee makes a §1981 claim alleging racial harassment should be whether the acts constituting harassment were sufficiently severe or pervasive as effectively to belie any claim that the contract was entered into in a racially neutral manner. Where a black employee demonstrates that she has worked in conditions substantially different from those enjoyed by similarly situated white employees, and can show

---

12. The Court's overly narrow reading of the language of §1981 is difficult to square with our interpretation of the equal right protected by §1982 "to inherit, purchase, lease, sell, hold, and convey real and personal property" not just as covering the rights to acquire and dispose of property, but also the "right . . . to *use* property on an equal basis with white citizens," Memphis v. Greene, 451 U.S. 100, 120 (1981) (emphasis added), and "not to have property interests *impaired* because of . . . race," id. (emphasis added).

In Shaare Tefila Congregation v. Cobb, 481 U.S. 615 (1987), we reversed the dismissal of a claim by a Jewish congregation alleging that individuals were liable under §1982 for spraying racist graffiti on the walls of the congregation's synagogue. Though our holding in that case was limited to deciding that Jews are a group protected by §1982, our opinion nowhere hints that the congregation's vandalism claim might not be cognizable under the statute because it implicated the use of property, and not its acquisition or disposal.

the necessary racial animus, a jury may infer that the black employee has not been afforded the same right to make an employment contract as white employees. Obviously, as respondent conceded at oral argument, if an employer offers a black and a white applicant for employment the same written contract, but then tells the black employee that her working conditions will be much worse than those of the white hired for the same job because "there's a lot of harassment going on in this work place and you have to agree to that," it would have to be concluded that the white and black had not enjoyed an equal right to make a contract. I see no relevant distinction between that case and one in which the employer's different contractual expectations are unspoken, but become clear during the course of employment as the black employee is subjected to substantially harsher conditions than her white coworkers. In neither case can it be said that whites and blacks have had the same right to make an employment contract. The Court's failure to consider such examples, and to explain the abundance of legislative history that confounds its claim that §1981 unambiguously decrees the result it favors, underscore just how untenable is the Court's position.

Having reached its decision based upon a supposedly literal reading of §1981, the Court goes on to suggest that its grudging interpretation of this civil rights statute has the benefit of not undermining Title VII. It is unclear how the interpretation of §1981 to reach pervasive postcontractual harassment could be thought in any way to undermine Congress' intentions as regards Title VII. Congress has rejected an amendment to Title VII that would have rendered §1981 unavailable as a remedy for employment discrimination. . . . The Court's lengthy discussion of Title VII adds nothing to an understanding of [the question of what §1981, properly interpreted, means]. The Court's use of Title VII is not only question-begging; it is also misleading. Section 1981 is a statute of general application, extending not just to employment contracts, but to all contracts. . . . The Court, however, demonstrates no awareness at all that §1981 is so much broader in scope than Title VII. . . .

Even as regards their coverage of employment discrimination, §1981 and Title VII are quite different. Perhaps most important, §1981 is not limited in scope to employment discrimination by businesses with 15 or more employees, and hence may reach the nearly 15% of the workforce not covered by Title VII. See Eisenberg & Schwab, The Importance of Section 1981, 73 Cornell L. Rev. 596, 602 (1988). A §1981 backpay award may also extend beyond the two-year limit of Title VII. Moreover, a §1981 plaintiff is not limited to recovering backpay: she may also obtain damages, including punitive damages in an appropriate case. Other differences between the two statutes include the right to a jury trial under §1981, but not Title VII; a different statute of limitations in §1981 cases, and the availability under Title VII, but not §1981, of administrative machinery designed to provide assistance in investigation and conciliation. . . .

C

Applying the standards set forth above, I believe the evidence in this case brings petitioner's harassment claim firmly within the scope of §1981. Petitioner testified at trial that during her 10 years at McLean she was subjected to racial slurs; given more work than white employees and assigned the most demeaning tasks; passed over for promotion, not informed of promotion opportunities, and not offered training for higher-level jobs; denied wage increases routinely given other employees; and singled out for scrutiny and criticism. . . .

Despite petitioner's stated desire to "move up and advance" at McLean to an accounting or secretarial position, she testified that she was offered no training for a higher-level job during her entire tenure at the credit union. White employees were offered training, including a white employee at the same level as petitioner but with less seniority. That less senior white employee was eventually promoted to an intermediate accounting clerk position. As with every other promotion opportunity that occurred, petitioner was never informed of the opening. . . . Petitioner claimed to have received different treatment as to wage increases as well as promotion opportunities. Thus she testified that she had been denied a promised pay raise after her first six months at McLean, though white employees automatically received pay raises after six months.

Petitioner testified at length about allegedly unequal work assignments given by Stevenson and her other supervisors, and detailed the extent of her work assignments. When petitioner complained about her workload, she was given no help with it. In fact, she was given more work, and was told she always had the option of quitting. Petitioner claimed that she was also given more demeaning tasks than white employees, and was the only clerical worker who was required to dust and to sweep. . . .

Petitioner further claimed that Stevenson scrutinized her more closely and criticized her more severely than white employees. Stevenson, she testified, would repeatedly stare at her while she was working, although he would not do this to white employees. Stevenson also made a point of criticizing the work of white employees in private, or discussing their mistakes at staff meetings without attributing the error to a particular individual. But he would chastise petitioner and the only other black employee publicly at staff meetings.

The defense introduced evidence at trial contesting each of these assertions by petitioner. But given the extent and nature of the evidence produced by Patterson, and the importance of credibility determinations in assigning weight to that evidence, the jury may well have concluded that petitioner was subjected to such serious and extensive racial harassment as to have been denied the right to make an employment contract on the same basis as white employees of the credit union.

III

I agree that the District Court erred when it instructed the jury [that Patterson had to prove not only that she was denied a promotion because of her race, but also that she was better qualified than the white employee who had allegedly received the promotion.] . . .

I therefore agree that petitioner's promotion discrimination claim must be remanded because of the District Court's erroneous instruction as to petitioner's burden. It seems to me, however, that the Court of Appeals was correct when it said that promotion-discrimination claims are cognizable under §1981 because they "go to the very existence and nature of the employment contract." The Court's disagreement with this common-sense view, and its statement that "the question whether a promotion claim is actionable under §1981 depends upon whether the nature of the change in position was such that it involved the opportunity to enter into a new contract with the employer," display nicely how it seeks to eliminate with technicalities the protection §1981 was intended to afford—to limit protection to the form of the contract entered into, and not to extend it, as Congress intended, to the substance of the contract as it is worked out in practice. Under the Court's view, the employer may deny any number of promotions solely on the basis of race, safe from a §1981 suit, provided it is careful that promotions do not involve new contracts. It is admittedly difficult to see how a "promotion"— which would seem to imply different duties and employment terms—could be achieved without a new contract, and it may well be as a result that promotion claims will always be cognizable under §1981. Nevertheless, the same criticisms I have made of the Court's decision regarding harassment claims apply here: proof that an employee was not promoted because she is black—while all around white peers are advanced—shows that the black employee has in substance been denied the opportunity to contract on the equal terms that §1981 guarantees. . . .

Justice STEVENS, concurring in the judgment in part and dissenting in part.

. . . I agree, of course, that *Runyon* should not be overruled. I am also persuaded, however, that the meaning that had already been given to "the same right . . . to make and enforce contracts" that "is enjoyed by white citizens"— the statutory foundation that was preserved in *Runyon*—encompasses an employee's right to protection from racial harassment by her employer.

In *Runyon* we held that §1981 prohibits a private school from excluding qualified children because they are not white citizens. Just as a qualified nonwhite child has a statutory right to equal access to a private school, so does a nonwhite applicant for employment have a statutory right to enter into a personal service contract with a private employer on the same terms as a white citizen. If an employer should place special obstacles in the path of a black job applicant—perhaps by requiring her to confront an openly biased and hostile interviewer—the interference with the statutory right to make contracts to the same extent "as is enjoyed by white citizens" would be plain.

Similarly, if the white and the black applicants are offered the same terms of employment with just one exception—that the black employee would be required to work in dark, uncomfortable surroundings, whereas the white employee would be given a well-furnished, two-window office—the discrimination would be covered by the statute. In such a case, the Court would find discrimination in the making of the contract because the disparity surfaced before the contract was made. Under the Court's understanding of the statute, the black applicant might recover on one of two theories: She might demonstrate that the employer intended to discourage her from taking the job—which is the equivalent of a "refusal to enter into a contract"—or she might show that the employer actually intended to enter a contract, but "only on discriminatory terms." Under the second of these theories of recovery, however, it is difficult to discern why an employer who makes his intentions known has discriminated in the "making" of a contract, while the employer who conceals his discriminatory intent until after the applicant has accepted the job, only later to reveal that black employees are intentionally harassed and insulted, has not.

It is also difficult to discern why an employer who does not decide to treat black employees less favorably than white employees until after the contract of employment is first conceived is any less guilty of discriminating in the "making" of a contract. A contract is not just a piece of paper. Just as a single word is the skin of a living thought, so is a contract evidence of a vital, ongoing relationship between human beings. An at-will employee, such as petitioner, is not merely performing an existing contract; she is constantly remaking that contract. Whenever significant new duties are assigned to the employee—whether they better or worsen the relationship—the contract is amended and a new contract is made. Thus, if after the employment relationship is formed, the employer deliberately implements a policy of harassment of black employees, he has imposed a contractual term on them that is not the "same" as the contractual provisions that are "enjoyed by white citizens." Moreover, whether employed at-will or for a fixed term, employees typically strive to achieve a more rewarding relationship with their employers. By requiring black employees to work in a hostile environment, the employer has denied them the same opportunity for advancement that is available to white citizens. A deliberate policy of harassment of black employees who are competing with white citizens is, I submit, manifest discrimination in the making of contracts in the sense in which that concept was interpreted in Runyon v. McCrary. I cannot believe that the decision in that case would have been different if the school had agreed to allow the black students to attend, but subjected them to segregated classes and other racial abuse.

Indeed, in Goodman v. Lukens Steel Co., we built further on the foundation laid in *Runyon*. We decided that a union's "toleration and tacit encouragement of racial harassment" violates §1981. Although the Court now explains that the *Lukens* decision rested on the union's interference with its members' right to enforce their collective bargaining agreement, when I joined that opinion I thought—and I still think—that the holding rested comfortably on the foundation identified in *Runyon*. In fact, in the section of the *Lukens* opinion discussing the substantive claim, the Court did not once use the term "enforce" or otherwise refer to that particular language in the statute.

For the foregoing reasons, and for those stated in Parts II(B) and II(C) of Justice Brennan's opinion, I respectfully dissent from the conclusion reached in Part III of the Court's opinion. I also agree with Justice Brennan's discussion of the promotion claim.

NOTES

1. Ms. Patterson claimed not only that she was harassed during her employment but also that she was laid off because of her race. Is it possible that the decision to lay her off is not actionable under §1981? After all, the majority holds that §1981 "does not apply to conduct which occurs after the formation of a contract." Taken literally, has the majority read the statute to require employers to hire on day 1 but allow them to fire on day 2? Although some district courts held in the wake of *Patterson*, that §1981 did not apply to discharges, the first appellate decision held that racially discriminatory discharges remain actionable. Hicks v. Brown Group, Inc., 902 F.2d 635 (8th Cir. 1990).

2. What about the possibility that termination would be post-formation conduct which "interfere[s] with the right to enforce established contract obligations"? The majority says, "The right to enforce contracts does not, however, extend beyond conduct by an employer which impairs an employee's ability to enforce through legal process his or her established contract rights." Does that mean that a discharge is not actionable unless the employer also barred access to the courts? If so, what is the point of court access for an at will employee?

3. In an employment at will situation, perhaps termination can be viewed as a refusal to enter into a new contract of employment for that day as is made with white workers. But, if that is true, isn't Justice Stevens's dissent clearly correct about racial harassment also? Does the majority's discussion about whether a promotion constitutes "contract formation" assist you in answering these questions?

4. Would it be fair to say that the majority has upheld stare decisis in theory but effectively overruled *Runyon* by its constrained reading of §1981?

If so, what is the point of stare decisis in the first place? Wouldn't a straight overruling of *Runyon* have been more honest?

5. If the Court was bound by stare decisis, why did it begin its analysis of the case at hand with the text of the statute rather than with the decisions which had earlier construed it? For example, McDonald v. Santa Fe Trail Transportation Co., reprinted at p.895, applied §1981 to a *discharge* which was alleged to have been racially motivated.

4. The Relationship of Section 1981 and Title VII

Page 921. Add at end of second full paragraph:

This question was resolved in Owens v. Okure, 109 S. Ct. 573 (1989), which unanimously held that §1983 claims are governed by general personal injury statutes rather than by statutes applicable to intentional torts.

When the application of *Garcia, Goodman,* and *Okure* results in a change in the limitations period courts previously held controlling in particular jurisdictions, the question of retroactive application of the Supreme Court precedents arises. Such application could either lengthen or shorten the limitations period that had previously governed. *Goodman* itself retroactively applied the statute it held to be correct, although it mandated a case-by-case analysis. The Court addressed the question again in St. Francis College v. Al-Khazraji, 481 U.S. 604 (1987), approving the Third Circuit's refusal to apply a shortened statute of limitations to render untimely plaintiff's suit, which had been filed within the time previously held controlling in that circuit. There has been a tendency of the courts to use retroactive application to the benefit of plaintiffs. Thus, retroactivity has been invoked where the new rule provided a longer period of limitations, Rowlett v. Anheuser-Busch, 832 F.2d 194 (1st Cir. 1987); Larkin v. Pullman, Inc, Pullman-Standard Div., 854 F.2d 1549 (11th Cir. 1988); contra, Foster v. Board of School Comm. of Mobile Cty., Ala., 872 F.2d 1563 (11th Cir. 1989), and no retroactive application has been found where the new law shortened the period. Malhotra v. Cotter & Co., 885 F.2d 1305 (7th Cir. 1989).

D. SECTION 1983

Page 934. Add at end of third full paragraph:

In Will v. Michigan Department of State Police, 109 S. Ct. 2304 (1989), the Supreme Court effectively extended state immunity by precluding §1983 suits for damages in *state* court against the state government or against state officials acting in their official capacities. Such defendants were not "persons" within the meaning of the statute. Nor will §1981 assist plaintiffs since Jett v. Dallas Ind. School Dist., 109 S. Ct. 2702 (1989), held, essentially, that such suits against state actors must be pursued under §1983. However, in Howlett v. Rose, 1990 West L. 75,259 (June 11, 1990), the Supreme Court held that, where other state actors were concerned, state courts could not refuse to exercise jurisdiction over §1983 suits, nor could such courts recognize state law defenses since §1983 creates a federal cause of action.

Page 935. Add at end of second paragraph:

Most recently, the Supreme Court has refined the extent of immunity by focusing on the clarity of the constitutional prohibition. In Anderson v. Creighton, 483 U.S. 635 (1987), the Court established that it is not sufficient for a defendant to know that constitutional rights are implicated; she must be aware at a sufficient level of specificity that her conduct violates such rights:

> The contours of the right must be sufficiently clear that a reasonable official would understand that what he is doing violates that right. This is not to say that an official action is protected unless the very action in question has previously been held unlawful, but it is to say that in the light of preexisting law the unlawfulness must be apparent.

Id. at 640. The appellate courts have applied this doctrine to exonerate individuals from personal liability in a wide variety of circumstances. E.g., Cygnar v. City of Chicago, 865 F.2d 827 (7th Cir. 1989) (affirmative action law not clearly enough established at time of action to subject individual to liability in reverse discrimination suit); Warner v. Graham, 845 F.2d 179 (8th Cir. 1988) (sacramental use of peyote by non-Indian members of Native American Church not clearly enough protected to impose liability on defendant for firing plaintiff).

Nevertheless, the focus of the Supreme Court on the objective reasonable official rather than the subjective state of mind of the actual defendant invoking immunity does not render intent irrelevant. In many cases, the constitutional right being vindicated is precisely (and only) a right against wrongly-motivated conduct. The paradigmatic race discrimination case — a refusal to hire — challenges a decision which, but for the intent of the decision-maker, would not be subject to attack, since there is no general right to government employment; rather, there is a right not to be denied employment because of one's race. For such claims, a decision on qualified immunity necessarily entails an inquiry into the defendant's mental state. The inquiry has been phrased as limited to factors bearing on intent but not extending to the defendant's knowledge of the state of the law. Poe v. Haydon, 853 F.2d 418 (6th Cir. 1988), *cert. denied*, 109 S. Ct. 788 (1989); Wright v. South Arkansas Regional Health Center, Inc. 800 F.2d 199 (8th Cir. 1986). *Poe*, however, may have taken away with one hand what it gave with the other: it suggests that a plaintiff must establish the prohibited intent by "direct" as opposed to "inferential or circumstantial" evidence.

Page 935. Add after *Wheeler* citation in fourth paragraph:

Further, although the statute speaks of territories, the Supreme Court recently held that neither the territory of Guam nor officers of that territory could be sued under §1983. Ngiraingas v. Sanchez, 110 S. Ct. 1737 (1990).

Page 936. Add new text before "E. Remedies":

The courts that have addressed this question have generally held that the same litigation structure applies to §1983 suits as to Title VII disparate treatment actions. E.g., Riordan v. Kempiners, 831 F.2d 690 (7th Cir. 1987); Kitchen v. Chippewa Valley Schools, 825 F.2d 1004 (6th Cir. 1987). See also Patterson v. McLean Credit Union, 109 S. Ct. 2363 (1989) (§1981).

E. REMEDIES

1. Legal and Equitable Relief

Page 937. Add the following at the end of the carryover paragraph:

Several recent cases have stated that the backpay award is equitable when sought as an adjunct to reinstatement, but legal when recovery of other compensatory, or punitive, damages are sought. E.g., Santiago-Negron v. Castro-Davila, 865 F.2d 431 (1st Cir. 1989); Skinner v. Total Petroleum, Inc., 859 F.2d 1439 (10th Cir. 1988).

Page 938. Add the following at the end of the carryover paragraph:

Recently, courts have attempted to formulate standards for determining the appropriate amount for punitive damages awards. For example, in Rowlett v. Anheuser-Busch, Inc., 832 F.2d 194 (1st Cir. 1987), the court said the jury

10. Reconstruction-Era Civil Rights Legislation   Page 939

should be instructed to balance such factors as the grievousness of the conduct, the solvency of the defendant, and the potential for deterrence of the verdict, and should be told the maximum reasonable amount allowed by such balancing. And in Edwards v. Jewish Hospital, 855 F.2d 1345 (8th Cir. 1988), the court said that the amount of punitive damages must bear a "reasonable relationship" to the amount of compensatory damages awarded, but the rule is inapplicable when only nominal compensatory damages have been recovered.

3. The Eleventh Amendment

Page 939. Replace the last full paragraph on the page with the following:

The Eleventh Amendment is applicable in a §1981 or §1983 action against a state or a state official in his or her official capacity. The Supreme Court has held that §1983 is the exclusive means for suit against state actors for violating §1981, Jett v. Dallas Independent School District, 109 S. Ct. 2702 (1989), and that the Eleventh Amendment is fully applicable in a §1983 action against a state actor, e.g., Quern v. Jordan, 440 U.S. 332 (1979).

The Eleventh Amendment has also had a substantial impact on the Supreme Court's interpretation of §1983. Under the Amendment's influence, the Court has held "that neither a state nor its officials acting in their official capacities are 'persons' under §1983" for the purpose of a cause of action for damages. Will v. Michigan Department of State Police, 109 S. Ct. 2304, 2312 (1989). Thus §1983 does not provide a cause of action for damages against a state or state official in her official capacity even when the Eleventh Amendment is inapplicable—for example, when the state has waived its immunity or when the action is in a state court.

PART IV

ANTIDISCRIMINATION EFFORTS THROUGH GOVERNMENT CONTRACTS

Chapter 12

Handicap Discrimination

B. THE SUBSTANTIVE PROVISIONS OF THE REHABILITATION ACT OF 1973

2. The Concept of Handicap Discrimination

Page 1004. Add the following at the end of Note 1:

A teacher who taught hearing-impaired students and had contracted AIDS posed no "significant risk" in the workplace, but his condition could be monitored to ensure that any secondary infections he contracts also pose no significant risk. Chalk v. U.S. District Court, 840 F.2d 701 (9th Cir. 1988).

APPENDIX

Page 1066. Add the following from §3 of the Age Discrimination Claims Assistance Act of 1988, Pub. L. No. 100-283, 102 Stat. 78 (1988), after the text of §626(e):

Notwithstanding section 7(e) of the Age Discrimination in Employment Act of 1967 (29 U.S.C. 626(e)), a civil action may be brought under section 7 of such Act by the Commission or an aggrieved person, during the 540-day period beginning on the date of enactment of this Act [April 7, 1988] if—

  (1) with respect to the alleged unlawful practice on which the claim in such civil action is based, a charge was timely filed under such Act with the Commission after December 31, 1983,

  (2) the Commission did not, within the applicable period set forth in section 7(e) either—

    (A) eliminate such alleged unlawful practice by informal methods of conciliation, conference, and persuasion, or

    (B) notify such person, in writing, of the disposition of such charge and of the right of such person to bring a civil action on such claim,

  (3) the statute of limitations applicable under such section 7(e) to such claim ran before the date of enactment of this Act, and

  (4) a civil action on such claim was not brought by the Commission or such person before the running of the statute of limitations.